UP ABOVE
THE CITY
DOWN BENEATH
THE STARS

To Mark

X.

UP ABOVE THE CITY THE CITY

DOWN BENEATH THE STARS

MAGAZINE, THE BAD SEEDS, INTO THE UNDERWORLD AND BEYOND

BARRY ADAMSON

OMNIBUS PRESS

Copyright © 2021 Omnibus Press
(A division of the Wise Music Group
14–15 Berners Street, London, W1T 3LJ)

Cover designed by Rehan Abdul
Picture research by the author

ISBN 978-1-913172-25-1
Signed Edition 978-1-913172-61-9
Special Edition 978-1-913172-57-2

Design and Typeset by Evolution Design & Digital Ltd (Kent)
Printed in the Czech Republic

www.omnibuspress.com

Contents

Chapter One

Manchester. Wednesday, June 11, nineteen fifty-eight.

It is dark inside the Room. Dark, dismal and eldritch.

A low, thumping, rhythmic, engagingly hypnotic boom blends easily into the ominous electronic sounds that drift all around me.

The commotion creates an intense, continuous atmospheric soundtrack, from which there is no reprieve.

Eyes open or closed, the effect is exactly the same.

This Boom-Boom Room has been my home for as long as I can remember. I can't put a date on it but believe me, it feels like forever.

I don't mind it so much. Everything I need seems to be right here but, lately, I've had thoughts about being someplace else. Somewhere I've never planned to go to.

It's a notion that has been gnawing away at me for some time...

Globules of light sail by, floating into an ever-expanding screen, before dissolving. The rise and fall of each beam offers some hope of another life outside of the Room. Some indication as to where I might be headed, perhaps?

I ask nobody in particular, *Is this a memory, a dream, the start of something new. Or is it something else altogether?*

More whirring, bumping and the occasional pulsing of lights but no answer.

The not knowing forms a troubling knot of anxiety in my jelly-baby belly.

For reasons I cannot comprehend, not for the first time, I am beginning to doubt myself and all that surrounds me.

The Room has rarely been as disheartening as it is now. The light dissipates and tenebrous shadows, coupled with the sheer loneliness I have gathered up over all the centuries I've been here, collude to chip away at my fragile mind.

It begs me to question if something other, something better than all this woeful ambiguity, might lie ahead of me, once I evacuate this claustrophobic, muscular, pear-shaped organ.

I try to accept my fate and hope my mood will pass.

*   *   *

Like an old friend, a sound I've become familiar with is audible from somewhere nearby. I recognise it instantly. I even know it by name.

The bass line from the song 'Fever', by Peggy Lee, has begun to play.

As troubles dissolve, it's just me, the bass, the drums and those oh-so-enticing finger clicks. In the darkness, a wry smile creeps across my lips as Peggy cantillates.

Never know how much I love you...

I fall under a kind of narcotic spell. The music takes a hold of me and consumes my every bodily cell, as my unborn self tunes into the arrangement.

There are no other instruments on the song except for the upright bass, drums and voice, all the way throughout. Without knowing this, you'd swear that there was a full orchestra playing. You may even need to go back and check if you heard me right, as the feeling from the record is so musically complete, despite its minimal construction.

*   *   *

I screw up my embryonic eyes, young hips swaying through the first of the three key changes, head slowly lurching back and forth to the beat. The way those toms punctuate the song, every time Peggy shouts

2

'fever', would almost cause me to fall over if I wasn't in here, sloshing around.

* * *

The key changes again for further elaborations on how this addictive phenomenon, a 'sickness' known as 'lust', is what's really making the world go around.

* * *

I bathe in the afterglow of the song, which, as it fades, promises to stay with me forever. I also realise that my anxieties have now completely faded too.

I'm free to speculate how long it will be before I reach the final stages of... whatever the hell happens next. And while I put those to bed quite quickly, one question remains like a lone child at the gates after the first day of school, waiting for a parent to arrive.

When will I finally get to meet whoever owns those mixed tones? Those tones of conflict, derision and laughter, those muffled inflections I hear in close proximity every day?

'Mum', 'Dad', 'Our Carol'. Those are the words I hear, repeatedly. Sometimes 'Lily', sometimes 'Barry', sometimes 'Our Kid'.

After much pondering, I finally get it: 'Mum' is Lily. 'Dad' is Barry and 'Our Kid' is Carol. They have something to do with this, I'm sure. It feels like a point of connection, whenever I hear their voices. Satisfied, for now, I yawn and listen to the sounds in the Room, before slipping into sleep.

* * *

It is now 7am and there seems to be more of a commotion than usual outside the Room. It makes me imagine crowds of... *people* gathered outside, waiting for some kind of show to begin.

The front door shoots open.

From a high angle, looking down on a terrace called Upper Medlock Street, the summer morning sunlight surrounds us as we spill out of the house, all four of us.

It's a kind of controlled chaos, with me hidden away inside my little Room.

I hear the familiar sound of car doors being opened and then slammed shut.

My mum (I assume it's her) is yelling at a couple of kids to 'Shove off!' as they ask if they can touch my dad's skin for good luck. This is followed by the sound of thickened footsteps as my dad (I'm sure it's him) makes his way around to the driver's side, jumps into the car and turns the ignition key.

'St Mary's here we come, Barry lad,' he says out loud. It would seem that my time has, indeed, arrived.

The mood is light enough, but I have this feeling, though. A feeling I heard Our Kid express recently as: 'Something's not quite right here.'

* * *

We are now inside the hospital.

There seems to be little movement in my arms and legs.

I can see their blurred image, but I can't exactly feel them.

They simply wobble and float around, no matter how much I will them to stay still.

I try to manoeuvre, to turn myself around, and as I reach around to pull on a rope attached to my belly, I fail to grasp it. I'm now looking for a way out but then, in the blink of an eye…

In a moment of radical midwifery, I am dragged out by my backside and flopped onto a stainless steel table, like the latest little catch hauled out of the ocean.

I dare not open my eyes, as the difference between here and the Boom-Boom Room is optically overwhelming.

Above me, a filament strip of light buzzes and slowly glowers out of the darkness. Strange electronic noises permeate the atmosphere – a kind of echo of where I've spent the last months. I begin to observe the world from below as several blurry faces now lean over and engulf me. My eyes attempt to widen as the faces make themselves fully clear.

Lily Maud Adamson, English, pale of freckle, thirty-five years of age.

Palbert Wellington Adamson, also known as Barry, Jamaican, as tough as old boots, thirty-three.

4

Carol Anne Adamson, an eleven-year-old cherub with light brown skin.

They don't quite seem to know what to make of the new arrival. They all look upon me as though examining a rare new breed of animal. They gaze at each other, full of apprehension and concern, as swinging doors swing open and a voice booms out loud.

'The boy has dyschondroplasia.'

Tibial dyschondroplasia (TD) is a metabolic disease of young poultry that affects the growth of bone and cartilage. Often occurs in broilers (chickens raised for meat) and other poultry which have been bred for fast growth rates. The tibial cartilage does not mature enough to ossify (turn into bone). This leaves the growth plate prone to fracture, infection, and deformed bone development. It is the leading cause of lameness, mortality, and carcass condemnations in commercial poultry.

Two nurses stare at my mum and lean into each other to whisper.

'Unplanned, I'm guessing?'

'An accident, she told me. I mean both arms *and* both legs dislocated like a diseased chicken? I ask you, who'd want that, the poor love?'

The booming voice is back.

'That's a different kind of dyschondroplasia. This one is also known as Ollier's disease. Now. Would you leave me with the family?'

* * *

The good doctor reasons: 'We can try and snap his arms back into the sockets right away, or probably wait until he is three. But he will require an operation known as an osteotomy to correct the hip deformities when he gets older. That's where we reset the hips, and he will have to lie in what we call a spica cast for a few months.

'Bit of a bind, as these casts begin at the chest and go all the way down to the ankle, with the legs spread wide for the hips to set by means of a metal bar which will go from here...'

He touches the inside of my left knee.

'...to here...'

My right knee.

He grins. 'The metal bar is known as a "witch's broom" – that's rather odd, isn't it?'

Still with my legs apart, he says, 'Don't worry, though. We'll cut a circle out of the cast around the genitalia and behind, so he can... you know. When he's older, we're going to have to start replacing his bones: hips and shoulder sockets in particular.'

He throws a blanket over me. 'All alright? I'll leave you to think about it.'

*   *   *

Lily, in particular, is completely beside herself. This, in her mind, is surely further hellish punishment for a life lost to a kind of... well, what is it? A kind of self-persecution for crimes committed?

The last baby boy, ten years previous, was pronounced dead on arrival. Then, a few years before meeting my dad, there was the lone miscarriage she suffered while pleading and bleeding with her own father, pleading that he allow her to leave her dank dwelling and come back home to my grandmother's absolute cruelty – a woman who wasn't even her own mother. And now this?

*   *   *

I'm wrapped in tight swaddling clothes and put into a cot next to my mum. The tightness of the wrapping is incredibly soothing; it also balms the sound of the whispering all around me as my eyes flicker in the harsh daylight. I look at her but she looks away.

The two nurses exchange glances with each other.

'Don't worry, love, we have cases like this all the time.'

'He'll be right as rain. You won't even know there's anything wrong with him.'

My mum looks at me lovingly, albeit with a slight grimace only I can see. I wish the swaddling were tighter, but at the same time, I'm consumed by an urge to run away. Which, given what we've all just been told, might be slightly problematic...

Another nurse brings my mum a cup of tea. I watch her drink, study her face and hands and look for myself in her blanched appearance. Her lumpy knuckles, full of golden rings that seem to have sailed onto her digits. Her nose and the hook of it. I know that hook, I'm sure.

6

My eyes close and I fall into a deep sleep, to wake up in another Room altogether.

* * *

I hear the cheering of many men in the distance as I look to see where I might be.

The walls are grey and there is little light. The sounds of struggle are all too clear and there are rats circling the periphery of my little eyes.

The stench is overpowering.

The sound of screaming from nearby pierces the cheering, which then gets louder.

Some men crash through the door and run towards me, shouting at me. They grab at me and then force me into some kind of foot contraption. One of them winks at me, baring his teeth.

I am at first in shock, then an incredible amount of pain as some hot liquid is poured upon me... my legs... my chest... I pass out.

* * *

There is more cheering as I'm dragged through a crowd. Returning from unconsciousness, from the torture I've already endured, I can see their angry, distorted faces baying for my blood. The sounds of neighing horses and rattling chains pervade my senses as the final disruption begins. Each horse is tied to an arm and a leg by my executioner; at the sign for them to bolt, I will be torn, limb from limb.

As the flag comes down, I wake with a gasp...

* * *

The next day, we lurch along the cobbled streets in my Uncle Norman's chariot.

My mum gazes out of the window, staring into a black and white sky. My dad turns the radio on and scrolls through an orgy of static, clipped voices and glitchy white noise, before finding something coherent.

The number one song of the day, 'Who's Sorry Now?' by Connie Francis, plays on the airwaves. My mother turns to the radio as if she is being called by name. She begins to sing, escaping into the 'all' of the song as I watch her from my sister's comforting arms.

Lily sings along, both opening and, at the same time, bathing her wounds in a kind of haunted self-deprecation; her pained voice is incredibly self-centred and yet a beautiful instrument in its own right. The lyric wraps itself around her every sensibility, as if the gods are communicating directly to her through the radio. It documents and informs her darkest feelings, manifest in every cell of her being.

She deftly moves Connie aside, in favour of somebody who's living the song in the moment, unscripted. Herself. Her vibrato is controlled and held spectacularly as she cadences the verses.

Whose heart is aching for breaking each and every vow?

She intuitively knows how a voice can grab hold of a person and turn them inside out. Make them surrender at the deepest level, as she is willing to surrender herself.

I can't help but notice that a large part of the song's power lies in the way it sounds. Connie's voice hovers in a kind of echo, the subconscious now made conscious through the sentiment of the lyric. In the background, other voices seem sympathetic as they 'ooh' and 'ahh'; at the same time they are mockingly victorious as the song's key changes up a tone.

The snare drum is now hit with a drumstick, whereas, in an earlier part of the song, it was softly stroked with wire brushes. This hitting of the snare, along with the key change, raises and pushes the emotional stakes beautifully, with Connie (and my mum) exalting in how glad they are that the person the song is directed to is, without a shadow of a doubt, sorry now.

We are all frozen in the grip of my mother's voice. The world outside Uncle Norman's car – staring, segregated, with a bottomless hatred – simply falls away at the sound of her singing.

You can hear a pin drop when the song ends. Bonded together by our sorrow, dismay, disappointment, rage, defiance, dignity, and my own early sense of alienation, the Adamson family is like a strange band of stars. A bizarre musical troupe.

As my brain is already beginning to understand how music soothes the suffering of those who make it (and, indeed, those who sing it), we arrive back home at Eighty-Eight Upper Medlock Street, Hulme.

Chapter Two

Hulme (pronounced hyoom) is an ex-industrial suburb to the south of the City of Manchester. It is known chiefly for its social and economic decline in the 1960s, 70s and 80s and its subsequent redevelopment in the 1990s as part of one of Europe's biggest urban regeneration projects. The area received its name from the Danish expression for a small island surrounded by water or marshland which, in fact, it probably was when it was first settled by Norse invaders from Scandinavia.

It was evidenced as a separate community south of the River Medlock from Manchester in fifteenth-century map prints. Until the eighteenth century, it remained solely a farming area, and pictures from that time show an idyllic scene of crops, sunshine and country life.

The area remained entirely rural until the Bridgewater Canal was cut and the Industrial Revolution swept economic change through the neighbouring district of Castlefield, where the Dukes Canal terminated and containerised transportation of coal and goods rose as an industry to support the growing textile industries of Manchester.

It was this supply of cheap coal from the Dukes' mines at Worsley that allowed the textile industry of Manchester to grow. The Industrial Revolution eventually brought development to the area, and jobs to the urban poor in Hulme carrying coal from the 'Starvationer' (very narrow canal boats), to be carted off along Deansgate.

Many factories (known locally as mills) and a railway link to Hulme soon followed, and thousands of people came to work in the rapidly expanding mills in the city. Housing therefore had to be built rapidly, and space was limited. Hulme's growth in many ways was a 'victim of its own success', with hastily built, low-quality housing interspersed with the myriad smoking chimneys of the mills and the railway, resulting in an extremely low quality of life for residents. Reports of the time suggest that even in an extremely residential area such as Hulme, at times air quality became so low that poisonous fumes and smoke literally 'blocked out the sun' for long periods.

The number of people living in Hulme went up fiftyfold in the first half of the nineteenth century and the rapid building of housing to accommodate the population explosion meant the living conditions were of extremely low standard, with sanitation non-existent and rampant spread of disease. By 1844, the situation had grown so serious that Manchester Borough Council (now Manchester City Council) had to pass a law banning further building. However, the thousands of 'slum' homes that were already built continued to be lived in, and many were still in use into the first half of the twentieth century.

eXHuLMe.co.uk

As we continue along the road back home, rows of those identical, Victorian 'slum houses' stand gloomy and forlorn.

We arrive at Eighty-Eight Upper Medlock Street, amidst a sea of whispering net curtains, parted by the same folk who will, in a few days, say, 'Aw, he's a little belter' once their judgment has simmered. By virtue of their nosiness, various cups of sugar will be handed out in exchange for their bestowing of good fortune on my parents' latest 'half-caste'.

Inside our brick-fronted, quintessentially Dickensian, two-up two-down terraced house, the wallpaper is nicotine yellow. There is a huge, metallic grey tin bath hanging on the wall in the sitting room, opposite the fireplace. The kitchen is tiny and there is a coal-hole outside, where every Tuesday the coal merchant drops sacks so that my dad can scuttle it onto the open fire. Also outside is a toilet.

My nose begins to turn upwards. My mum pinches it playfully. 'Maybe we should call him Little Lord Fauntleroy?' she says to my dad. 'Get the kettle on, love, will you?' She turns to my sister. 'I'm bloody parched.'

Our Carol hands me to my mum, who holds me at arm's length while my dad takes a photograph. My sister heads off to the kitchen, fills the kettle with water, whacks the gas on the stove up, lights it, plonks the kettle on it, comes back into the living room and takes me back from my mum.

She rocks me a little and smiles at me, as I've become a little unsettled.

My dad spins the dial of the radio. He's an information junkie; a man who sits with a thesaurus and a dictionary by his side, hoping never to get fooled by something he doesn't understand or, worse, to be called a 'savage' for not understanding how a particular word relates to the world at large, or to the world of ideas.

My mum, of course, is all about the song.

She couldn't give two hoots what people think of her – or at least that's what we're meant to believe. Truth is, she cares what everybody thinks probably just a little too much.

My parents light up the first of forty cigarettes they will each smoke today – and every day for the rest of their lives. The kettle begins to whistle. My sister runs off into the kitchen to finish making the tea.

A wailing saxophone shifts the scene. Then a rock'n'roll 'Yakety Yak' riff rasps and cuts through the smoke-filled air. My mum becomes giddy with excitement.

'Give him 'ere, Our Kid.'

My sister's and my dad's faces light up.

My mum, hands bracketed under my dangling arms, dances me on her knee, jumping me up and down as the sax blares across the changes in the song.

'Gently, mind his legs,' says my sister, head popping out of the kitchen with an expression of concern. My mum shoots her a look of disdain, not wishing to stand corrected.

At this point in the record, a voice belonging to no less a personage than Lord Rockingham cuts through as the music stops dead.

Hoots mon
There's a moose loose aboot this hoose

My dad nods his head to the beat. He is propped up on one arm of the armchair my mum sits in. His leg is crossed so that his right ankle rests on his left knee. He wears a black woollen donkey jacket, with black dry wax patches across the shoulders and elbows, dark brown corduroy trousers and a pair of Dunlop rubber Wellington boots with a front zip.

On his head, at a rakish angle, sits a dark green flat corduroy cap, and he keeps a short dark green pencil behind his one visible ear for filling out betting slips and sizing up woodwork jobs. He draws on a Senior Service cigarette, its white paper standing out against his black skin as he blows the smoke high into the air and away from my face.

'Hoots mon': an interjection usually meaning 'Hey, man.'
'There's a moose loose aboot this hoose': 'There's a mouse loose about this house' – a standard cliché highlighting Scots' pronunciation.

This popular mix of Scottish patriotism, self-effacing humour and wordplay travels south of the border and jumps out of the radio. Now the family can embrace something close to home.

Especially my dad...

My dad and Uncle Norman, around nineteen forty-six.

Scotsmen originally surveyed Jamaica as the foundation site of the slave plantations. To this day, its legacy resonates in place names such as Glasgow, Hampden, Argyle, Glen Islay, Dundee, Fort William, Montrose, Dumbarton and St. Andrews. Of the one hundred and seventy-three place names in Greater Kingston, a quarter can also be found in Scotland or are based on Scottish family names: for example, Hamilton Gardens, Stirling Castle, Gordon Town and Elgin Street.

Many of the Scots emigrants in the eighteenth century were temporary sojourners. However, there are many examples of Scottish men having children with their slaves and settling permanently. The husband of one of Robert Burns' mistresses chose to remain in Jamaica on his plantation, with his 'ebony women and mahogany children'.

Many Jamaicans are therefore directly descended from Scots, and this heritage is reflected in their surnames. Former slaves also adopted the names of plantation owners after Emancipation in eighteen thirty-eight. Common Scots-Jamaican names include Adamson, Campbell, Douglas, Reid, McFarlane, McKenzie, MacDonald, Grant and Gordon.

Despite all this, the descendants of Scots in Jamaica have been termed the 'Forgotten Diaspora' by Scots-Jamaican Professor Geoff Palmer, of Heriot-Watt University in Edinburgh.

Born in Kingston, Jamaica on August 5, nineteen twenty-seven, my dad comes to the UK in nineteen forty-four, at the tender age of seventeen (his papers say he is nineteen), following older brother Jimmy as one of six thousand black men volunteering to join the RAF.

After meeting my mum towards the end of the war at a dance in Manchester, he doesn't ever go back to Jamaica.

We never speak directly of this Scottish connection and my mum shows a complete disinterest in tracing her own ancestry, let alone his.

When his passport runs out, he will never renew it. Any talk of 'back home' is not allowed. Later, I will often try to glean information about a history that seems to have just... disappeared.

His response to any question from my enquiring mind is, '*Bwoy...* you nosey, you know?'

But I manage to get some info from Our Kid.

My dad's four brothers and three sisters were disowned, at my mother's request, when they wouldn't stop asking him to send money 'back home'. His relationship to his brother Jimmy is drenched in guilt, as he missed a message that Jimmy was about to die of TB not long after the war. My dad never got to say goodbye to him.

*　*　*

'Hoots Mon' is a rare moment of coming together, where we celebrate our dislocated history with lighthearted self-mockery.

The song comes to an end.

My dad says, 'I'd better be off, Lil.'

He leans into my mum, who puckers up. As they slowly navigate towards each other, they kind of peck each other on the lips as opposed to the cheek and then smile into each other's eyes.

They are bonded by adversity.

My mum knows my dad's sense of dislocation all too well, and my dad understands my mum's certain kind of crazy.

I sit between them. My observation and understanding of both of them is only just beginning.

'See you when I see you, love.'

'Yeah, I'll see you when I get back, love.'

As my dad reaches the door of the living room, he turns to look at my mum and me. He casts a quizzical gaze as she looks into my eyes and speaks softly.

'Monday's child is full of grace.'

I smile.

'Tuesday's child is fair of face.'

I chuckle.

'Wednesday's child is full of woe.'

I wait and I watch. She rubs her nose against mine like the Eskimos do and says nothing more.

My dad pulls up the collar of his donkey jacket and heads out into the heartland of industrial England.

HIs journey to work is markedly funereal.

The spirit of Manchester's populace is still hunched in mourning for the Manchester United football players who lost their lives in the Munich air disaster – on Thursday, February 6, nineteen fifty-eight, a few months before I was born. Their star player was Duncan Edwards and, years later, whenever I talk to my dad about the skills of George

Best, he will always steer me back in the direction of the 'great Duncan Edwards'.

The team were on their way back from Belgrade after drawing three-all with Red Star in a European Cup game when the crash happened.

Manchester was a city in shock. United and City supporters came together in a grief that touched everyone. As they mourned those who had died, they also prayed for those still seriously ill in hospital: manager Matt Busby and his beloved star player.

Edwards came out of his coma after two days and was showing considerable improvement. He was speaking to his girlfriend, Molly Leach, who had flown from Manchester to Munich, and managing to eat a bowl of soup.

However, the next day the *Manchester Evening News* ran the blunt headline 'EDWARDS WORSE'. He had six times more nitrogen in his blood than is normal and an artificial kidney was rushed from Freiburg University clinic, in a last-ditch attempt to save his life. After three attempts, the kidney began to wash the impurities from his blood and hope returned. But not for long, as the procedure had to be reinstated and repeated to worsening effect.

On February 24, a dark cloud hovered over Manchester and beyond as news filtered through that Duncan Edwards had lost his fight for life.

The final death toll was twenty-three, including club officials and journalists.

Another Manchester United star player, Bobby Charlton, said, 'He was the best player I ever saw, or am likely to see in my lifetime.'

My dad wholeheartedly agrees.

From this foul drain the greatest stream of human industry flows out to fertilise the whole world. From this filthy sewer pure gold flows. Here humanity attains its most complete development and its most brutish; here civilisation works its miracles, and civilised man is turned back almost into a savage.

Alexis de Tocqueville, *Journeys to England and Ireland*, 1835

* * *

Glover's Cables (WT Glover and Co) is a cable factory situated in Trafford Park, just a stone's throw away from Old Trafford, home of the great Manchester Utd and those 'Busby Babes'.

Walter T Glover established his wire manufacturing company in 1868, occupying premises at the Bridgewater Street Iron Works in Salford. W T Glover & Co, known as Glover's, originally made cotton-covered and braided, insulated copper wires for use on bell, signalling and telephone circuits. As trade developed, the company moved to the Springfield Lane Cable Works in 1880. At this time, factories and larger private homes were beginning to install electric lighting, which required better insulated cable. Glover's started to manufacture cables covered with between one and three layers of rubber strip, waterproof tape and compounded cotton braid. In the late 1880s, Glover's began to make lead-sheathed cables for underground use. The company became a limited company and moved to Trafford Park in 1898, securing the exclusive rights for the supply of electricity to all the roads, streets and premises of Trafford Park...

During the 1950s, Glover's developed high voltage submarine power cables, used to link centres of population with sources of generation. The parent company formed a subsidiary, BIC (Submarine) Cables Ltd, to manufacture and install the Glover's cables. Glover's submarine cables linked England and France, and the north and south islands of New Zealand. Increasing competition from other cable manufacturing companies resulted in the south side of Glover's Trafford Parks works integrating with the newly formed Wiring and General Cables Division of the British Insulated Cables Company (BICC). The Trafford Park factory closed in 1970, but the Glover's brand continued as part of BICC.

Science Museum Group

* * *

The year is nineteen sixty-one. I am growing at a rate of knots, yet even though I'm three years old, I can still barely walk.

My dad comes home every day from Glover's Cables and takes a jar of Swarfega off the kitchen shelf and vigorously scrubs his hands. Swarfega is a dark green, gelatinous, thixotropic substance used to clean grease, oil, printer's ink or persistent hydrophobic dirt from the skin. Working a small amount into the dry skin, as with other such cleaners, can be more effective than soap or other common cleansing products. Swarfega is ubiquitous in environments where this kind of dirt is common, such as garages and machine shops.

This particular day, after he's scrubbed his hands to within an inch of their life, my mum hands him a letter. They both look at me with strained smiles.

A few days later, me and my mum travel on three buses to Pendlebury Children's Hospital in Salford.

On arrival, I look to my mum for reassurance as the overbearing smell, a mixture of some other cleaning product plus something rather sickly – possibly pertaining to death – combines to create a feeling of dread I can never get away from whenever I visit the place.

We see a doctor who moves my arms around, asserting that the limited movement is indeed down to dyschondroplasia. An appointment is made for me to come back next week.

On the way back, we stop in town and I am carried into Woolworths in Piccadilly, in the town centre, before we get the last bus.

My mum buys me some Dinky Toys, Matchbox cars and a small Meccano building set.

I'm all smiles again. I can't wait to get home to tell my dad and Our Carol about the great day we've had.

Next week, we repeat the same bus journey and arrive once again at the hospital, where that same strange smell hits me in the guts.

I'm told to lie down on a bed and my mum is telling me, 'Shush, it'll be alright.'

I feel a slight prick as I stare into her eyes.

I wonder if I'm not headed back to the Boom-Boom Room, as I'm whirring around and floating through time and space. I can't feel anything anymore. Sounds are reverberating and echoing as the image of my mum fades into the distance.

The next thing is I'm in my mum's arms and mine are incredibly sore, as is my throat, and I'm as hazy as anything. The doctor is talking but I cannot understand anything he is saying.

My mum carries me out into the cool evening and, with each bounce in her arms, I wonder if I'm going to be sick. As we don't stop off in town, I realise we aren't going to make it to Woolies.

The house feels comforting and the familiar noise of the radio soothes me a little. My dad takes me from my mum's arms, with Our Kid trying to see what's going on.

She keeps asking, 'Is he okay, Mam?' and I'm put to bed. I might really be sick now, as a queasy feeling comes over me.

My arms are aching so much. I can't hear the song that's playing. The sound is all wishy-washy, so my little brain (which hurts a lot) fails to find a place in my head where I can concentrate on the melody, the arrangement, the singing and the lyrics. Especially the lyrics.

My sister pours water into my mouth and now all three of them look down on me with worry. I wonder why I feel distant from each of them.

I also wonder why we are called Adamson and not something more African.

Adamson coat of arms.

Chapter Three

I float around my room, levitating above my parents and Our Kid.

They slowly crane their necks upwards to follow me as I disappear through the roof, hovering now above Upper Medlock.

The slates on the rooftops are silvered by the light of the hanging moon.

I soar higher.

I'm so high that lovely Manchester becomes a city of tiny lights, diminishing, the further away I float from it.

* * *

I joyously whisk my way upwards, then further afield, through the European continent and beyond, into the future at a rate of a hundred miles an hour, without a care in the world. I fly high above the clouds and into the silence of the stars.

An orchestrated soundtrack carries my lifeless body as, lost and content at the same time, I become attuned to the feeling.

But surely this feeling of *wild out there* – where I now seem to be floating – isn't the same as feeling *wild in here?*

The light on the horizon is deep orange and blue.

It arcs this new world, and I'm filled with lightness as I cast my eyes downwards. My chest swells with the luminosity that now surrounds my world, and my own sense of belonging.

I desire to be taken higher, yet something begins to claw at my mood, a restlessness, as I see a flash of my former self – back on that metal hospital table, wrapped in swaddling clothes. My head is literally in the clouds as the soundtrack becomes dissonant, warning me of a possible storm ahead.

*   *   *

I begin to nosedive.

The surface of the earth shifts beneath me as I plunge towards it.

My seemingly endless wellbeing becomes punctuated with noise.

Shouting, scurrying, the smell of burning toast, the clomping of footsteps and that damn radio, blasting out Brian Poole and the Tremeloes' hit, 'Do You Love Me?'

I open my eyes to nineteen sixty-three.

I ease myself out of my tiny bed, located in our tiny front room, and put my feet on the ground. After a fashion, I begin to walk. My right leg is some three inches longer than my left, so I lean over. I am lop-sided and limp heavily.

My body pulsates underneath my skin as I move towards the bedroom door and pull it towards me. I leave the room now and turn to face the stairs. Behind me, the front door is open and I'm drawn to the noise from the street. Slowly turning my head towards the piercing morning light, I take several steps towards the door but something stops me from leaving. I turn back, towards the stairs. Behind me, a surge of high wind grabs the front door and slams it with a bang.

My shoulders leap up to my ears. My sister runs out of the front room to see what the explosion was. Seeing me there, gawping at the stairs, she comes towards me.

The scene darkens. A bright light emanates from the top of the stairs. The Cole Porter song 'You Do Something To Me', with its swirling orchestral crescendos, begins to play.

Me and Our Kid look at each other with a mixture of anticipation and foreboding, as Mario Lanza's voice, accompanied by my mum's, soars way up high. She stands at the top of the stairs, not a million miles away from a Cinderella, and she is going… not to the ball, but to begin her first day of work as a registered nurse. Her crisply starched blue and white uniform is topped off by an even crisper white nurse's hat.

20

My mum's first day as a registered nurse, nineteen sixty-three.

She glides down those stairs, looking to the stars.

Tell me why should it be
You have the power to hypnotise me...

She spins into the front room, where the curtains are drawn. Me and my sister's mouths are on the floor as we watch her pirouetting across the carpet. We are totally captivated.

The song ends and my mum curtsies. We clap furiously as she takes a bow. This could be the first time we've seen her smile in quite a while, so we clap even more, letting her know how wonderful she is from the very core of our beings

My mum now flings the curtains open and we are blinded. We stare into each other, wide-eyed. We know what's coming next. My mum waltzes into the kitchen and we are beside ourselves with excitement.

My sister jumps up and runs across the room, to turn on the radio. The song that plays has jangly guitars and starts with its chorus; we both join in, singing and grinning into each other's faces.

My mum appears with two plates of sandwiches. Thick slices of white bread the size of doormats, filled with layers of butter and heaps of white sugar. We are given these sugar butties as a reward for her great mood. We munch on them like there's no tomorrow and then bounce up and down like lunatics as The Searchers stomp through 'Sweets For My Sweet' on the radio.

*　　*　　*

Another Friday night.

Three kettles boil in a frenzy on the stove. I'm hoping I will go first tonight. My dad drags the metal bath, the tin tub, off the wall and places it dead centre of the living-room floor. He then throws some coal on the fire.

My eyes drift towards a scar he carries down the left side of his face. It looks like a knife, or a razorblade, sliced him from just in front of his ear, down to beneath the middle of his lower lip.

The no-talk rule around my dad's past, the total erasure of it, means I have to pick my moment to ask him about what happened. That moment isn't now.

Maybe I should wait for one of those days when he takes me to the barber's for a haircut, where he seems less hyper-vigilant. Where we are surrounded by people of his race, who shout and laugh out loud in a language I can barely understand, but try to imitate obsessively when alone, to perfect the dialect and diction – just in case I should ever need it.

He's leaving for Belle Vue racetrack, for the dogs, after which, if he wins, he might bring home something from the newly opened Kentucky Fried Chicken place.

But not before he's hacked the heads off a couple of rats he's seen in the kitchen. He grabs a razor-sharp spade...

My dad prides himself on making his own tools for work, buying the steel and handcrafting the wooden handles to fit his various-sized saws and screwdrivers – and his finest weapon, this spade.

The swishes and clunks let us know that the sparks are flying. He will emerge any moment now, victoriously holding the headless vermin by their tails and exclaiming that he'll drop them off in the bins at the back, before heading off for a night with Bomber and Uncle Norman – two mates from the RAF.

*   *   *

I don't go first, I never do, which means that after my sister has her bath, I have to jump in. It's always lukewarm and flakes of white scum float around the edges.

Tonight is no exception.

I take my clothes off and cover my privates.

My mum says, 'Oh for God's sake, you haven't got anything I haven't seen before!'

I get in and sit, shivering.

I count those calcium and magnesium particles and follow their path, making sure they stay right away from me.

To complain to my mum again would be foolish, it'd only get me a thick ear.

The saving grace here is Cussons Imperial Leather. My mum knows that this creamy, luxurious-smelling soap is the Adamson extravagance that takes the whole family away from the reality of an ever-cold house, the rats and trips on a dark night to the outside toilet.

From a grainy, flickering black and white television screen, PJ Proby sings, 'Hold Me'. A new escape plan begins to materialise. Instead of toys after Gartside Street/Pendlebury hospital visits, I will ask for the tools of my newly foreseeable trade: a red velvet suit, Cuban-heeled shoes and a white shirt with frills down the front.

(Within a year, this is how I will dress daily. If not, then you'll find me wearing a grey, collarless Beatle suit with a black plastic wig – the Cuban heels work well with this outfit too.)

My mum lifts me out of the bath and plonks me on the floor. As she rubs me down, my head never leaves the TV. My body twists as my mum tries to move me with each rub of the towel. 'Keep still, will you?'

Clouds of Imperial Leather talcum powder burst around me like dry ice as I bop along to the song and my mum smiles.

The show finishes, and now Prime Minister Harold Macmillan dispatches his unflappable pragmatism, keeping his hands on the nation's purse strings even though we've 'never had it so good'.

My sister turns the television off and, of course, turns on the radio.

Covered in talc, I am suddenly a little white boy.

Tommy Steele's 'The Little White Bull' comes on and all three of us sing along. My mum leads the charge, with me and Our Kid responding at the end of each line.

Once upon a time there was a little white bull (little white bull)
Very sad because he was a little white bull (little white bull)
All the black bulls called him a coward just cos he was white
Only black bulls go to the bullring, only black bulls fight

The song is from a musical comedy movie, *Tommy The Toreador*. It's a whimsical tale of bravery, of how colour differentiation and size shouldn't stop you from getting where you want to go.

Tommy Steele is masterful in his storytelling skills, using his cockney accent to narrate the more endearing parts and then employing almost middle-class tones to emphasise the seriousness of the message. Then comes the dramatic twist, where the little white bull is overwhelmed but has a try anyway.

I become a little overwhelmed myself. Tears begin to roll down my cheeks like tyre tracks on a light layer of snow as I look at my mum. She opens her arms to me.

'C'mere, love.' She wipes my face of the residual talcum powder and, as the song draws to an end, looks me right in the eye and sings...

You're gonna be a great little bull
The best... in... Spain

'Right, you two, off to bed.'

Carol walks me to the front room. At which point, my dad walks through the door armed with a box of Kentucky Fried Chicken (he won!) and my sister asks if we can stay up a bit longer to have some. We wait for my mum's answer. My dad smiles wryly, knowing it already.

'Go on then.'

We huddle around a small table and marvel at this new invention: 'Colonel Sanders' secret recipe'. Turns out that my dad won quite a few bob tonight. He goes on about the 'odds' and 'dead certs', and we all nod at how amazing those odds and dead certs must have been, grabbing another leg or breast to chomp on the skin and the meat. After this treat of treats, my mum says, 'Right, this time I mean it, teeth, wee and bed.'

Tucked in and free to dream, some hours into the early morning I'm shaken awake by Our Carol.

The room is on fire and she is desperately trying to get me out of there.

She manages to do so as my mum and dad are running down the stairs.

Next day, the police come to the house, with most of the street watching, and tell us that we were the victims of an arson attack. If it wasn't for the quick thinking of Our Kid, 'Who knows what would have happened?'

I move upstairs to the much quieter back bedroom, for safety reasons, but miss the sounds of the outside world calling to me in the night, when I was facing the street.

* * *

Every day my mum drops me off at Emden Street Primary School. On one of these days, I fall from a wheelbarrow and split my nose open. In the same year, I take my brown toy elephant that squirts water from its trunk. There is a nozzle on the end and I wonder if I can squirt water by taking the nozzle off the trunk and inserting it in my own nose. I shove it all the way up but nothing happens; then I realise that I can't get it out.

Next, there is an unplanned trip to the hospital, where the nozzle has to be pulled from right up inside my nose by a doctor.

My mum is as nowty as anything as she drags me home, saying, 'It's always bloody me, me, me with you, isn't it?'

I turn to my dad, who does not look good at all. He is weak and frail and looks to the floor. When we get home he goes to bed.

25

The doctor comes over and it turns out my dad has pneumonia. He tries to tell my mum something but she shushes him and tells him to go back to sleep.

He is this way for two weeks. Finally, when he's better, he tells us the story of how he picked the winning pools numbers for that week and wrote them down, and that they were in his donkey jacket pocket.

He wanted to tell my mum to fill out the coupon and take it to the corner shop. I never did find out how much money we would have won.

Not long after his illness, my dad surprises me by returning from work with a pair of beautifully handcrafted claves. I have no idea what these two rounded blocks of wood are for, but I knock them together. He watches my mind come alive and he smiles, telling me that the next time the song 'It's Now Or Never' comes on the radio, I should play along with Elvis.

* * *

He reads the paper as my mum knits one and purls one. At the sound of the slow, serenading vocal opening of 'It's Now Or Never', I grab my claves, now never more than two feet away from me, just in time for the opening chorus. Making sure I stay in time and stop before the first verse, I begin again as Elvis croons.

My parents exchange a glance of satisfaction. My dad flicks the broadsheet to straighten out the part he is reading. My mum gently inserts a knitting needle into a ball of grey wool.

She then stretches and lets us know that the constant pain in her back is still there, by way of a particular kind of groan.

She stands before my dad and, as she does most nights, says, 'Give us your pegs, love.'

My dad whips out his front two teeth, which are fitted to a denture plate, and hands them to my mum. She then pulls out several of her own, in a motion half-spat and half-manoeuvred. She waits for me to recoil in horror as she laughs, exposing her gums to me, before bursting into song:

All I want for Christmas is me two front teeth!

* * *

Nineteen sixty-four is an incredible year for music. The UK charts are just overflowing with songs that can lift anybody out of their everyday. To completely forget yourself, you only have to turn on the radio to catch any of these songs…

'Glad All Over' – The Dave Clark Five
'My Boy Lollipop' – Millie
'Hippy Hippy Shake' – The Swinging Blue Jeans
'You Really Got Me' – The Kinks
'Where Did Our Love Go' – The Supremes
'Not Fade Away' – The Rolling Stones
'House Of The Rising Sun' – The Animals
'Twenty Four Hours From Tulsa' – Gene Pitney
'My Guy' – Mary Wells
'Baby I Love You' – The Ronettes
'Oh Pretty Woman' – Roy Orbison
'Downtown' – Petula Clark
'Walk On By' – Dionne Warwick

Beside myself with excitement, with any number of these songs whirling around my brain, I pop to the shop for my mum. Hurriedly limping down the street, I decide to cut past the broken-down house.

I slow down as I remember what my friends say about 'never going inside that place', that in the basement 'there's this horrible ghost that'll get you'. I lean into the window, where the sunlight ends, and the musty smell creeps around my nostrils. The loudest thing I can hear is how quiet it is.

I take out one of my all-protecting, horseshoe-shaped magnets, mostly red with its magnetic strip exposed. This simple toy brings me so much joy: how it picks up my dad's nails when he is fixing things around the house, or my mum's needles when she is pinning up a hem and accidentally drops them on the floor, calling out to say she has a job for me.

I have two magnets and the best thing about them is that when I put the ends of both together, they jump apart. I really like slowly pushing the bottom part of the horseshoe and watching the other magnet jump away. I swing it around my finger, as though it is a real horseshoe tossed onto a stake in a pitching game. My mind is temporarily in the Wild West as the magnet spins out of my control, slipping off my finger.

It lands in the basement of the broken-down house. My knees begin to knock slightly and my mouth becomes dry. I can see the magnet – or half of it anyway – as it lies in the dirt. It is brushed by a chink of sunlight that bounces off a piece of broken glass.

I have to go around the corner and down the stairs, into the basement where my magnet is on the floor, or... I could just leave it and go home. I mean, I do have another one.

But like my mum says, they are a 'pair that fit together perfectly' and I do love playing 'attract and repel', as she calls my little game.

I creep around the side of the house and find the door, which eases open with an uneasy creak. Dust floats around in slow motion like tiny flying bugs as the light catches and fades across the staircase with my every tentative step.

Finally, I reach the bottom of the stairs and know that I have to make a right turn. I duck down. If I sneak around the corner, I can grab my magnet and run back up the stairs.

I look around the corner and see the tiniest glint on the floor. I steel myself to dart across and get it. I then hear my name: 'Barry!' This loud whisper stops me in my tracks and my heart beats like thunder.

I crawl across the room, eyes focused on the magnet, but there is somebody in the corner of my eye. I grab it and turn to see a man, taller than anyone I've ever seen before, tattered but glowing. He moves towards me and I run.

I run like the wind, across the room and back up the stairs, down the street and straight into Eighty-Eight Upper Medlock Street, eager to tell my tale of narrowly escaping a hideous death at the hands of a ghost.

I push the front door open and gasp for air. In the front room, sitting beside my mum and dad, are two men, swaddled in black funereal coats.

On the table are pictures of children, and then other pictures of school buses with children waving from the windows.

On the floor sit several pairs of black, shiny children's shoes, which match the men's mournful coats.

My mum and dad look away as the men suggest I try the shoes on. I notice that on one side of each pair, the heel is marginally bigger than on the other side by about two inches. I furrow my brow as they talk about the brochures and 'future happiness', pointing at the smiling children in the photographs. I look again at the side of the bus, seeing the words, 'SCHOOL FOR THE DISABLED'.

I surprise myself, my parents and, indeed, the two 'undertakers' with the conviction of my grievance. I am *not* to be carted off in built-up shoes, dumped on a bus and taken away from everything, I protest.

The two morticians gather their wares and scamper out of the door.

I'm waiting for a good verbal hiding, but instead I'm presented with a blow-up Yogi Bear punch bag and a pair of boxing gloves. Yogi is an anthropomorphic animal who appears in television cartoons and comic books.

The boxing gloves are brown plastic and my hands instantly sweat when I put them on. My dad is blowing up Yogi Bear while my mum says, '*It's a nice day for a pic-a-nic, Boo Boo!*'

I imagine those two men flying around the outside of the house like the vultures they are. I check the skies from the windows.

I also start to imagine the discussion they've had with my parents: 'He would benefit greatly from attending the school. After all, he would be with others just like him.' Or, 'We can take him off your hands right away if you like?'

The bag is fully inflated now and wobbles at the slightest touch. It can be punched hard and then bounces back up, as my dad demonstrates.

I hit Yogi hard and, indeed, he bounces backwards, and forwards, but I'm feigning interest now. My parents leave the room and my mind wanders back to the two men.

How long has this been planned?

Was I going away for good?

Have my parents agreed to some kind of terms, or are they going to be paid for me to be taken away?

I slam Yogi and he bounces back, catching me in the face. He smiles at me; my parents laugh next door. My sister, now home, joins in with them.

In my mind, one of the two men becomes Yogi. I hit him and he begins to laugh, as do the children on the bus.

Their laughter fills the room, as does the laughter of my parents, the other man and my sister.

'It's always me, me, me with you, isn't it?' I say to Yogi, before landing a right hook.

As Yogi keeps on smiling, I pull off the gloves. He moves back and forth as the seconds tick away. I can just about make out, through misty eyes, the sharpened pencil that I pick up and drive home into the bear.

I watch him deflate with a deafening hiss, the smile never leaving his face.

My parents and my sister stand at the open door.

My mum sighs.

My dad picks up the deflated bear and my sister shoots me a look of confusion, before they all walk out of the room.

I stare at the pencil and breathe hard.

Chapter Four

For generations of children, eating marmalade on toast at breakfast was all about saving up tokens. Once they had collected enough, they could be exchanged for a 'Golly' badge issued by manufacturer James Robertson and Sons.

These small enamel brooches came in a wide variety of figures, from cricketers and musicians to commemorative figures issued to mark national events like the 1937 coronation. All featured the company mascot, Golly, a black-faced golliwog figure with frizzy hair, white eyes and bright red lips.

The idea of the Golly mascot was dreamed up by Scotsman John Robertson, whose father, James, had founded the family business in Paisley in 1864. On a visit to the United States, he came across many young country children playing with little black rag dolls apparently made from their mothers' old black skirts and white blouses. Their name for them was 'gollies'.

When Robertson returned to England, he began work on creating a mascot and trade mark for his company, and by 1910 it was appearing on all its literature.

However, it was a skilled Birmingham enameller who first came up with the idea of producing badges featuring Golly, and in 1928 he made the very first, the Golly golfer. It proved a sensational success, giving Robertson's a high profile among consumers and ensuring that children everywhere became caught up in the race to collect new figures as they appeared.

The figure itself changed over the years, with the original 'pop eyes' replaced by more subtle side-glancing eyes in the 1970s, but by the end of the twentieth century over twenty million gollies had been sent out, ensuring them a place in British culture for many years to come.

In 1983, the Greater London Council opted to boycott Robertson's products as offensive, and five years later the golly disappeared from TV advertising. When Robertson's retired Golly in 2002, however, the company insisted that the decision had nothing to do with charges of racism. Commenting, 'we are not bowing to political correctness,' it said: 'We are retiring Golly because we found families with kids no longer necessarily knew about him,' adding: 'We have to move with the times.'

Jane Bakowski, *Kent Online*

* * *

In the kitchen, bread caramelises under the grill. The sugary smell creeps up the stairs like an ethereal vapour from a genie's lamp, snapping me and Our Kid out of our zombie-like state.

We go bounding down the stairs, two at a time, both hoping the other might slip up and get crushed in the rush.

This route has been practised over and over, so that the last few steps can be leapt over and a safe landing – without looking, gobbling up the toast being our total focus – will be achieved.

I beat my sister and land with a thud, ignoring the shooting pain in my right hip.

We scramble around the tiny kitchen table.

Our Carol pours herself a cuppa and says, 'Mam, where's me dad?'

My mum plonks the toast onto the table, along with a cream-coloured butter dish and a brand new pot of Robertson's Golden Shred marmalade. In animated fashion, she bursts into song:

Look for the Golly!

This is the song from the Robertson's advert on the television.

'Your father's outside, supposedly seeing to the car. But not if 'er across the road has owt to do with it.'

I grab at the marmalade jar to get at the tokens. If I get enough, I can trade them for 'collectables': enamel badges of the Robertson's mascot, the same Golly that I look for on every jar.

I carefully peel off the token and slide it into my trouser pocket, reminding myself to put it inside a book upstairs.

Our Kid snatches the jar out of my paws. I'll get her for that later.

My mum is at the sink, washing up.

I wait for what seems a lifetime until Our Carol's knife has left the jar and dollops of marmalade smother her two pieces of toast. I yank the knife off her and lather mine.

We exchange a fretful glance while scoffing down those pieces of golden heaven.

My dad appears and tells us the car's packed to the brim. We're ready for the off.

As we pile into the car, a curtain twitches across the road. My mum spies the nosy neighbour and yelps at her like a terrier: 'Oi! You can wind your neck in an' all!'

As we pull out of Upper Medlock Street and onto Salutation Street, my dad tuts and shakes his head. My mum says, 'Well, who the bloody hell does she think she is, the Queen of Sheba? Gawping at you like that all of the time!'

I offer the alternative viewpoint: maybe she was just seeing what was going on, or looking out for the postman? Using her parent superpower, my mum turns her head around in slow motion, one hundred and eighty degrees.

'Mind that.' She points to her nose.

'Shut that.' She points to her mouth.

'And you won't get that.' She holds up a fist to my face.

My dad unexpectedly sneezes, louder than an exploding house, almost causing the car to fall off its wheels. Me and Our Kid crack up with laughter as he apologises to my mum for the earth-shattering volume. She turns her face away from him and bemoans 'what I have to put up with'.

But we are leaving Manchester, and soon we are in full voice. Me, Our Kid, my mum and dad launch into…

We're off
We're off
We're off in a motor car
Sixty coppers are after us and we don't know where we are

DISSOLVE TO:

EXT. A6 NORTH SOUTH ROAD – LATE MORNING

A brown and beige Hillman Imp cruises along the A6. Singing can still be heard coming from inside the car.

We fell
We fell
We fell in a dirty well
Sixty coppers are after us and they fell in as well

Sunlight bleeds through the fingertips of the trees cradling the A6 as the family heads further north via the M6 Preston bypass. The children sing at the top of their lungs while shielding the harsh light from their eyes.

…Sixty coppers are after us and we don't know where we are

CUT TO:

'Alright, you two, I think we've had quite enough of that,' says my mum.

Our calls of 'Are we there yet?' are accompanied by knowing winks. We laugh without fear of reprisal as I bounce up and down in the backseat.

The Beatles' 'A Hard Day's Night' comes on the radio as my mum and dad light up. I whisper to Our Kid that we should call her 'Fag Ash Lil' and my dad 'Andy Capp'. My sister bursts out laughing as we pick up the song.

My mum draws on her Benson & Hedges as my dad flicks his ash into the car ashtray. Me and Our Kid wave our arms, half-dancing, half-dealing with the billowing smoke that fills the car with its windows closed. We continue to dodge the stabs of sunshine.

It'll soon be George's guitar solo – which we'll both try and sing – with its simple seven-note opening and some incredibly tricky triplets, played against a four-four time signature. I can see his smile of satisfaction as he executes this bizarre yet wonderfully catchy piece of playing.

Our version sounds like we're just making daft noises, which my mum's sideways glance attests to. But we pretend we're John, Paul, George and Ringo, blasting out the part before the middle-eight refrain.

We get to the end of the song as we arrive in Morecambe, giddy at the prospect of what amazing possibilities the day might hold. Morecambe is unlike anything I have ever seen before, a full-colour movie set that screams 'FUN!'

We find a place to park by the seafront. My legs are almost kicking out of the car door with anticipation. Then we hear a noise.

A hard splat beats down on the roof of the car. This is followed by another, and very quickly by another. We now see huge droplets of rain on the windscreen.

Outside on the street, holidaymakers like us gather one another up, covering their heads and each other with newspapers, running in all directions. The noise becomes deafening as the rain bashes off the windows at an incredible rate. My mum pulls a handful of plastic folded rain-bonnets from her purse.

'Lucky I brought these,' she says, handing them out. On seeing my horrified grimace, my dad gives me a smile.

I make a grab for the plain see-thru one, lest I get landed with the polka dot or the pink one! My dad takes the polka dot and giggles like a child as my sister lunges at the plain one. I get the pink one.

Our Kid whacks me on the arm, letting me know I lost.

'*Owwww!* Mam!?'

'Will you two stop it for heaven's sake!'

The rain doesn't let up for a moment. My dad says, 'There's a cafe across the road, let's go there. Everyone stay together.'

It continues to pelt down as all four of us exit the car and run. We dodge the crowd as though they are bullets. My dad scrapes me up out of the way of a man who'd otherwise splatter me.

We burst through the doors of the cafe.

The scene freezes. It's as though this is a moment from *The Magic Boomerang*, the television show where a young boy can stop time by launching a boomerang high into the air and freezing everything around him until it comes back.

With time stopped, I walk around the cafe and examine some of the customers. They seem to be all of furrowed brow. One woman is whispering into a man's ear as he's about to gobble down the egg and bacon mounted on his fork.

I walk around the counter, where two women are in a frozen conversation. One of them is looking over the other's shoulder. Another woman in a flowery pinafore is filling an urn from a boiling kettle.

I work out the trajectory of looks coming our way, trying to discern the levels of intrigue over straight-out judgement. Looks to be about seven-to-three in judgement's favour.

I return to my position within the family unit and we are back in real time. There are clattering noises and the sound of a woman's voice. She addresses my mum.

'Is it for the four of you, love?'

Eyes are darting around the room. Some stare in astonishment.

'Aye, that's right, love,' she replies.

Our clothes are dripping wet. 'Hang your coats up over there if you want. Still cats and dogs outside?'

'Buckets and spades,' my mum offers.

The rain does not stop, even after double egg and chips all round. I ask my dad if he knows what we're going to do now.

'Well, Barry lad... I did see an advert for the Odeon Cinema.'

My body begins to vibrate.

'Says there's a double bill at the moment of the, uh... what was it, Lil?'

She rubs her chin; our eyes widen. 'I'm not sure... was it the new Beatles film?'

'Oh yeah,' my dad says.

'Or was it the new James Bond film?'

'*Goldfinger*?' I shout out, a victory worthy of scoring an away goal.

My mum shushes me, leans in and says, 'Behave, you, or you'll stay in this bloody cafe for the rest of your life.' She raises her head and her voice. 'Can we get the bill, love?'

The waitress rubs her hands on her pinny, then heads towards the till.

'Right, I'm just popping to the little girls' room,' says my mum.

* * *

For a while now, I've been worried that I'm going blind in my right eye. If I cover my left then it's difficult to see. I don't want to mention it, as I think it'll make me even more of a burden than I am already.

It is strange, though, like somebody has poked me in the eye with a blunt stick. Shapes converge and there is no sharpness or focus on anything in particular as my brain tries to make sense of all the optical confusion.

My mum comes back from the toilet and notices me staring into space, with my right eye drifting inwards towards my nose.

'Will you stop your bloody squinting, Skenning Emma?'

I shoot her a look that says, '*Skenning Emma? Who's she when she's at home?*'

'Barry,' she says, pointing to my eye, 'something's not quite right here.'

I'm under scrutiny as the cafe, its sounds and its people swirl around my head.

My right eye drifts towards the middle again as I fail to control it. I can feel it shutting down until I become almost single-lensed, like a camera.

My dad and my sister stare at me. He seems perplexed as to what the problem is. She doesn't seem that interested at all.

'Can't see anything, Lil… Hang on, what's that?'

They all move in closer. I feel as though they're observing me from the same perspective as they did back at my birth.

My dad has noticed a stye on the lid of my right eye. My mum moves him out of the way to study me. She takes off her wedding ring and starts to gently rub the lid of my eye.

'There. That should take care of that.'

My eye drifts again.

As I turn away, stye stymied, she shoots a quizzical eyebrow at me that says, '*We are gonna get to the bottom of this, young man.*'

My sister tells my mum she's going to the toilet now. My mum tells her, 'Keep your hand on your halfpenny,' and winks at her.

Our Kid sees me trying to figure out if there's something provocative about that. I'm staring into space again when she returns.

'I might have to go again when we get to the cinema,' my mum says.

'How come?' I ask.

'Because, Big Ears, there I sat brokenhearted – paid a penny and only farted.'

'Right, come on then,' my dad says. 'Let's head for the hills.'

The bonnets reappear as we dodge puddles. I learn a new word from my Dictionary Dad: precipitation.

* * *

'Can we get popcorn?' I ask.

'We can all share one,' says my mum.

The dim light of the cinema offers up otherworldliness. Hushed tones herald the anticipation of something much bigger than this washout of a day. My dad's return with popcorn signals a total blackout as the massive screen now illuminates the entire room.

Flashing, distorted images quickly settle into the spiralling numbers four, three, two... Then a scene from ancient Greece glows from the screen: an amphitheatre with a flight of stairs, adorned with Ionic orders and roof, all white against a bright blue sky, framing the words 'PEARL & DEAN'.

Orchestral music swells...

This is a few years before the greatest twenty seconds of music to ever grace the screen, Pete Moore's 'Asteroid' with its futuristic hook of *'Pah-pah-pah-paaah pah-pah-pah-paaah pah-pah-pah! Pah-pah-pah pah-pah-pah-pah-paaah-yaaaaah!'*

Nonetheless, the scale of the screen, the level of volume and the feeling of being at the centre of a glamorous continental excursion take us to a world far away from the one we're used to.

Several adverts for various products grace the screen: Silvikrin shampoo; TSB banking; still images of a local tandoori restaurant; and then, my favourite, Hamlet Cigars, where a highwayman's shenanigans get thwarted but he doesn't seem to care. He takes out a packet of said cigars and an amazing piece of music begins: a version of Johann Sebastian Bach's *Air On The G String* played on jazz bass, drums and piano. The bass walks calmly as the highwayman lights up, the piano plays single-note figures and the drums, touched lightly, swing it in the coolest way possible as a voiceover says, 'Happiness is a cigar named Hamlet, the mild cigar from Benson & Hedges.'

The Pearl & Dean logo reappears to round off the adverts, accompanied by the sound of a scratched-up record fading into the distance. The screen begins to dim, and with our hearts in our mouths, we are plunged into total darkness. Out of this darkness a lion roars, crowned by the words 'Metro Goldwyn Meyer'.

At the first roar I am totally shocked, due to the sheer volume and the size of the lion. I am also thrilled to my bones.

A circular graphic scrolls across the screen.

A three-chord blast of music, ending on a blood-tingling low note, heralds a silhouetted spy (Bob Simmons) walking in the opposite direction.

The music now hooks into a four-note string loop with bongos, over which an electric guitar theme now plays.

It is just brilliant. The spy fires a gun, the screen bloodies, the graphic lowers and dies.

Then the film begins. Night. South American holdings surrounded by water.

The music breaks down from theme to score as James Bond appears in a wetsuit, complete with a duck on his head for undercover disguise as he swims to shore.

After getting rid of a patrolling guard, he breaks into the secured building and plants a bomb on some nitro tanks. Bond then discards the wetsuit to reveal a white evening suit; placing a rose into the lapel buttonhole, he slides into a nearby nightclub.

As he checks his Rolex the bomb blows, destroying an operation of which he declares, to a low-key cohort, that there will be no more 'heroin-flavoured bananas funding revolutions'.

Bond then goes to his hotel room (after being warned not to), where a dancer who was at the club is bathing.

They kiss.

He spies an assailant, reflected in the eyes of the dancer while kissing her.

He spins her around and she gets hit on the head, instead of Bond – who then throws his assailant into the bath. As the assassin grabs Bond's gun, 007 chucks an electric fire into the bath, killing his foe.

He then proclaims that the whole incident is 'shocking!'

The girl on the floor is coming to. Grabbing his jacket to leave, Bond further adds, 'positively shocking.'

I am already out of my tiny seven-year-old mind and the title sequence is only just about to begin. Out of the blackness once more comes the theme music by John Barry, still the most striking ever heard.

A golden hand carries double exposures of the villain of the piece, Auric Goldfinger, played by Gert Fröbe. It visually spells out the title of the film.

Producers Albert 'Cubby' Broccoli and Harry Saltzman take first credit, continuing in this lurid style as Shirley Bassey begins to sing 'Goldfinger'.

Bond, played by Sean Connery, also appears in double exposure, against a statuesque woman made of gold (Margaret Nolan).

The sequence continues, introducing Honor Blackman as Pussy Galore and Shirley Eaton, who plays Goldfinger's girlfriend, Jill Masterson.

Harold Sakata as Oddjob, Goldfinger's servant, drives through this stylised opening sequence, but the emphasis is on Bond. It establishes him as a sex hound while simultaneously linking him with heroic stunts and spectacular deaths.

The whole film is amazing.

My little life is changed forever.

I am stunned as the lights come up and I'm asked if I need a wee before the next film starts.

As far as I am concerned there is no next film. The images and music of *Goldfinger* have transported me out of the ordinary, out of the everyday, into another world I never thought could exist.

I pull a Golly token out of my pocket, stare at it and feel like I could do anything. That one day I could be the first Golly in space, or James Bond, or the man who makes the music, or the film.

As I sit in the car, the world seems to have completely opened up before me. All I have to do now is walk through a door to discover a whole new world of danger and excitement. This new knife-edge is where I feel I need to be, to truly live my life to the fullest.

* * *

I visit my step-gran with my mum. She lives alone at fourteen Shelley Grove, in Droylsden, a few miles east of the town centre, in a house that constantly smells of baking. The mood, as always, is uneasy.

After my mum's birth to another woman, my grandad, George Wright, put his foot down, declaring to his wife Lottie, 'The child is to grow up under our roof' – much to her chagrin. I choose to ignore stories

My mum, my step-grandma and my mum's half-sister Doreen,
around nineteen forty-six.

of how badly my gran always treated my mum, who, as a punishment,
was forced to remain in a cupboard under the stairs for long periods of
time. Lottie felt that this was justified.

On this day my cousin David is also visiting with his mum, Doreen,
my mum's half-sister. He also has a younger brother, Peter, who I've
met before but, being a bit younger than me, I've not really spoken
to much.

There is another family divide, not only by blood. The fact that my
mum is married to a black man is unacceptable – especially to David
and Peter's father. Ronald Frederick Bowler, ex-army, now a butcher,
worked his way up from slaughterman in an abattoir to cutting up
animals in his own shop by the time the boys came along. His position
on race relations (or lack thereof) means we can never visit David and
Peter, or Auntie Doreen; likewise, they can never come and visit us. My
gran's is like a neutral ground, where at least I get to see them and they
me – hence the tension.

My mum wages a kind of war between herself and my gran, with
Doreen looking on – acquiescent but offering support to her mum (her
real mum) in her gestures, not without the odd curt word.

41

My grandad George Wright (second left, back row), my mum (centre, back row), my aunt Doreen (second right, back row) and my step-gran Lottie (third right, front row) on a trip to Great Yarmouth, nineteen forty-eight.

I see something of myself in David. Like me, he is used to being on the receiving end of something which might destroy another person entirely: hurtful words that need to be instantly forgiven, in order for life to continue.

Even so, I eye him at a distance.

He is white and I am not, so I examine the differences between us. I don't want to get close to him, because I'm going to be the next James Bond, or John Barry Adamson, writing all the music and quite possibly starring in the films too, so I need to keep away from anything deemed 'normal', like a family, I tell myself.

I'm sure that if I were to share my dreams with him, with anybody for that matter, I would be instantly ridiculed and would experience a kind of humiliation. It's best I keep to myself and, let's face it – who needs all this family tension when I'll be off saving mankind, disarming nuclear missiles and the like?

I relocate to the front room. I've brought a pile of comic books with me for just such an occasion.

I plonk them on the floor and lean against a chair. The silence is incredibly calming, with only a grandfather clock keeping time and punctuating the silence every now and then. On the hour a bell tolls, reminding me that my own grandfather died a few years before I was born. I can see him, though – and is that an old, stale odour of pipe tobacco amidst the baking and pinafore smells?

I leaf through my comics and transport myself via *Captain America*, *The Amazing Spiderman* or *Superman* to other worlds that seem to fit my way of thinking.

These comic books satisfy my mind and make sense of everything. Alone and quiet, I can fantasise my way out of a general discomfort I find hard to describe. I want to join in with everybody, believe me, but... something always stops me from diving in. I'm always watchful, deciphering looks, moods and the way that people talk. I feel like I can

David and Peter outside their dad Ronald's butchers shop, nineteen sixty-nine.

see beneath what they are saying, to the truth about them. To the reality of what, in fact, they are *not* saying.

My cousin David walks in and sees the comics.

He asks if he can join me, sharing my discovery of escape.

I can see that we are the same in this moment.

We now both sit in silence with the clock ticking, occasionally tolling.

I look up every now and again to see if he is as serious as me about what we are doing: leaving the world behind, trading it for something else altogether.

By the look on his face, I can see that he is.

Chapter Five

The 1966 FIFA World Cup tournament was played in England between 11–30 July. It was the eighth World Cup, the first having been played in nineteen thirty. England defeated West Germany four–two in the final to win their first World Cup title; the match had finished at two–all after ninety minutes and went to extra time, when Geoff Hurst scored two goals to complete his hat trick, the first and – as of twenty eighteen – the only to be scored in a World Cup final, with spectators storming the pitch during the fourth goal.

England were the fifth nation to win the event, and the third host nation to win after Uruguay in nineteen thirty and Italy in nineteen thirty-four. Brazil were the defending champions but failed to progress from the group stage.

Matches were played at eight stadiums across England, with the final held at Wembley Stadium with its capacity of ninety-eight thousand, six hundred. The nineteen sixty-six event featured the highest number of teams of any international tournament to date, with seventy nations participating. Prior to the tournament, the Jules Rimet gold winner's trophy was stolen but recovered by a dog named Pickles, four months before the tournament began. The final, which was broadcast domestically by the BBC, was the last to be shown entirely in black and white.

* * *

'The Sun Ain't Gonna Shine Anymore' by the Walker Brothers cuts through this, the wettest of summer days, where boredom hangs like a dark cloud.

My sister yells at me to get out of her room, as she controls the radio these days and plays seven-inch singles on her Dansette portable record player.

I fly downstairs as my dad hurries himself from room to room. When I find him, he is bursting to express his feelings to somebody, anybody.

He haphazardly throws some items into a small suitcase.

'You just don't know what this means, Barry lad!'

Indeed, I don't.

I ask him, 'Are you going away, Dad?'

'Eh?'

'The suitcase. Are you going somewhere?'

'Not me, Barry lad.'

I breathe a sigh of relief.

'We are, though.'

'Eh?'

'Your uncle and aunt have invited us to Oldham to watch the match. England in the World Cup final – can you imagine that? It's going to be flipping amazing, son.'

I'm confused, as I thought we weren't allowed to go see them at their home. I ask, 'Will David be there too?'

My dad looks at me and offers a quizzical eyebrow. 'Oh, I see, you're thinking of your Aunt Doreen and David and Peter? No, we're not going there, son.'

'So who are we going to see?'

My dad tuts, then says the usual: '*Bwoy*, you nosey, y'know?' He doesn't pay much mind to my question. 'Don't worry about it, Barry lad. You'll get to know them after you meet them all.'

I look at his scar and wonder if this is the time to ask how he got it, as he's in a good mood. But maybe that's too much of a personal question. Might it cause him to think about something in his past that he doesn't want to?

I slouch off to my room and sit on the bed.

The Batman outfit I'm wearing reflects back to me in the mirror.

I am all-powerful in my disguise, invincible. And with an iced lolly stick stuck in the spokes of my bike, I'm ready to noisily 'bomb it' through the mean streets of Oldham, catch all the criminals and bring them back to the Gotham City of my mind, Moss Side police station.

Instead of keeping my disguise on, though, I have to put on shorts, a short-sleeved shirt and brown plastic sandals that I really do not like. We get into the car. I have no idea where Oldham is, but I go along with it, as my dad is the happiest I have seen him for quite a while.

My mum is in a good mood too, singing and flailing her arms around in the passenger seat to the Lonnie Donegan song on the radio, 'World Cup Willie':

He's World Cup Willie
We all love him too...

I have never been in a pub before.

The smell of stale beer and cigarettes is immediate and overpowering.

My new 'aunt and uncle', the landlord and landlady, greet us with excitement.

Through all the noisy business of the bar, I see the boy who turns out to be my 'other cousin', Mark, who just stares at me. He's several years old than me, and seems really angry about something.

'Mark, get over 'ere,' his mum says. He lurches towards us, to be told who I am and to look after me.

We leave the bar and go into the lounge, where at least it's quieter. Mark seems miles away, as my mum likes to say about people when they don't seem interested in anything you're saying to them.

I brought comic books for us and an Action Man, some Dinky cars and a replica James Bond Aston Martin DB5, complete with ejector seat, guns that fire from under the headlights and a shield that pops up to protect the back windscreen.

Mark offers a smile, but it doesn't seem to be about anything I've just told him. I think that as he's older, like my sister, it's difficult to find the same interests. Carol stopped playing cars with me ages ago. He seems like he can't be bothered at all.

The door bursts open and in come the grown-ups, dancing and laughing and singing 'World Cup Willie', while trays of food and drinks clatter around. The black-and-white television is turned on and commentator Kenneth Wolstenholme enthuses about the game ahead.

Mark suggests we go outside to the garden. We strike up a conversation about school and friends and television. He tells me his favourite programme is the wrestling: Saturday afternoons at 4pm on ITV, *World Of Sport*. I see why he is glum now. The BBC have taken over his world with the football, so he'll miss out on his weekly fare of Mick McManus and Jackie Pallo.

Mark wakes up somewhat as he describes the rules and personas of the game, a bit like my dad when talking about Manchester United.

'I can show you some of the moves if you like?'

'Alright, that sounds like a laugh.'

He immediately puts me into a headlock, while explaining how difficult it is to get out of such a manoeuvre. His arms squeeze my jaw and my neck, making it difficult to breathe. I am leaning forwards in his grip, so my balance is completely off. As he recalls a fight between two of his favourite wrestlers, I fear my legs will give way. He lets go and I rub my neck, take a deep breath and carry on listening to what he is saying. After all, we're making friends now. This I understand.

Mark talks of Jackie Pallo, blond hair tied back into a ponytail, and Mick McManus' jet-black hair. He seems to find this fascinating, playing with his own hair. I suspect he's imagining himself to be one of any number of professional wrestlers. He flexes his arms in front of himself and looks at the muscle building up under his shirt, his eyes switching from bicep to bicep. He talks about a particular fight as if he himself is one of the wrestlers in question. He describes the colour of the corner being blue, shouting out, 'Seconds out. Round two,' and making the sound of a bell, 'Ding ding!'

He grabs me and begins to wrestle me again. My nose is squashed against his chest and there is a mustiness about him. I realise from the headlock, and now this, that he hasn't washed for a while.

Mark goes on about 'half-nelsons', 'full nelsons', 'armbars', 'chicken wings' and 'the cradle'. He presses on, explaining falls, submissions and knockouts. He now has me pinned to the ground, his knees pressing heavily into my shoulders. I cannot move, and the more I struggle, the worse the pain is. I tell him to get off but he just grins and presses harder, asking me if I submit yet. I grin back to let him know that I know it's just a game – but okay, that's enough now.

He stares into me from above, spittle forming around his mouth. I'm not sure if my shoulders aren't going to snap as he asks me if I give in.

'Say you submit.'

He senses my resistance and presses me again. Harder.

'Say it.'

'I...'

He presses even harder, causing me to moan.

I find the stubbornness to stare him dead in the eye and say nothing, as though letting him know he can do anything to me and I won't give in.

His gaze narrows and he presses me for all his worth. I conclude that he is far more powerful than me and that this, in his mind, is not a game.

'Okay. I submit.'

He laughs out loud and then leaps off me. Holding his arms in the air, he circles me, making crowd noises and soaking up his imagined applause. He commentates on his own win: 'The winner by submission and champion of the universe...'

I can't breathe properly from the weight of him being on my chest for all that time. My shoulders feel like they did when I came back from the hospital a few years ago.

I turn over onto one side to help myself up. A single tear rolls down my cheek and I catch it with my shoulder, so as to hide it. I then turn fully face down and see a beetle on its back. It struggles to right itself and I know that if it stays like that, it will die. I flick the beetle over and it scurries off into the undergrowth. I manage to lift myself off the ground and stand up as Mark circles me like a vulture.

Mark's mum appears, shouting, 'C'mon, you two, the game is about to start.'

In my mind it already has, with Mark as the clear winner. Now it's me who has lost interest in everything. I let him go ahead of me so I can come back to myself. I'm not hurt that badly but, because of the way he didn't let up, he's no friend of mine. I decide to keep away from him for the rest of the day, as if I don't know him. Which is true, after all.

* * *

We settle down in front of the tiny black-and-white television in the lounge. England, managed by Alf Ramsey and captained by Bobby Moore, win the toss and elect to kick off. My dad is to the left of me and Mark's dad, in a white string vest, is to my right. Our mums come in and out with sandwiches and drinks. Behind me, near the window and almost behind the curtain, sits Mark. He bites his nails and spits them onto the floor.

After twelve minutes or so, a cross comes into the English penalty area which an England player misheads to one of the other team, who gets his shot on target. The shot goes in – making it one-nil to West Germany. My dad slaps his knee and turns away from the television. Mark's dad holds his arms in the air in disbelief

Not long after, the Germans concede a free kick, which Moore takes straight away, Geoff Hurst levels the score with a downward glancing header. My dad comments about them both being 'West Ham greats'.

After seventy-seven minutes, England win a corner. Alan Ball delivers the ball to Geoff Hurst, whose shot finds Martin Peters, who produces another shot which beats the German goalie from eight yards to make the score two–one to England. I turn to look at Mark, who can only grin and spit another nail out. His mum sees him and gives him a quick slap behind the ear. He acts like he's been beaten up and leaves the room with a '*What you looking at?*' crumpled face.

Germany are really going for an equaliser in the closing moments. Late on, England concede a free kick when big Jack Charlton goes up for a header with one of theirs. The kick hits the wall; the rebound falls to another German player, who shoots across the goal face. The ball deflects across the England six-yard box, the Germans move in and level the score at two–all, forcing the match into extra time.

Hurst turns on a sixpence and shoots from close range. The ball hits the underside of the crossbar, bounces down and is cleared. The ref is uncertain if it is a goal and consults his linesman, who indicates that it is.

One minute before the end of play, the Germans send their defenders forwards in a desperate attempt to score a last-minute equaliser. Winning the ball, Bobby Moore picks out the unmarked Geoff Hurst with a long pass, Hurst carries on running with the ball and scores, unbelievably, moments later. I jump around with my dad and my mum, and my 'auntie' comes rushing in, to see what all the fuss is about. Mark's dad is crying.

The final goal gives rise to one of the most famous calls in English football history, when the BBC's Kenneth Wolstenholme says: 'And here comes Hurst... Some people are on the pitch... They think it's all over, well, it is now.'

* * *

The mood in the room, the pub, the town and the whole country is one of complete ecstasy. A constant whirl of noisy happiness is all that can be heard. It's like all of our Christmases really have come at once. Everybody is just so overjoyed. My dad has a constant grin, when he's not bellowing out loud. My auntie is beside herself, drinking and dancing and pretending to be a Tiller Girl, off *Sunday Night At The London Palladium*, kicking her legs high into the air.

Trays of sandwiches pass by like cars on a motorway. The clinking of glasses is a continuous racket, along with songs of celebration. The pub fills up more as day bleeds into night.

I need to find my mum. I open the door from the lounge into the pub but can't get any further, as a sea of legs won't allow me to pass.

'Where you going?' Mark asks.

'To find my mum and dad.'

In the lounge is a jukebox that plays forty-five-rpm singles. It glows in the darkening room. Our Kid would love it.

Mark walks over and presses some of the buttons. He then leaves the room.

I walk over to the jukebox, which begins to awaken. A robotic arm pulls up one of the discs and places it in the centre. The sounds of humming and scratching anticipate what is to come next.

Trumpets blare out, playing a mariachi theme. (I worry that the volume is a bit too loud.)

Then a voice, loud and low, begins to sing:

Love is a burnin' thing...

I have never heard a voice like this before. I am transfixed by it and how it appears to be wrapped in a strange kind of darkness. The music

51

is light and bounces around the room, yet the voice is filled with a reflective doom.

And it burns, burns, burns…

Mark comes back into the room carrying a metal tray. On the tray there are six or so small drinking glasses, filled with a yellowy liquid. He has a couple of packets of crisps as well, which he throws at me.

'I saw your mum and she says I'm to look after you.'

He pushes buttons on the jukebox. The record starts again.

'Here, have one of these – it'll put hairs on your chest.'

'What is it?'

'Sherry.'

I have no idea what sherry is, but he is smiling and holding one of the small glasses with what looks to me like wee in them. He drinks it down in one.

'*Whooooo!*' Mark begins banging his hand on the arm of the sofa. Dust flies up as he tries to stay in time with the music. He sings along and holds one of the glasses in front of my face, staring at me like he did when I first saw him in the pub. He drifts out of focus as the tiny glass becomes as big as his face. The music echoes and reverberates. I take the glass and swallow the wee.

My mouth and chest burn as the music surges on. The noise of the bar fills the room as my mum opens the door. Before I have time to ask when we're going home, she is grabbed by the waist and pulled back into the bar, rolling her eyes and laughing.

She screams, 'Get off me, you daft 'apeth!'

The song plays again, and as it does, I notice the interval between the two mariachi trumpets as they harmonise what feels like a description of sentimental love. Meanwhile, Johnny Cash tells his dark tale of inevitability.

I drink another sherry. The room glows around the jukebox. I really want to go home now. I feel a bit sick too, and want my mum to come back. I stagger to the door of the pub and open it, but I'm pushed back by the sheer volume of people stood in front of me. I close the door again.

The jukebox stops. Mark stares at me in the silence, like he might want to fight me again.

'Your mum said to tell you that you're sleeping in my bed tonight, that okay?'

'Yeah?' I pause, my head swirling. This is the last thing I want – but there again, who doesn't like a sleepover? A chance to be away from the familiar and have a laugh.

'C'mon then.'

He leads me upstairs. The noise of the pub turns into dull thuds, muffled singsong and handclaps.

He opens the door. The bedroom is the size of the bed. Everything matches. Pale flowers, cold linen. The room totally smells of him. His must.

He closes the door. Walks around me. I open my duffle bag and get out my winceyette cotton pyjamas.

My Action Man looks up at me from the floor. I reach to pick it up.

From behind me, I can hear him getting into bed. 'You won't need that.'

I turn to face him. He has pyjama bottoms on but no top.

'Why?'

He slips under the sheets. 'Because I have a much better game we can play.'

I watch him and remember the way he pinned me to the ground when we played *World Of Sport* in the garden earlier.

'Not more wrestling?'

He laughs. 'No, not more wrestling.'

He looks at me more softly than he has all day. 'C'mere and I'll show you.'

I climb in bed, still dizzy from the sherry. I feel like we're finally becoming friends.

He puts an arm around me. His skin is warm beneath its mustiness as he pulls me towards him.

I look up at him and he seems lost in thought.

He says, 'Hey?'

'What?'

'You, er... ever sucked anyone off?'

I have no idea what he is talking about.

'It's really great fun.' He laughs again.

He pulls the front of his pyjamas down. His willy is big and floppy.

I begin to pull away, but that increasing wrestler's grip around my shoulders reminds me of his strength.

He pushes at the base of his willy with his free hand, causing it to get bigger and the skin to go back.

'Go on, try it.' His hand reaches up and grabs my neck as his willy stands up, all by itself. 'I said go on!'

I'm reminded of him pressing me to submit, as his hand now cradles the whole of the back of my head and he begins to push it gently but surely towards his stomach. He squeezes me a little harder now as my head is aimed further down, just past his bellybutton. Into my tiny mouth goes his fat and rather quite smelly World Cup willy.

* * *

The following morning, after brushing my teeth without looking at my reflection in the bathroom mirror, I get dressed. I button my shirt up, smooth myself down and walk downstairs as though in slow motion. My mum and my auntie laugh out loud about last night. The pub is a complete mess. Folk are running around cleaning it up and my dad is shaking hands with strangers. I walk beside him to the car but he doesn't see me. He throws the bags into the boot and I climb into the back. I don't hear the door close or notice any difference between the inside or outside of the car. We drive away and the family that we've just visited – who in fact are simply friends of my mum, not related to her at all, or to me – are huddled together and waving us goodbye. Mark smirks at me when his mother prods him to appear more affectionate, as they disappear into the distance. My mum sings along to the Lonnie Donegan song on the radio and I see myself as if from outside the car for the whole journey – as though looking through a cinecamera.

I dare not look back at the lens. The only sound I hear is that of the darkly churning reels, endlessly repeating a stalking filth that now plays over and over and over again in my mind.

Chapter Six

Within weeks of the World Cup final…

I'm wearing a pale pink, 'flesh-coloured' eyepatch, to help with a lazy eye (amblyopia) that became apparent in Morecambe last year. After being looked at by the optician earlier this year, it was decided I must wear said patch for several hours each day so that my eye corrects itself and gains strength.

I also have some glasses which look like the bottom of milk bottles. I hate wearing the patch, as when my one good eye is covered up, I can hardly see. Plus I look strange with it on, and feel even stranger.

I hold my right hand up in front of my face. I can see it but have to focus really hard, as I never see it clearly.

The background swims around without moving as my eye tries unsuccessfully to work out the distance between objects and colours, and the spatial relationship they hold with each other.

Too much of the patch and my head begins to hurt. I feel slightly sick so I take it off, but feel the need to close both of my eyes for a moment.

As I do this, shapes start to dissolve. The image of my hand fades into the distance as I begin to feel a bit better; it's safe to open my eyes again.

I walk up the stairs to visit my sister. I just want to be near her, I suppose. I'd love to tell her about what happened in Oldham, then she could tell my mum and dad and they could go there and 'sort it out'.

But my sister's in a mood, and tells me to get out as soon as I'm in the doorway.

I go to my own room, sit at the bed and stare at the wall. I'm considering which toy to play with when the door opens. My mum and dad stand there, with Our Kid in the background. She's crying but trying to pretend she isn't.

'Time to go, son,' my dad says.

'Go where?'

Terror leaps up and grabs me by the throat. I remember the sign from those vultures' pictures: 'SCHOOL FOR THE DISABLED'.

I begin to cry and tell him, 'You said I didn't have to go to that school. That I could go to a normal school because I was so brave. You *said...*'

My mum asks my dad, 'What's he on about?'

'I dunno,' he says

I cry out in a kind of defeat.

My dad looks me in the face and says, 'You not goin' to no damn disabled school.' He rises from his kneeling position and kisses his teeth.

My mind begins to race once more. I see flashes of the pub. Mark with his weight on my chest and then his willy in my mouth.

There's a ringing in my ears and my vision is so blurry. '*They don't know anything about Mark,*' I tell myself. '*None of it.*' I look to the floor and almost whisper, 'Not back to Oldham?'

My dad pauses for a very long time, leaving me on the edge of my seat. My sister turns away and my mum sighs.

'No, son. To the hospital.'

I look at my mum and she makes an apologetic face. I wonder why.

'C'mon, let's be 'avin' you, my love.'

'Don't worry, son, we're all coming with you.'

I want to ask if I'm in trouble for some reason, but I can't.

I also want to tell them about Mark, but I can't.

Nothing makes sense. '*Is it because I didn't say no to him?*' I think almost out loud.

* * *

We set off once more for Pendlebury Children's Hospital. Usually it's just my mum that takes me for check-ups, but here we are, all four of us. I must admit that all of us being here makes me feel safe and protected.

But I can't help wondering why Our Kid is so upset, still trying to hide her tears from me. '*Maybe she doesn't like hospitals,*' I reason with myself. I remember that, in fact, neither do I. Well, not much anyway...

As we arrive, the atmosphere is creepy. Sounds echo everywhere, whenever a kid raises his or her voice. The smell of the place pulls at my nostrils.

My mum chats to the receptionist. We can see kids with broken arms and legs; some others are in wheelchairs, wearing dressing gowns and pyjamas. All are with their parents, as though there was a big fight at school and they all had to come to the same hospital afterwards.

A nurse comes and asks us to follow her. We are taken to a ward where other children are. I wonder if we aren't visiting somebody – maybe one of my mum's friends' kids?

'If you'd like to get changed?'

She pulls a curtain around us. Only then do I notice that my mum's bag is not her usual one as she takes out some pyjamas and then a smaller bag. As she looks inside of it, I can see a new toothbrush and a tube of toothpaste.

'*What's happening?*' I ask myself. I'm a little concerned as to why I'm here. '*Surely not my arms again?*'

My dad helps me get undressed, his massive hands gently undoing my buttons. 'C'mon,' he says.

'If Mark has broken my arms, then I'll walk to bloomin' Oldham and give him what for,' as my mum might say.

I get into bed as my mum smiles at me, rubbing my hand. My dad tucks me in.

Then the curtain that was pulled around us flaps back open as two nurses appear.

'Right then,' one of them says, all smiley, 'what's your name, handsome?'

I look at my dad.

'Barry.'

'Barry? That's a nice name.'

She winks at my dad, out of sight of my mum, thank God.

'Barry, I'm just going to pop this into your mouth, okay?'

She produces a thermometer, flicks it up and down, then eases it in. She looks at the upside-down watch pinned to her uniform as the other nurse wraps something around my arm, pumping a rubber ball which begins to squeeze my arm tightly, deadening it for a bit.

Then it deflates and my arm comes back to life. The first nurse takes out the thermometer and reads it, mumbling to herself.

'There. All done,' says nurse number two. 'You can leave this lovely lad with us now, he'll be fine.'

I feel a bit odd as they're saying all these nice things about me. At the same time it feels good, as lately I've not been feeling so good about myself.

I look for my mum and dad to say, '*No, that's fine – we'll stay with him.*' Instead, they ruefully rise and sigh. Once more, my sister begins to cry.

My mum gives me a look that says, '*I wish I could do more to help you right now, son – but I can't.*' I'm now getting more than a tad worried.

The curtains are quickly thrown back by the nurses. The knowledge that everybody is about to leave – except me – takes hold.

I begin to panic. My breathing becomes faster and I'm welling up. I want to ask them not to leave me here, or at least maybe my mum can stay?

'You'll be alright, love.' My mum holds my hand again and kisses me on the cheek. 'We'll be back tomorrow.'

My dad pushes his face in mine. Head of the herd, he looks me in the eye and nods to me to be brave.

The ward is really big. At one extreme is a huge window which seems to take up that whole end of the room.

I turn and watch my parents and sister walk away, towards the other end of the ward. Towards the exit. They fade into the distance as the light in the room also begins to dim.

* * *

Hours seem to pass before some electric lights come on, first around the nurses' station, and then up and down the ward as we have our tea.

I keep seeing my parents and Our Kid leave, over and over again, every time I look towards the nurses' station. Now I know I did something really bad in Oldham, and so here I am – in loads of trouble. Who to tell? Who to ask if I'm right?

The clocks go back this weekend. I wish I could. I wish I could go back and change everything. I wish I had a magic boomerang and could stop time. I'd go back in time and run downstairs, tell my mum and dad that I'm sick and can't go to Oldham, World Cup or not. Then Our Kid could stay with me and we could have listened to music all day.

'Right, everybody, get yourselves tucked in. Lights out.'

The electric light fades to nothing as the moonlight from the window illuminates the whole room.

Some of the kids who were screaming and running around now dart into their beds. A nurse stands at the end of the ward, ready to shush anybody who says a single word.

We all sit in silence for a moment.

'Goodnight, children.'

'Goodnight!'

There is a flash of lightning.

The room lights up momentarily, causing the kids to gasp out loud.

After a few more moments, thunder begins to rattle and rumble. The kids begin chattering away.

There's another, much bigger, much brighter flash of lightning. Some of the kids begin to call out loudly to each other and a chant begins.

'ONE!'

'TWO!'

'THREE!'

Then louder, as more kids join in.

'FOUR!'

I look towards the nurses' station. Two nurses smile and shake their heads at each other. Then they look around at me and stop smiling altogether.

'FIVE!'

On five, there is an enormous thunderclap and all the kids cheer and laugh. Except me.

Another bolt of lightning and the shadow of the Victorian window-frame, which is arced around the top, leans across the whole ward. Then it flickers and crashes with the lightning as all the kids start screaming.

The chanting begins again, slow and determined.

'ONE!'

'TWO!'

'THREE!'

'FOUR!'

'FIVE!'

'SIX!'

Another huge explosion of thunder. This one seems to envelop the whole ward, which sends the other kids into an absolute frenzy. Some jump out of bed and run to the window, yelling. Some dive under the covers.

I realise that if we get to TEN, then the whole hospital might blow up. The storm is a great excuse for the other kids to show off their free will; they no longer care about being told off by the nurses, who carry on watching, laughing, yet still giving me worrisome looks. I start to shake as the next bolt changes the ward to a stark black-and-white nightmare. The chanting becomes faster and even more energetic.

'ONE!'
'TWO!'
'THREE!'
'FOUR!'
'FIVE!'

'SIX!'
'SEVEN!'
'EIGHT!'

Tears roll down my face at the loudest thunder I've ever heard. The scene is a gruesome free-for-all as kids scream and jump on their beds, pulling each other about. I sink beneath the sheets and wait for it.

Wait for it...

* * *

It is morning and everything seems quite normal. The hospital is still here and, more surprisingly, so am I. There seems to be little or no damage to the structure of the ward. The big window at the end of the room remains intact.

It feels to me somewhat like an episode of *The Avengers* television show – where all the stuff that was happening has been revealed by Steed and Mrs Peel as some sort of elaborate hoax, leaving them free to sip champagne and wait for Mother to call.

The smell of breakfast punctures the musty atmosphere. The kids that were going nuts are sat up in their beds. Some read comics, some eat cornflakes or let the fat off the bacon slip down their throats.

I'm starving. I look to see if I'll be getting breakfast anytime soon.

The hospital radio plays all the hits and 'Hold Tight!' by Dave Dee, Dozy, Beaky, Mick & Tich blasts through the ward. I take on the song's energy and worry seems to walk out of the door.

Two men dressed in white walk towards me. They are pushing a cart. At last, breakfast.

They stand beside my bed now. The breakfast is covered with a white tea towel. One of them asks me how I am.

'Fine, thanks.' I will be, after I bash the heads off boiled eggs and get some cornflakes down my neck.

'Good lad.' He pulls back the tea towel to reveal a metal and glass hypodermic needle, which sits in a shiny, odd-shaped tray.

My eyes widen as I remember these two men now. From when they had their black coats on and came to the house with their built-up shoes and brochures.

My fear comes back.

I don't know what this is and I want my mum.

He holds the needle up and a tiny droplet of liquid escapes, running away down the side.

My mood changes. I smile inwardly because I now understand that very soon, like James Bond, I will be strapped to a table with my legs far apart. A laser will gradually creep up between them, threatening to split me apart unless I admit my crime.

My new mission is to say nowt.

He moves up next to me. 'Right. This will make you go to sleep and you'll be fine after that.'

'*But I've just woken up?*' I think to myself.

'Can you take your arm out of the sleeve of your pyjamas?'

The other man now smiles at me, which I assume means, 'We've got you now, there's no escape. The fireworks you saw last night weren't the end, my friend, they were just the beginning...'

'Sure,' I say, sounding really unsure.

The needle goes into my arm. I drift into another world as the hospital radio DJ announces:

'I'm going to play a special song for a young lad by the name of Barry Adamson. The song is requested by his sister Carol. She says to wish you all the best and she'll be there waiting for you when you're back on the ward.'

I – I love the colourful clothes she wears
And the way the sunlight plays upon her hair

That churning, phasing organ is so light as the Beach Boys' 'Good Vibrations' permeates the whole scene. Carol Kaye's bass figure, orchestrated high up the scale, comprises offbeat, plucked figures subtly beneath an intro and first verse combined.

As the needle is pulled out of my arm, I see Our Kid and her smile and wish she was here.

I hear the sound of a gentle word
On the wind that lifts her perfume through the air

A choir of woodwind surrounds the lead voice, holding the chord as a flute figure descends. Drums pepper the introduction and a tambourine cheekily leans into the gap between the beats. I nod to myself when the stomping unexpectedly takes the chorus beyond the realms of what seems possible:

I'm picking up good vibrations
She's giving me excitations
(Oom bop bop good vibrations bop bop
Excitations bop bop)

An eerie sound plays on a bizarre instrument, a theremin, which manipulates soundwaves by hand gestures. It plays a five-note figure as basses and cellos modulate a six-note pattern over four beats. The backing singers assuredly validate the song's sentiment by adding the words 'bop bop' to the line. They're telling us this is a *very good thing.* It lifts itself up further by changing key, not once but twice, reasserting itself even more.

I look down upon the ward from way up high as I float around. I'm becoming the singer in the second verse. The other kids and the nurses and the two men wave to me. I wonder how they can see me, but if they can, then all of this must be very real. And there is no pain in my body. No pain.

Close my eyes, she's somehow closer now
Softly smile I know she must be kind
When I look into her eyes
She goes with me to a blossom world

The chorus plays again for them all to sing along to, before a departure heralded by a fairground piano trips us into somewhere else. The theremin plays low as the choir builds upon itself.

I don't know where but she sends me there
(Ooh my mind what elation)

The song breaks down completely and unexpectedly, with a church organ and maracas keeping the beat.

Gotta keep those lovin' good vibrations a-happenin' with her

The bass steps in and walks beside the vocal and the maracas. A homeward-bound harmonica figure marches into the distance by way of an audacious fadeout. The song would seem at this point to be over, but a chorale of voices blares out a single chord and then pauses. Then the chorus doubles up with extra voices:

Good good good good vibrations
(I'm picking up good vibrations)
Good good good good vibrations
She's giving me excitations...

The cello figure is made louder and the vocal melody is now played on the bass. This comes to an extraordinary full stop by way of a vocal line, a mere utterance which turns into a brand-new outro section:

Na na na na na, na na na
Na na na na na, na na na (Ba da da, duh da, da)

This figure becomes almost religious, accompanied by gospel-like voices which suggest the highest point has been reached. The drums come back in; the cellos and theremin play us out; the bass plays the chorus line to sum up all that has gone before.

The song fades out... the world fades in.

* * *

I slowly open my eyes.

Above me, filaments of light buzz and glower out of the darkness. Figures move around in a blurry slow motion, amidst chattering and whispers.

I feel the need to get up and go to the toilet, but I can't seem to raise myself off the bed. Lifting my head feels strange too. Maybe I should call out for a nurse?

I decide I'll get up and walk to the nurses' station, to see if I can get something to eat as well. It feels like ages since I ate anything.

I begin to lift myself off the bed but nothing happens. I pull the sheet back and see that I'm wrapped in a plaster cast, which starts under my arms.

64

As I pull the sheet back further, I see that the cast goes all the way down to my ankles – with a 'witch's broom' between my legs, just like the good doctor said at my birth. There's also an opening around my willy and my bum.

My mum, dad and sister are walking towards me. My sister is still crying. I wonder if she's actually been this way since yesterday.

I begin to sob a little too now as I realise I'm locked in a jail made of plaster. I wait for the moment to tell my mum that I'm really, really sorry and ask her to forgive me.

'Sorry for what? Don't be so bloody daft.'

I cast my eyes over my plastered white body.

'C'mere,' says my mum.

She cradles my head. I pop one eye open and see my dad as he looks down at the cast, trying unsuccessfully to keep himself together as he swallows several waves of sorrow.

Chapter Seven

Me at home post-operation, nineteen sixty-seven
(as portrayed by actor Leo Tetteh).

The theme from the US television show *Branded* blares out across the room.

The drums roll ominously as Union soldiers march across the parade ground of the cavalry fort. Six-foot-five Chuck Connors (as Captain Jason McCord) stands tall and erect, his face expressionless, as a colonel (played anonymously by John Howard) mercilessly strips McCord's insignia and buttons from his uniform. The colonel breaks the captain's sword over his knee, pointedly throwing the two pieces outside the fort.

Court-martialled out of the service, McCord stoops to retrieve the broken sword and walks away into the desert. He decides, as the solitary survivor of a massacre, to keep silent about its real causes and preserve the memory of his revered General Reid – who was the real coward. He also hopes to prevent further Red Indian hostility.

My mum asks me if I'll be okay as I tuck into a Sherbet Fountain. This is a yellow cardboard tube of zingy sherbet with a liquorice straw poking out of the top.

I glance down at the paper bag beside me on the side table. Perched between my Action Man's legs are two double lollies (chalky, fruit-flavoured lollipops) and a packet of Refreshers.

The *Branded* theme song plays out, and I don't yet realise I'm alone as a huge gloop of sherbet slides down my throat.

A gunfight in a saloon sees the local sheriff killed. The townsmen stand but do nothing, despite a lone woman's pleas. She takes the sheriff's gun and marches into the saloon. McCord turns the sheriff's body over, which gets the attention of the townsmen. Inside the saloon, a young punk asks the deputy if he wants to try his luck.

The sherbet dip is becoming all wet and the straw is clogged. I carefully undo the package and make sure nothing falls out, suck the sherbet from the outside of the liquorice and then split it into two, licking the remaining sherbet from inside and chewing on the liquorice.

The lone woman stands now with a gun fixed on the punk, explaining that she knows this guy killed her husband. McCord steps in and takes the gun from her. He challenges the gunman and shoots him dead. The townsmen want him to be sheriff now.

The yellow packet is now open on my cast, which serves as a table across my chest. I'm in two minds whether to pour its contents down my throat or to make it last as long as I can.

McCord offers them two weeks. The lone woman explains that she was married to the sheriff who was killed. As the new sheriff, McCord will become the target of every gunman around.

With the liquorice all chewed up and gone, I decide to wet my forefinger and stick it into the sherbet. It's a sherbet magnet which I suck all the remainder from.

McCord sets about enforcing the law by removing the guns of all those who want to impose their own gun law on him. He's reminded that his time isn't long as a crowd builds to await the arrival of the father of the punk he killed. The bereaved dad challenges the new sheriff and tells the whole town the story of McCord's cowardice.

A sherbety finger enters my mouth. The remainder has been scraped up onto my finger, now serving as a spoon.

McCord tells the father to get out of town – which he does, although he also leaves McCord's reputation in tatters. The townsfolk want him gone and find new ways to challenge him, calling him a 'sneak up'. The punk's father sends a note saying that tonight he'll take on McCord. McCord quits as sheriff and tells the father he is leaving town, but not before a gunfight. McCord wins and becomes a hero in their eyes. But he says he's no hero at all, before leaving town...

The theme song plays out as I listen for the sounds of Lily, Carol or Barry. But none of them are in the room.

The cast is itchy, around the top of my legs on each side and in the middle of my back. I wish it had hinges, like a door, so that I could open it and move around, walk about even – or like my mum often does, pop to the shops.

That's what she said she was doing anyway. Is that her in the kitchen?

'Are you sure you're going to be okay?'

When did she say that? Hang on... *did she even say that at all?*

I'm convinced I hear her chatting to herself in the kitchen, her slippers gliding across the floor as she hangs onto them, lest they fall off – which sometimes they do, when she exclaims, 'Bugger!'

'Mam?'

I listen past the telly – try to listen further afield.

'Mam?'

I grab a double lolly but can't get the wrapper off as fast as I want to. The sides of my legs are itchy again and I want to close them together, but I can't. I want to look around the house, but I can't.

I eventually undo the lolly's taut wrapping from underneath. Finally I get the two-tone dome into my mouth, dragging my teeth along the chalky surface till it breaks down. I become absorbed in this act, like my life somehow depends on it.

The *Black & White Minstrel Show* is now on the telly.

Something hits me in the gut. Behind all the smirking and singing is something else that arouses anger. It's as though I'm looking at myself but not me at all. As though the perception of me is that I'm some kind of... joke?

Or is it that I have qualities these men must try to ape by wearing dark make-up and wigs, in order to show their appreciation of me and those like me – my dad in particular?

I don't know. I'm confused by the whole thing.

My mum comes back from the shop. I loosen my grip on the lollipop. She throws her bag on the couch and comes over to me

'Eh, what's the matter, love?'

I try to hide what is inside. 'Nowt...'

She walks over to the television and turns it off in a huff, just as those Black and White Minstrels sing 'I Wish I Was In Dixie' with a parade of showgirls.

These white men with burnt cork on their faces put on a great show alright. But now, something in my stomach (maybe the sherbet) causes me to feel nausea. I have this pain and shortness of breath, as though there's not enough air in the room for me, and the minstrels, and the showgirls, to breathe.

My mum stares at me as I hold the broken remnants of the lolly and stick in my hand. I look at the lolly as though it's just appeared out of nowhere.

'Right, I think we'd better start getting you outside.'

* * *

Days later, there is a commotion at the front door; multiple voices, including my mum and dad's. I try to listen to what's being said, just as the door closes and the sound of the street is scooped away with a slam.

'It's bloody ginormous!' says my mum.

'I know. Well, it's better than being stuck in front of that bloody television all day,' offers my dad.

'Where's it gonna sit?' she asks.

My dad looks around for a solution. 'We'll just have to leave it here.'

I am picked up and carried to the corridor, where there is indeed a ginormous, almost coffin-like wooden pram. It fits my cast like a glove, both in width and length. Bespoke, I guess, is the word I'm looking for.

'Made to measure, like a suit,' my dad says, reading my mind and winking at me.

I am regally carried and rested on a bed of pillows and blankets, covered in a thick, crocheted cream blanket.

My dad glows with pride. 'That fits him nicely.'

I realise that he and the lads at work have crafted my personal chariot themselves.

With the cast hidden, me and my mum venture outdoors.

There is no hiding from the late October sunshine as I adjust to the natural light. Being royalty in my own mind, I wave to all and sundry as people ogle at the size of what is essentially just an oversized pram.

My mum's expression is one of ice. Pushing the pram brings a certain kind of attention beyond what she is used to. She is quite eloquent about where folk can 'shove it'.

We reach Embden Street School and push through the gate, where all at once the children surround me, gazing at the pram in awe and wonder.

I look around all their faces as the noise becomes cacophonous. I catch one face, the only one who doesn't think at this point that I'm worthy of such attention.

'Who are you?'

'I'm Barry.'

'I'm Willie Trotter.'

Willie Trotter calls out to some other kids, then runs away to get on with whatever game they were playing. I am transported out of the school.

The camera rises high above us and then the scene fades out. As does the soundtrack of the kids' voices and their laughter, echoing into the distance.

* * *

Time passes so slowly.

I have an itch that's unbearable, right in the middle of my lower back. My mum and dad flip me over and she slides a knitting needle down inside the cast, to try to scratch the itch.

70

Almost, but not quite.

I'm wriggling inside, dying to get out, like a caterpillar whose time is long overdue.

'Let's get you back to the hospital,' she sighs, ever so slightly.

I'm in the hospital now, flipped over like a sausage at a barbecue. I see a nurse with what we might call a pizza cutter, hand-held in the same way but plugged into the wall so that the cutting bit whirs around like a dentist's drill.

I feel the pressure where the square of cast is being cut away. I hope she doesn't open me up like a tin of beans. Finally, the drill stops and a waft of air touches my back for the first time literally in weeks. I reach back and have a good old scratch, overdoing the sounds of relief for my captive audience.

The nurse says, 'While I've got you here, I might as well have a look at your scars.'

Flipped back over again, as my back panel is already removed, she begins cutting an oblong shape at the side of my upper thigh: operation site number one of two. The pizza cutter whirs at high speed, throwing dust into the air as she carves away as if excavating for buried treasure. I imagine myself to be Tutankhamun.

'Right then, let's see what we've got here.'

'*Ohhhh!*' They both jump back and my mum covers her nose. 'What the bloody 'ell?'

'It's okay, they've just become a bit infected. I'll take the stitches out and redo them.'

I hear my mum whisper to my dad, 'It bloody stinks.'

I wish I had a Refresher chewy bar, or some Fruit Salads and Black Jacks.

After the stitches are redone and the area cleaned, I'm ready to go home. An appointment is made to come back a few weeks later and have the whole thing removed.

* * *

Come the day, I lie in wait in the waiting room. I see a train of other kids with broken arms and legs, splints and crutches and slings. Then there's me with my cast signed by the Embden Street kids, about to be cast off forever. My excitement, shared by my mum, rises as each glum-faced kid hobbles into the nurse's room, where the now familiar buzz of the pizza cutter assures us we're definitely in the right place.

The first kid, with the broken leg, has a plaster cast billowing cotton wool from above his knee, where he's clearly been picking at it. After being in the other room for what seems like no time at all, he walks past us with only a slight limp and a grin as wide as a street. His mum wipes tears of what was once apprehension but is now joy from his face.

With most of the arms and legs done with, I am the last-but-one. The kid with the broken arm in a sling rifles through books and toys and tosses them onto the floor, his mum paying no mind. Nodding in my direction, she says, 'Be glad to get rid of it, I bet?'

A nurse appears. 'Barry Adamson?'

The nurse and my mum carry me as the other mother looks on, slightly incredulous. I am placed under blinding light on a metal table. As before, the cutter whirs into life again. To my relief, the witch's broom is immediately cut in two. No more will that particular spell be cast upon me.

Everybody in the room seems to understand this. From the underarm of the cast, I'm sliced down the right side from chest to ankle, and then the other side is also cut.

The nurse smiles. 'Almost there now.'

With the top of the cast removed and the bottom pulled out from under me, the moment of truth arrives as I'm lifted onto the floor.

I am naked and shrivelled up like an old man. I seem a lot thinner than I remember. My skin is completely dry and flaked. I'm quite embarrassed by that and can feel eyes upon my body.

I feel all wobbly as my mum holds her arms out to me and the nurse lets go of mine. I stand amidst the bright lights and white specks of plaster dust, with PJ Proby singing the song 'Somewhere' in the distance.

I attempt to take one small step for man, but fall forwards, crashing to the ground.

The nurse and my mum pick me up. My mum says nothing, swallowing her expectations.

The nurse explains that I'll need my strength to build up all over again because of the length of time in the cast, 'which is very different to a broken arm or a broken leg'.

She gives my mum a comforting smile and a series of exercises she can help me with.

The other kid, the one with the broken arm in the other room, yells out, 'Yeah!' as his cast is removed. This is followed by much clapping and cheering.

Chapter Eight

The white men with their jauntily angled flat caps – some bespectacled or with Woodbine cigarettes protruding from their gobs – move in. They wear billowing denim trousers and tweed jackets over light plaid shirts.

They smirk to each other as the wrecking balls and spades do their work. Dust begins to rain on what once was deemed unfit to reside in – and now definitely is. The place that was once our uncomfortably comfortable dwelling at Upper Medlock Street, Hulme.

'They're getting rid of the lot.'

'About bloody time an' all…'

Our suitcases are packed, standing stoically on the last chunk of pavement we can find. We look up at my dad for strength and guidance as he surveys all that he is about to leave. Having mastered a way of life that has seen him shift from total outsider, man of colour, a gentleman to be feared rather than trusted, he is now almost a part of what we call 'society'. He is accepted enough to be acceptable, even to some degree by himself.

His six-foot-odd frame is rooted to the spot as he murmurs blue murder beneath his breath.

The focus shifts to my sister who asks me, aged nine, what I think about The Beatles' new double EP, *Magical Mystery Tour*…

The title track has a now typical Beatles-esque opening, with piano and guitar chords supporting a brass-band figure over a called-out

74

announcement. Ringo hits a joyous beat, setting up the song for the trip we're about to take:

Roll up
Roll up...

The vocals begin, shifting and phasing over the so solid backbeat. The feeling is one of disorientated anticipation, due in particular to the phasing effect on the vocal.

Phase shifting was first achieved using tape recorders, but by now is done largely with electronics. A phase shifter splits the signal and alters one part relative to the other, so that when they are recombined there is that weird swooshing sound caused by interference between the two parts, like the drums in 'Itchycoo Park'.

A flanger adds delay circuitry to create more pronounced effects, heard mainly in psychedelic music. Rhythmic phasing involves parts playing against each other where the beats go in and out of sync over time.

This effect adds to the experience of movement. There is a motion which affects the brain and creates a slightly churning sensation in the stomach. It's a kind of satisfying apprehension which attests to the movement that is about to take place in our lives.

My memory is recording it like splendid Super 8 colour film stock. Walls begin to crumble as the good folk of Hulme move from coughing to clapping. The dust swirls, becoming sparkly now, creating a luminous flight path where we begin our ascent. We're on a magic swirling ship of the mind.

Our lungs fill up with air and we are carried off; swirling around the clapping crowds, me and Our Kid's eyes are wide open. My mum gives a regal roll of the wrist as she looks down on her thronging mass.

The Beatles' song restarts, with the opening repeated. At a cruising height of thirty thousand feet, it changes speed and floats for a further four bars, with one more added to reorientate and establish a new, much slower tempo. (Most likely an edit of another version that was equally brilliant.)

We look behind us as the digger men strut in line beside their machines like soldiers. They throw their caps into the air and catch them, bowing to the womenfolk who spin around. A glimpse of stocking can drive these workmen into survival-of-the-fittest mode. They leap into the air in unison, make exaggerated gestures and step away from the scene as the dust begins to settle. Meanwhile, The Beatles' magical mystery tour continues to echo in the background.

The song comes to an end but the music continues as the clouds part. In waltz time a piano mulls around, leaving us to ponder our future long after the music has faded.

There's a stillness as we descend, our feet finally setting foot in front of number nine, Longport Avenue, Withington.

We see families appear at their front lawn gates. They point and speak to each other from behind their hands. The scene is hazy despite an electronic soundtrack, suggesting the arrival of an unfamiliar species in a world that has been without change for quite some time. Which, in and of itself, creates a curiosity among the people who are already here.

I look at my dad and see how black he really is, set against this new vista of whiteness. A burnt effigy of the beautiful and the damned, he lifts his head and stands tall. Some of the women are blushing; some of the men are suggesting that they go back inside now, arms around the kids. Dying to take them away, take them today…

My mum wades into the womenfolk, to make herself welcome and, no doubt, to mark her territory for anyone who'd even think for a minute that her man could be taken. Captivating and charming, she skilfully reads every thought, word and gesture of her newfound friends – offering kindness, support, but at the same time sending a *woe betide you* message that comes across as a sardonic interest in others. She is dizzying and dazzling in her approach, knowing when to pull and push at exactly the right time.

I smile at one of the girls about my age and she exposes her buckteeth, smiling back at me from her freckled face. I feel a warm glow inside as she introduces herself as Pamela.

* * *

Withington, although only a few short miles away from Hulme and Moss Side, looks and feels like another country. Our new house is testimony to this, beginning with a front garden, ten feet square, and a privet hedge. To the right is a pathway that divides the house next door and leads onto a ginnel, a narrow passage between houses. Walk down here and you arrive at the back of the house, where there is another garden, bigger than the front one. Then, turn left and you are at the back door that leads into the kitchen. Behind this is the living room, with a front door on the right that leads to the street, nearby, a stairway going up to three bedrooms and a bathroom.

Mine and my mum and dad's bedrooms face the street, while Our Kid's room, massive, looks out onto the back garden.

Mine is known as the boxroom as half of it's taken up by a boxlike shape. I'll never find out what it's for, but it has a solid top and concrete base. It just stands there, three or four feet square in dimension.

We all meet upstairs, coming out of our respective rooms, with mock-royal affectations.

'After you.' 'No, after you.' 'No, really – *after you.*'

We all crack up laughing as my mum swans down the stairs, holding an elongated cigarette holder.

'Eh, our Barry! Found this the other day. Whaddya think?' We laugh.

* * *

I create a map of the area. Longport Avenue is situated between Goldbourne Avenue at one end and Elmstead Avenue at the other. The avenue bends and there is a passage leading to Whitchurch Road, which connects Goldbourne Avenue again at one end and Meltham Avenue at the other end, a short walk from Elmstead. Whitchurch Road finishes at Princess Road at one end, with its ginormous Hough End Fields, and at the other there is Burton Road by Withington baths. Burton Road leads into Withington Village. These are my chosen perimeters.

I glide into Longport Avenue.

With my legs less gammy, I observe my realm and decree: 'This is my manor and my kingdom. It is from where I shall rule my people. Ye shall all be beholden unto me, for I am the King.'

I carve the initials 'KBA' (King Barry Adamson) into the garden gate and get a right old crack round the lughole for doing so.

Later, that day, by way of retaliation, I work out that I can use the blackberries and raspberries that grow at the bottom of the garden to fake my own death. Squeezing the juice all over my face, arms and legs, I lie on the kitchen floor. I'm simply amazed that everybody just

Me, Longport Avenue, nineteen sixty-eight.

walks past me, or over me, without noticing their King in such dire need.

The next few months see me walking much better. I'm also attending a new school: Old Moat Junior, situated on what was, in eighteen forty-five, the site of Withington Old Hall. No trace remains of the old house but the remnants of the moat are under the school in Old Moat Lane.

In the same way that Withington, with its noble heritage hanging around its neck, seems a world away from the one I've been used to, so do these kids.

I love them all.

Immediately.

They shine.

The girls smell so nice and they are all beautiful. They also have the greatest names:

Alison Beggs.
Carla Mellor.
Nina Kachinszky.

On the first day I fall head over heels in love with them all. My mind is totally preoccupied with them, as much as it is with all the day's

Miss Doody's class photo, nineteen sixty-eight.
Me, second row from the back, far right.

interactions and revelations. They seem untouchable, each in their very own way.

All of them are Super Brains. I gawp at them idiotically as they waft around in their own worlds, protected from us stumbling, bumbling boys. Their lofty demeanour only enflames my already heady mix of reverence, adoration and a certain idea of servitude.

Us lads bond over similar jumpers and playground fights. I take on Tony Martin, that big blond guy in the middle of the second row from the back with the white V-neck.

As we fight, I notice his cheeks flush and a flash of fear that I'd have bet our house on him never ever knowing. He's revealing his vulnerability. My compassion ramps up and I worry it could cost me the fight, stopping me going in for the kill.

Miss Doody (on the left, arm constantly bandaged) separates us and clips me around the ear. She orders me to stand behind the lines that form in the playground, our prerequisite for heading back under her control.

I march back, thinking about Karen Hutchkinson, Julie Stewart, Carole Crump.

The Chris Montez song 'The More I See You' becomes the soundtrack to my years at Old Moat Junior School. I daydream that I'm singing it to the girls as I dance my way through the playground:

EXT. OLD MOAT JUNIOR SCHOOL PLAYGROUND – DAY

BILLY OLDBURY picks out some notes on the vibraphone as the vista widens to show all the kids in the playground: BARRY FITZGERALD nonchalantly strums along on guitar as KAREN HODGKINSON hits the drumkit.

BARRY ADAMSON, charming and ever so charismatic, dances his way past the school gates as the introduction plays out. The lads in his year look up, somewhat reverential of his dashing good looks and sharp dress. They clap in unison along to the beat, nodding to each other, conceding that Barry has *it* over anyone else.

Form tutor MISS DOODY is on the piano. CLOSE UP on her hands as she moves across the keys with dexterity, a jazzy lilt to her style. She sends Barry a wink to let him know this is where the vocal comes in. Barry turns on his heel and sings directly to camera:

The more I see you
The more I want you...

CLOSE-UP on ALISON BEGGS as she gives Barry one of her famous 'Who do you think you're looking at?' looks as he circles her. But as he continues singing, she breaks into a smile.

Barry turns his attention to the *wondrously beautiful* CARLA MELLOR, who turns away from him in mock disgust as the song plays on. Barry feigns a broken heart, and so she starts to warm to him.

Miss Doody thumps the piano, rounding off the sequence. We recall the story of how Chris Montez & co decided to shift the key up a tone and, instead of more words (because none were written), to sing:

La, la, la, la, la
La, la, la, la, la…

PREFECTS spill out of the toilets, dancing and clapping. Then they stand behind Barry as all the kids do the same dance. They coolly keep time to the beat as the camera follows Barry slipping out of the school gates to resume a 'normal life'. He looks back on all the singing and dancing and salutes everyone, before turning away and heading off into the distance.

FADE OUT.

* * *

I walk home down Old Moat Lane, slip into Doncaster Avenue, then shimmy down Whitchurch Road and down the passageway that is my gateway to Longport Avenue.

As I reach the end of the passage, I glance up at the Morans' house and wonder what Billy and Pauline are up to. There is a smell of stale biscuits creeping down their stairs as Pamela Butcher, she of the freckles and buck teeth, says hello to me.

We exchange awkward but sweet stories. I document how we've been getting on since we moved here.

'Better go in, me tea's on the table.' She flushes bright pink and I notice her knees turn slightly inwards as she walks away in a frilly skirt and blue cardigan with white sandals.

I turn and wave to Ken, the haemophiliac next door, and wonder how it must be to watch out that you don't bump into anything, lest you bleed out. He's a bit older than me and, understandably, he's incredibly sensitive.

A few of the lads are kicking a ball around. I kick it to Martin Penny. He shimmies like George Best and exudes footballing greatness. His brother Carl zooms past on a bicycle, as though to the Tour de France, complete with all the gear.

I enter the house. My mum is cooking chops so it must be Tuesday.

Before heading up to my room, I look to the coat stand to see if my dad's flat cap is hanging there. It isn't, which means he isn't home either, so I miss out on smelling the inside of it and the strange closeness and comfort that this brings me.

I haul myself up the stairs as 'All You Need Is Love' by The Beatles blares out of my sister's room. She has had her room painted white – from the walls to the carpet to the bedstand.

All white.

Pristine.

Shiny.

Unsullied.

Gleaming.

Perfect.

Untouchable.

Me and Our Kid, Longport Avenue, nineteen sixty-eight.

Chapter Nine

My dad has secured three tickets to see Manchester United play Polish side Górnik Zabrze, in the quarter-finals of the European Cup at Old Trafford. But instead of unparalleled joy, he seems preoccupied with something else altogether. I'd have thought the very fact of this event alone ought to supersede all else.

I align my feeling with his, though, playing down my excitement as he leaves the room. My mum walks in with her brow furrowed, lighting up a cigarette.

Tales Of Mystery And Imagination is on the television. At the conclusion of tonight's episode, two children rip out the hearts of their parents and throw them in the fire. I can't believe my mum and dad let me watch that. It's an image (and idea) that will probably remain with me for some time.

The usual cry of 'Right, you, teeth, wee and straight to bed' echoes around my head as I try to shake the image off. I head out of the room, close the living-room door, inhale my dad's cap and scoot upstairs to brush those pegs, then change into a plain white vest and my Winceyette cotton pyjamas.

My dad is there already, lighting a Valor paraffin stove-lamp heater on this chilly February evening. The stove has a column that lifts off to reveal a burner, with controls at the side to regulate the flame. He sets it alight, adjusts the controls and eases the column back onto the stove. I jump into bed as he says, 'Night, Barry lad.'

'Night, Dad,' I say. 'Are you looking forward to the match?'

'Course I am,' he says unconvincingly. He looks to the floor and leaves the room.

Instead of dropping off, I'm wide awake.

The stove casts a light from the flames onto the ceiling, like a shimmering flower. The pattern from the flames, reflected from the top of the stove, dances gently and hypnotically above me.

The smell of the burning paraffin creeps into my nostrils. I inhale it and turn on the small radio I keep in my bed, tuning into Radio Caroline. The theme tune to the 'Baby' Bob Stewart show soothes me.

'Image' by Alan Haven is a slow orchestral piece that features a Hammond organ at its heart. A quickly repeated four-note figure rolls across a sumptuous vista of cool drums and a wash of strings, punctuated by slinky, stabbing guitar chords.

'Baby' Bob's Mid-Atlantic tone by way of Liverpool is, as always, captivating and instantly recognisable. Several hits of the day make the airwaves. I try, but fail, to settle in. Then he plays an older song, 'Not Fade Away' by the Rolling Stones.

The song is a brazenly sped-up cover of a Buddy Holly and the Crickets song. It leaves me no choice but to celebrate the sheer panache, bravado and gall with which it rips through the tiny speakers of my radio.

Harmonicas and shakers drive the rhythm into a controlled frenzy. The song stinks of mischief and mayhem, summoning up enough *duende* to make anyone lose their way. It is utter genius and Jagger spits out the lyric like a poke in the eye:

I get out of bed, remove my pyjama top and strut around with imaginary flames, mimicking Brian Jones' superb mouth organ between my empty hands. In any other context, a song about real feelings of love might seem as mushy as the peas I hope we'll have with our chips on Friday. But here, with the Stones uprooting the primal instinct, it's anything but.

Offbeat claps accompany the demented skiffle. I climb onto the box in my room and make it my stage as the harmonica solo and guitar blast through it at a sweltering pace.

In the dark with the mighty Stones and their whirling flames around me, my fears are laid to rest. No longer am I stalked by the sickness of Oldham, or the plaster casters of Pendlebury Hospital – or indeed, the ripped-out hearts of *Mystery And Imagination*. Standing on the box, I can see the whole street, more or less. My total domain.

Just then a light comes on in Fran Orpington's bedroom. I duck so as not to be seen, but remember that I am a little dark boy in the darkness, lit only by flames that emanate from my stove.

She begins to undress.

I am transfixed as she takes off her clothes.

I believe that she can see me but that she carries on anyway.

She pulls her knickers down.

The flames grow higher and higher.

* * *

One spring morning in Longport Avenue, we kids fall around laughing as the bread van pulls away at full speed, crates jangling like sleigh bells and loaves threatening to topple off. The milk/bread man pushes his cap back and flicks us two fingers, snarling, which makes us laugh even more as we return the gesture.

Don't eat Rowland's bread
It'll make you shit the bed
You'll fart like thunder
(No bloody wonder)
Don't eat Rowland's bread
(traditional)

Pamela Butcher blushes out her conflict between delight and disapproval.

Martin Penny plays keepie-uppie with a leather football.

Ken the haemophiliac picks at a scab on his arm.

Fran Orpington regains her royal repose in a woollen two-piece jacket-and-skirt suit.

I am aching to tell her everything about the other night, to see if she feels the same way. But I'm disturbed as to why I can't look her in the eye. Why I keep my own towards the ground.

We go our separate ways. I see Fran chatting to Pamela and gulp down a wave of nausea. I did not, and could not, turn away from watching her undress from the boxroom. I feel my heart being ripped out and thrown into the fire by the other kids.

I limp down the ginnel to the back door, where there's a stack of milk and orange bottles. I grab an orange juice, shake it furiously and watch the bits move around before popping the green foil top. I also smirk at a loaf of Rowland's bread – which I prefer to Mother's Pride, if I'm honest.

INT. THE ADAMSONS' KITCHEN. LONGPORT AVENUE. MID-MORNING

Barry enters the kitchen and sees that his mum is in a trance. She doesn't notice him as she's engrossed in singing the Engelbert Humperdinck song 'Release Me'. She smokes a Benson & Hedges cigarette at the same time as she stares out of the window.

BARRY'S MUM

To live a lie would be a sin
Release me and let me love again

In close-up, she toys with the chain around her neck.

Over her shoulder, in a wider connecting shot, Barry tiptoes across the kitchen floor. He stops in his tracks when he hears...

BARRY'S MUM

I can hear you, you know?

Barry looks around to see the side of his mother's face as she continues looking out of the window, almost snarling now. The Humperdinck record sounds like a bizarre orchestral warp on the soundtrack.

BARRY'S MUM

You and that bloody radio of yours.
I should take it off you. See how you get on then.

BARRY

I'm going to my room.

CHAPTER NINE

BARRY'S MUM
    Go on then. Bugger off. You make me sick.

She turns on the tap and extinguishes her cigarette in the water, causing it to sizzle and burn out in a TIGHT CLOSE-UP.

FADE OUT.

* * *

Match day arrives and a swarm of people descend on Old Trafford, including me, my dad and my sister. I am suspended between, almost carried along by, these two giants. We seem to wade through endless crowds.

Kick-off begins and there are legs everywhere. I can't see a thing.

My dad lifts me so I can just make out George Best, holding his shirtsleeve between his fingers and palm as he dribbles past player after Polish player. I also glimpse the swept-over hair of Bobby Charlton as he runs through the middle, and see a toothless Nobby Stiles fearlessly go in for a heavy tackle before I'm put back down again.

Time seems to merge. I have no idea how long the match has been going on for.

Then the crowd surges and I lose sight of my dad and sister. I expect to see them at any minute, but as the gap in the crowd closes I'm pushed to the outside.

I'm alone, with everyone else cheering. Behind the crowd, I try to figure out how to get back into the stands. It's impossible, but as I begin to walk to the inside parameter of the ground, I hear an announcement over the tannoy: 'WILL BARRY ADAMSON MEET HIS FATHER AND SISTER BY THE CLOCK?'

They might as well have said, 'Substitution for Manchester United: number seven, George Best, is to be replaced by number twelve, Barry Adamson.' In my mind, I'm now running out onto the field.

Matt Busby has given me my instructions: pick up the ball from Nobby and get it through to Brian 'Kiddo' Kidd – who in fact scores in the eighty-ninth minute, giving us a two-nil lead over Poland.

My dad is tempted to scold me, but his relief at not losing me (plus his mood at United winning the match) seems to take over.

* * *

I come home from school one day to see a gleaming white Ford Console Capri outside our house. I surmise that Uncle Norman must be visiting. (I always think there's something a little bit shifty about Uncle Norman. The fact that he doesn't ever make eye contact with anybody is a bit strange.)

I run into the house and collide with laughter. My mum and dad, Norman and his rather exotic wife, and Our Kid are having an afternoon soirée. It all seems incredibly grown-up and I feel immediately awkward. But I sit down invisibly next to Our Kid where, unseen, I am free to observe. I particularly observe Norman's wife: tall, black beehive hairdo; severe eyeliner that whips into a sharp end at the outer corner of her eyelid; white-crocheted mini-dress that you can actually see through. (I try not to look.) She holds court, flitting unselfconsciously from subject to subject, matter to matter. Our Kid is fascinated with her hair and my dad is just… fascinated.

My mum studies her and is unusually quiet, dragging on her cigarette and staring at her as if taking a scan of her soul. An hour or so later, we all go outside to see them off. Norman glows with pride as he opens the car door for his wife. He tells my dad not to forget meeting up at the club with him and Bomber on Friday.

They take off and my dad waves briefly before going back inside. Me and Our Kid wave until they are out of sight. Looking around for her, I assume my mum has gone in to make our tea.

* * *

Later, my dad goes out and my sister goes to meet her friend, Doreen, in Moss Side. '*It's just me and me good ol' Ma,*' I think to myself. My mum sits in front of the telly with a box of Maltesers chocolates. I ask her if I can have one by way of leaning my hand towards the box. She slaps my hand and tells me, 'Get lost.' I sit there for a while, watching her until she tells me how 'more-ish' they are. Unwittingly, I see a box of bald black men, their heads shining in the fading spring light: Moorish.

I run upstairs and look across to the Orpingtons' house, but Fran isn't in her room. I take out my Action Man soldier and undress him. I look in my collection of paints and clay and find a black gloss modelling paint and a brush. I begin to paint Action Man black.

On this, the day of my tenth birthday, I wake up to find a wrapped-up parcel outside my door. I open it and the package contains a briefcase. Concealed inside the briefcase is a spy kit, made up of a gun and a camera. Attaching a stock and a silencer transforms the gun into a sniper rifle.

It is called a Secret Sam.

It is the toy that dreams are made of.

I couldn't be happier.

Secret Sam spy toy.

After playing with my Secret Sam for what seems like ages, I'm escorted over to the Morans' house and there, leaning against the wall, is a blue two-wheeler bicycle that belongs to Billy Moran.

'You've had your eye on a bike for a while, eh?' says my mum.

'Yeah,' I say.

'Well then, this bike' – she points to the one leaning against the wall – 'is now yours.'

Me on my tenth birthday, with my 'new' bike.

It's Wednesday night and my dad says, 'Barry lad, wanna go to the dogs?' To which there is only one answer. (Apart from jumping up and draping myself around his neck, with him saying, 'What the hell?')

We head for Kirkmanshulme Lane, Gorton, home since nineteen twenty-six of the Belle Vue Dog and Speedway racing track.

Once inside the oval stadium, the crackle of electricity is highlighted by floodlights and perfumed by the smell of hot dogs. The bookies employ tic-tac signalling, as though communicating the odds to the deaf.

My dad meets up with Norman and Bomber, who speak in a heavy patois I cannot understand at all. They seem to be complaining about their respective bosses, all looking very cool as they chew toothpicks. They only remove them to kiss their teeth after running somebody else down.

As the dogs are steered into their traps, anticipation builds as the mechanical hare they will chase completes a circuit around the track. All is quiet except for the sound of electricity. Then there is a huge cry as the dogs are set free and run like billy-o. Everyone is screaming for the dog they've bet on – especially us.

I ask if I can go to the toilet and my dad, reassured as I've been here before, simply nods in my direction. Once in there, I sit down and notice a photo pinned to the wall by a drawing pin, next to the toilet paper.

It's of two naked men. One is behind the other with his arms under the front man's armpits. He is lifting the arms of the man in front so that he cannot move.

No doubt this is a wrestling move. A headlock?

This picture may give me an answer as to why Mark was so into wrestling me. I can't stop looking at it while I'm in the toilet, for some reason, and I feel strange. So much so that I carefully fold it up and take it with me.

My dad and his mates are bemoaning their losses as the last race finishes. So we head on back to Withington in my dad's Ford Corsair, which I think Uncle Norman got for him. It will turn out later to be a stolen car – well, two actually, fantastically welded together. My dad will have to get rid of it after an unnerving visit from the police...

* * *

I start playing out with a new friend from Old Moat, John. I feel very comfortable around him; we just talk about everything for hours.

He doesn't know much about music, so I tell him about the songs I like. He's more practical than me and knows stuff like how, when you climb a wall and want to get down, you don't just jump off – you face the wall and sort of push yourself off, landing with your knees bent to absorb any shocks.

I try this but end up kneeing myself in the face. I expect to get laughed at, but John merely asks if I'm okay and says to keep trying, I'll get the hang of it.

We discuss at length a kid who was climbing the railing the other day, how he slipped and the spike went through his wrist. He was left dangling there until the ambulance came. They had to saw through the metal spike and take it along with him to the hospital, so that they could remove it there.

I ask John if he wants to come to ours for his tea one day and he says yes. So after school we walk past his on Whitchurch Road, where he drops his bag off.

Back at mine we play cricket in the garden, then have sandwiches and Ribena. I ask my mum if my cut-off jeans have been washed. She tells me she did all my clothes the other day.

'By the way…' she says. She places on the table, where John is sitting, the photograph of the two naked men I found in the toilets at Belle Vue. 'I think this is yours. I found it in your pocket.'

I'm not sure where to look. I think about Mark. About his smell.

John looks at the picture, then at me. He says that he should get back to his for his tea, instead of having it here.

After that, I never really see him again. At school he smiles at me, but whenever I try to talk to him, he says that he has to be somewhere and runs off.

I tell my mum about John avoiding me these days after she asks me, 'What's the matter, son?' She tells me not to worry because I'll always have her. Then she holds her arms out and says, 'C'mere, love.'

After hugging me and kissing me, she gives me a Penguin biscuit, covered in chocolate.

'Thanks Mum,' I say, all wide-eyed.

'Go on, get out of me bloody sight,' she tells me.

* * *

Later, I meet up with this other kid from school.

When he asks me what I like, I say the usual stuff about guns and knives and cars and sport. But even I'm totally surprised at what comes out of my mouth next, when I say that I really like birds and birdsong.

He looks at me as though I've just landed from outer space, scanning me for a few seconds to check whether I'm completely mad.

I realise I should have kept my gob shut, as my mum often tells me to.

He then says, 'Me too.'

I'm relieved somewhat as we cross the road and I think that maybe he'll join the Conservation Society and pick up litter with me.

'I like the sound that pigeons make,' he says. 'They say: "*Look at the coons... Look at the coons...*"'

Chapter Ten

It is the day of my sister's twenty-first birthday.

Fran Orpington and her mum have offered to make me a bespoke, Ben Sherman-style, red-and-blue checked, button-down shirt so I can look cool at her birthday party. I have to go over there for a fitting and I cannot wait to put it on.

I've been looking forward to the party at the local hall since winter began. Even though it's cold outside and the shirt is short-sleeved, I have to wear it. After all, I planned it this way.

'Do The Funky Chicken' is a novelty song by Rufus Thomas. It is also a dance. The song has what's come to be generically known as an 'infectious funk beat' and a bass line that owes its strut to a James Brown workout, as do the guitar chords.

The brass section, however, gives it its musical opulence, transcending it above a mere accompaniment to Thomas' buffoonery – the man himself begins the record making chicken noises – and into a stone-cold classic that cannot – once you've got over the idea that this must be a joke – be ignored.

The live footage of a bald, splendidly blasé Thomas dressed in a grandiose combination of pink suit (with short trousers, I might add), pink cape and white patent leather boots at his crowd-winning Wattstax charity music festival performance, seals his place in musical history, forever.

I just have time to blast the record and to practise the dance routine. The brass figure takes off as, like a chicken, I'm flapping my arms and legs all over the place.

My mum opens my bedroom door. 'What the bloody 'ell? Lord bless us and save us!'

'It's the funky chicken,' I say, flailing around the place.

'The funky what?' She squints, watching me go through the routine with intent as my focus increases. 'Oh, you bloody fool,' she says.

I carry on dancing, perfecting my moves to the groove of the song.

My mum looks at her watch – 'Right, time to get a move on' – and leaves me to it.

I leg it downstairs, out of the front door and across the road to knock at the Orpingtons. My shirt looks great. The button-down collar is really something and I feel like the coolest kid on the street. I thank them, blushing at Fran, who winces at me, then I'm back into mine to grab a cardigan and around the corner to the hall. On entering, I'm struck by the booming music coming through the speakers.

Our Kid looks amazing, her hair backcombed into a beehive.

I grab some sandwiches. When anyone speaks to me, I wait for them to tell me how great my shirt is.

An announcement is made about how wonderful Our Carol is and how much of a delight she is to be around. It's also noted that I'm here and I've been practising a new dance, which is sure to become the latest craze. Maybe I'd like to perform it now?

'What?'

All eyes are on me as 'Do The Funky Chicken' begins to blast through the room. A crowd of people start to surround me, egging me on.

As the collar of my shirt begins to go all floppy, they get closer. I'm surrounded by people clapping to the beat, telling me to 'Go on!' They are almost upon me, like a herd of zombies.

I stop being able to breathe for a moment, see a gap and run past them, just when it seems I'm about to be devoured. I bolt out the door like a headless chicken.

I arrive back at my empty house in a blur and run upstairs to my room, where I throw the shirt onto the floor, climb into bed and pretend to go to sleep.

On the radio, in the dark, Emperor Rosko plays 'In The Ghetto' by Elvis Presley. At the end of a verse, several black girl backing singers make the title line a refrain, while French horns pay a three-note motif.

The song ends, and I switch the radio off again as snot bubbles from my nose and my face is sodden with tears.

My head is still whirling around like a carousel. I try to think of nice things, like my mum's new car, a gold-coloured Hillman Imp. I repeat the numbers and letters of the licence plate, over and over:

FNF 506D... FNF 506D... FNF 506D... FNF 506D... FNF 506D... FNF 506D...

The carousel starts to slow down, and I fall asleep.

* * *

Several sleeps later.

We have an art class and I excel at making clay heads. The girls think I'm great and the boys really *do not*. I buy sweets and hand them out mostly to the boys. This one kid laughs at me and asks if I can bring sweets in every day.

I'm reaching for the bag of Everton mints to begin handing them out, when another teacher walks in and whispers something to Miss Lawson. She calls me forward and the other teacher takes me outside, in silence.

The teacher explains to me that my mum has been involved in a car accident and while she's okay, she's also in hospital. I'm asked if I'm okay. I say yes and sit quietly in the head's office, staring out of the window, waiting for my dad to pick me up.

I walk into the hospital, holding my dad's hand. The ward where my mum is looks just the same as the one I was in, with the children replaced by grown-ups. My mum looks defeated as she can barely sit up, not able to look at me or my dad. He goes to hug her but she winces, explaining that her top half is bandaged and she needs to rest up for a bit.

There is one sweet left. I roll the cellophane wrapping paper slowly between finger and thumb in my pocket, popping it into my mouth to feel the cool mint sensation over my tongue. The boiled sweet rattles temporarily against my back teeth before I crunch down hard, smashing it to smithereens to enjoy the chewy toffee inside.

* * *

The postman delivers the *1969–70 Burlington Autumn/Winter Mail Order Catalogue* and I am beside myself with excitement. Burlington, like Peter Craig, Janet Frazier and Littlewoods, sends out home-shopping catalogues that my dad takes delivery of twice a year. They offer credit facilities on the never-never, which means you put a small deposit on the goods you want and then pay a small monthly fee for twelve, twenty-four, sometimes thirty-six months, without interest.

These three-inch-thick tomes are packed with everything you could want, from the latest fashion clothing and accessories to household goods, electrical items, gifts and jewellery. As always, kids' toys are at the back.

When at last I get my grubby mitts, as my mum likes to say, on this complete guide to shopping (I am, inevitably, always the last person in the family), I head straight to my room and straight for the lingerie section.

The pictures of women in their corsets, bras, knickers and stockings are captivating.

I peruse these pages for ages. I like the feeling in my belly. If anyone walks into the room, I can always flick to the toys at the back – which I invariably do anyway, as there are so many things that I want from that section, not just for Christmas but *right now*.

My dad's also got his eye on something. Within days of the catalogue arriving, a brand new Alba stereo hi-fi record player, housed in a teak veneer cabinet, arrives on our doorstep.

Once in place in the front room, he produces an LP, *Late Spot At Scott's* by the Tubby Hayes Quintet. He takes the record out of its sleeve and examines it. Holding it in both hands, moving it this way and that, the light catches the grooves so that he can see if there is any dust or scratches.

He blows a puff of air across the twelve-inch vinyl disc, looks across its surface and hums a note of satisfaction.

We watch him in silence as he places the record onto the turntable and turns a dial to select whether to play a seven-inch single (forty-five revolutions per minute) or an album (also known as an LP, short for long player, for which the dial needs to be set at thirty-three and a third rpm). He activates the console, the record drops onto the rubber mat and the arm with the needle moves to the beginning of the album. It all happens in a very magical slow motion.

'Bloody 'ell, the suspense is killing me,' my mum says. The needle hovers above the record then drops onto it.

Before the *wow* there is *flutter*. Noises of static and frequencies picked up by the needle. But when the record begins, it's as though Tubby is in the room with us as he speaks:

'Good evening, ladies and gentlemen, welcome to the Ronnie Scott Jazz Club in London, where this evening you're gonna hear a session of music by my quintet, and before we start playing, we'd like to introduce you to the musicians in the group.'

Tubby himself plays the tenor saxophone. He introduces the band: Gordon Beck on the piano; Freddie Logan on bass; Alan Ganley on drums; Jimmy Deuchar on trumpet.

Tubby dedicates the first song to a recent trip to New York and calls it 'Half A Saw Buck'. I'm dying to ask my dad what that means, but I don't have to as after another round of applause and Tubby saying, 'One, two, a-one-two-three,' everything makes sense. A horn riff blasts through the room and I am transported to an America of the mind...

I have never heard anything like this before. It's as though my dad had kept this hidden in a drawer somewhere that I didn't know about.

After the intro, there are a series of complicated establishing phrases. Tubby takes a mind-blowing sax solo, worthy of anything that comes out of America, so my dad reckons. A trumpet solo follows and then drums lead the turnaround back to reiterate the initial phrases.

He then takes us through the next track, 'Angel Eyes', switching it up from tenor saxophone to vibraphone for a James Bond/John Barry-style slow workout arranged by drummer Alan Ganley, which is mesmerising.

The trumpet plays the lead. The vibes make a delicious, satisfying, haunting sound as Tubby takes a dexterous solo. My dad is enraptured too. We both seem to go to another place, different to the reality we experience day to day. Tension seems to lift and a feeling of peace surrounds the room as Gordon Beck takes a piano solo. My dad taps his hand gently on his knee as the intro returns and the song comes to a mysterious end with a floating chord.

Tubby then says: 'We'd like to conclude the first set this evening with an original composition which I've written for the group and it's entitled "The Sausage Scraper".' The audience laughs, as do me and my dad.

'The Sausage Scraper' is lighthearted but as cool a slice of jazz as you could ever wish to hear, the best track so far on the record (if you have to pick one). You get the sense that everyone – the band, the audience and, indeed, us listeners – is settled in for the evening, with nothing to worry about at all, until…

The record sticks. The needle has stuck in the vinyl's groove, due to a deep scratch, and a jarring three-note repetition jars again and again until my dad gets up and moves the needle past the sticking point. It drops onto a fluttering, abrasive and wonderful Jimmy Deuchar trumpet solo.

It takes quite a few bars to get back into the same space, but by the time Jimmy's solo finishes and you can hear Tubby off-mike say, 'Yeah,' Gordon comes in for the most brilliant solo he's played so far. We're back to where we were before and then some more.

A bunch of stripper beats and melodic phrases round the song off before the band easily slides into accompanying Tubby, so that he can wrap up side one of the album and announce the band again. (Note Freddie Logan's walking bass.) He announces that the band will be back after a break; then they conclude with an astonishing display of melded-together virtuosity, sending the needle straight into the centre of the record.

Tubby Hayes on the cover of *Late Spot At Scott's*.

The arm lifts up and I watch it settle back into its cradle.

I look at the upturned, fresh, smiling face of Tubby Hayes on the cover of the album and imagine his life to be far, far different from mine. But somehow, through the music I've just heard, there is definitely something similar about us on the inside. It's as though I intrinsically understand his need to make the music he is making.

But suddenly I'm choking on something.

My mum and sister appear, wearing wigs. My mum is spraying her wig with copious amounts of Elnett Satin hairspray, from the largest gold can I've ever seen. The smell of the spray consumes the whole front room.

My mum heads for my dad's knee and plonks herself, rather heavily, on top of him. 'What do you reckon, love?' she teases him.

My sister is laughing, as is my dad. But the afterglow of listening to the record has, to my mind, been disrupted.

'Face on him!' my mum says.

I leave the room and go upstairs, in order to breathe normally again.

* * *

There is a new publication out now called *The Book Of Life*. It's a collection of magazines that, purchased weekly, eventually becomes an encyclopaedia. I badger my parents to subscribe and it becomes my connection to the universal world beyond my family. I spend hours in my room leafing through it, trying to absorb everything beyond what I already know.

Which leads me to ask my mum, 'What's a clitoris?'

'What's a what, love?' she replies but doesn't look at me.

I'm forced to say it again, even though I know she's heard me. She also knows that I have an idea, based on *The Book Of Life's* explanation, of how a woman reaches orgasm. It's something else I'm preparing myself to ask her about as she fills her basket of washing.

'What's a clitoris?'

Without looking at me, she says, 'It's something that women have, love.'

Every weekday morning, after my dad leaves for work, I slip between the sheets next to my mum for twenty minutes or so, before she gets up and dressed for work. She notes that I am 'as snug as a bug in a rug'.

When she gets dressed, she asks me to cover my eyes while she pulls on her knickers, bra, stockings and then finally a silk slip, before putting on her dress. Her translucent skin, the look of her lingerie, the sound of her putting it on and the scent of her lying next to me, stays with me all day.

As I make my way to school, down Longport Avenue, down the passageway, onto Whitchurch Road and up to Old Moat Lane, I pass John's house and flick him the V, without a thought or care about what happened in our kitchen with that bloody stupid photo anymore.

* * *

I've now also joined The Man From U.N.C.L.E. Club. In my own mind, I'm already a long-serving member and have been ever since James Bond opened my eyes to another world…

The Man From U.N.C.L.E. is an American spy-fiction TV series that follows two secret agents, played by Robert Vaughn (Napoleon Solo) and David McCallum (Illya Kuryakin). They work for a secret counterespionage agency known as U.N.C.L.E., which stands for the United Network Command for Law Enforcement. Their boss, Mr Waverly, is played by Leo G Carroll.

Being finally initiated into the fold means so much to me. Everything about it is amazing, from the theme tune to the characters and the capers they get up to every week. The main objective of U.N.C.L.E. is to rid the world of THRUSH (Technological Hierarchy for the Removal of Undesirables and the Subjugation of Humanity). They are the bad guys, who basically believe in a master-and-slave type of world dominance and must be dismantled at all cost. U.N.C.L.E. has agents worldwide dedicated to stopping THRUSH.

Solo is fundamentally charming, confident, efficient and, like the character of James Bond, has an innate weakness for women. He also looks fantastic in the clothes he wears and he knows it. He's practical and shows no emotion as he goes about his job. Kuryakin is Napoleon's sidekick. He is intellectual, somewhat intense and listens to jazz in his spare time. Quite the opposite to Napoleon, he also likes to fence, which is something I'm curious about. I think that one day I might take it up as a sport – that's if my hips allow me to.

I stand somewhere between both of these characters: sometimes I'm all about Napoleon, but in other episodes I feel I'm like the slightly overanxious Illya.

So I'm now an agent, a member of the inner circle, and I have a certificate that attests to it. I've also been granted an ID card and a badge (the same number as Napoleon Solo's), which I will carry with me at all times.

The Man From U.N.C.L.E. club ID card and badge.

Chapter Eleven

My world continues to exist through *The Book Of Life*, where I learn about everything, including the environment. And so, I join the Conservation Society...

The Conservation Society was a British environmental company, established by Douglas MC MacEwan in nineteen sixty-six. It was formed in response to what were seen as basic ecological constraints on continued profit making and population growth in the United Kingdom. I do my bit by picking up litter (while also spying for U.N.C.L.E., of course – which my membership of the Conservation Society provides perfect cover for).

I come home from one such outing to hear sounds emanating from my sister's room. They're musical but with strange echoes, punctuated high notes and a swirling effect. I knock on her door (something I now do always) and after I'm told to come in, the sound changes into an electric piano and backbeat with predominating tambourines. Then a woman's voice sings.

Underneath these lines, the bass bounces and other voices set an eerily focused atmosphere by singing reverberated '*oohs*'. Then a chorus adds those other voices.

I see a record sleeve – or two, actually – bearing two words that jumps out at me: TAMLA MOTOWN. Our Kid, sensing my interest, says that this track is called 'Reflections' by Diana Ross & The Supremes. My sister has bought *Motown Chartbusters Volume 1* and *2*, and although some of these songs are not foreign to me, hearing them all 'under one roof' feels like a whole new world of listening. I join the dots between a song I heard her play a little while back, 'Reach Out' by The Temptations, and what I'm hearing now. It's the same world, the world of Tamla Motown.

Together, we spend the rest of the day listening to these two collections over and over and over. I digest every word, every musical phrase, every harmony, until it feels like I made them all up myself.

*   *   *

With the summer of nineteen sixty-nine drawing to a close, with a new school beckoning from around the corner, I pedal my bike as fast as I can down Whitchurch Road.

I've been round to Julie Stewart's house. Knowing I would probably never see her again, I tried as hard as I could to imprint an image of her beautiful face into the recesses of my mind, in the hope of never forgetting her. The same goes for Alison Beggs and Karen Hodgkinson.

The lads on Longport Avenue tell tales of horror about my new school. How I'm to have my teeth kicked in every day by the kids in the year above, hunting for new flesh like rabid animals. Or how, because the school symbol is a bee (the insect emblazoned on the front pocket of our school-uniform jacket), it provides the perfect opportunity for older kids to punch you hard in the chest. Then they will explain that they were helping you by eliminating said bee.

The main horror for me, though, is that I wasn't picked to go to either Wilbraham or Chorlton High Schools. My own school was thrown into the mix at the last minute, in case all else failed. It was suggested first to my parents and then to me; I think I might have smirked at the idea as I was signing the papers, as though any outcome was fine by me.

It's in Moss Side, a stone's throw away from the Hulme of my early childhood. I feel like I know what to expect, though the fearmongering from my friends only adds to an idea that I'm going backwards, not forwards.

The big day arrives. I decide I'm going to be okay, as my blazer is thick and my grey jumper provides adequate padding. Surely I'll be able to roll with the most hostile of punches? In fact I might even be able to retaliate, if I absorb the initial blows which, without doubt in my mind, are surely coming.

104

My mum drops me off at the lower-school playground and waves, smiling. I watch her Hillman Imp disappear into the distance, down Denmark Road towards Lloyd Street.

I turn around to face the playground and witness absolute mayhem. It's as though I'm watching a mainly black St Trinian's movie for both boys and girls, and the whole show is in full swing.

I must be the only still object, as I'm hoping my cap stays on. (Nobody else is wearing one.) I await that punch in the chest that will put me to the ground. Instead, I'm faced with Carmel Thomas, who squares up to me. I observe her as though she's the first truly black girl I've ever seen.

She kicks me in the balls. Hard. She then lets out a ferocious laugh as I sink to my knees.

By way of the whistle, everybody at last stops to draw breath. A teacher with dark hair, a pointed head and spectacles, whose name is Mr Provost, says, 'Welcome to Ducie High school.'

Intelligence is above everything, to my mind. So I'm plagued by a sense of self-doubt as to why the world of students who attend Wilbraham and Chorlton has failed to embrace me with open arms. I feel a kind of loneliness come over me, a sense of separation if you will. Every kid seems boisterous and wild to me. I can't seem to gel with anyone, black or white.

This subsides when I see Paul Campbell, Jimmy Tucker and Trevor Dwyer. All three boys are mixed race, the same as me. Now the playing field seems to level out somewhat. My designated classroom is pointed out and my anxieties are dissolving a little. I follow the herd and take a seat towards the back, near the window facing out to the corridor, in case I need to escape.

As usual my name, because it begins with an A, is read out first on the register. Nobody can deny the sense of importance this gives me in the eyes of the other kids. Everybody knows that being first is something that cannot be competed with. I have a certain smugness about it that I've perfected in covering up.

Back in the playground, I see Carmel Thomas whirling around like a deranged Bash Street Kid, wreaking havoc among those who so much as look at her. She captures me but, having faced her worst already, she gives me a kind of '*Got you*' grin, to which I grin back to say, '*Yes, you really did.*'

In that moment we seem to bond in some way, as if I understand what motivated her to kick me in the balls. It's something she recognises and appreciates, when actually I remain petrified of her and I'm just looking for ways to defuse any future attack.

I lean against the railings at break, watching one kid who walks back and forth across the playground, counting his steps until the bell rings to go back in. I still wait for that punch. It doesn't come by home-time and I sigh relief, jumping into my mum's car, cap shoved away in my bag – never to be seen again.

*   *   *

Soon after starting school, I get a paper round. It gives me a feeling of independence, plus a few bob in my pocket to buy records on Fridays from Paul Marsh's on Princess Road, before heading home to blast them out on the Alba stereo.

One such is 'Get Up (I Feel Like Being A) Sex Machine' by James Brown. The bass line is played by a seventeen-year-old Bootsy Collins; he plays the same notes repeatedly throughout with an exact precision I've not heard before. It is totally mesmerising.

The paper round also sees me deliver to one woman who insists I ring the doorbell and takes the paper off me by hand, often wearing only a pink see-through negligee. I try to pace the deliveries and save her for last, before I cycle back to the newsagents to drop off my sack and sprint home, singing the song's 'get on up' refrain.

All this with Bootsy's bass playing off-beats in my mind, causing my body to sway as though kicked gently behind the knees.

I borrow the catalogue and go to my room, heading straight for the corsets, bras, knickers and stockings. Something stirs in my groin but I don't know what.

I just hope it's not a clitoris.

This sensation travels into my stomach and feels warm. I close my eyes and see Julie Stewart's face. I want to reach out and grab her, pull her close to me.

The weight of the catalogue makes it constantly fold itself shut. When I open it again, startled by its closure, it feels like being caught for doing something I shouldn't. So I turn back to the toys and begin breathing easier, without the feeling that I might pee myself.

*   *   *

I'm more confident in front of my mum these days. So when she asks me, 'What the 'ell have you got to be happy about?' I mock the way she speaks.

'I'll wipe that bloody smile off your face in a minute!' she says.

I roll my eyes and chomp down hard on a piece of buttered toast. She throws a knife into the kitchen sink and I can tell immediately she's angry, above and beyond the normal.

I want to ask her if she is okay and explain myself to her, but it's too late and I'm running for my life upstairs.

She is in hot pursuit. She's also picked up a bamboo feather duster, which I guffaw over, but then I see she's more concerned with the bamboo than the duster.

She reaches me at the top of the stairs. I pause briefly so that I can receive a verbal warning – then we can get on with the day again.

Instead, she begins to rant and rave and thwacks me several times across the legs with the bamboo. Each thrash is harder and more mortifying than the last. As I look at her aghast, she tells me, eyes aflame, 'Go on, get out of me bleedin' sight before I bloody well kill you!'

*　*　*

I've been going to school on my own lately, across Hough End Fields where I wait for the bus from Wythenshawe, which takes me close enough to school.

Hough End used to be an airfield in the early nineteen hundreds, so I'm told. Flights would land from places like Oxford and, later in the century, regular services flew to London and further afield – Berlin or Moscow. Had Manchester Corporation been successful in getting rid of the land, Alexandra Park Airfield (as known then) would have become Britain's first municipal airport. Instead, it remained undeveloped until it was laid out as playing fields in nineteen forty-five.

I walk to the end of Whitchurch Road and look across to Hough End from Princess Road. This mighty piece of land is protected by four lanes of traffic, two heading north and two heading south, giving access in and out of the city.

After the tricky manoeuvre of looking both ways at the same time, I make it across this unapproachably industrious road and feel the open plain begin to envelop me. The pay-off is always worth risking my life for. As I walk out into this vast nothingness of grass, I wonder how long it would take to reach those trees in the far distance.

I start to run. My legs feel strong again, like they can actually carry me, but I'm never sure if they can. I drop the ball I've been carrying all the way from home, across 'Prinny' Road, as though it's a precious baby. Now I lob it into the air and smash it hard with my foot, sending it high into the clouds.

The Old Trafford crowd go wild!

I leg it after the ball, trapping it as it lands, and then I spin around. I make my way towards the goals, the ones that have been left up for the school matches. I'm back in the game.

This way and then that way, I shimmy past several defenders and eyeball the goalkeeper into believing I'm putting it to his right. As I move to his left, I simply slide it in. I turn away from the ball, no longer concerned with the need to retrieve it. The team surrounds me, congratulating me and marvelling at my skills. I glance up at the crowd and wink to my dad, who, clapping coolly, nods his head in a way that says, '*Well, you did tell me, but clearly I didn't quite believe you.*'

I make out it was nothing and dismiss my team's attentions by calling out, 'C'mon, lads, there's still plenty of time for them to get one back!' I clap my hands as I make my way back to the centre circle, shouting again, 'C'mon, lads!'

I lean forwards, putting my hands on my knees, and try to catch my breath. Then I walk through the empty goal to get my ball back. The wind whips around my head as dark clouds gather.

I head back, tapping the ball in front of me until I get to the main road and navigate my way across, back into Whitchurch Road and down the passageway, where pats on the shoulders are accepted. I hope my mum has cut some oranges into quarters for when I get back to the dressing room.

Through the front garden and the ginnel, I hear my mum and Our Kid shouting. I can't make out the words but their anger is evident. As I reach the back window, I see my mum screaming at my dad. Then she slaps him across the face and arms. My sister joins in and he stands there, unflinching, accepting what is happening.

I enter and the scene slows down, as though I'm watching a film. Their voices are now an echo as my sister and my mum, both in tears, continue to hit my dad. I can make out that Norman's wife has something to do with this. The penny drops. My inner cinecamera shows cutaways of her beehive hair and slashed eyeliner, then my mum's pensive and aggressive states of late.

My dad turns and stares at me as blow after blow from my mum and sister rains down on him. I want to say something but I cannot.

I walk through the house and upstairs to my room, reaching for a footie magazine that has a picture of the Manchester City team on the back. I begin to memorise each of their names by heart:

Corrigan.

Book.

Pardoe.

Doyle.

Booth.

Oakes.

Summerbee.

Bell.

Lee.

Young.

Coleman.

I stare into each of their faces and hold my breath as I try to black out.

*   *   *

I down my second dragon's blood and move onto the dance floor. 'Venus' by Shocking Blue blasts through the Pop Inn club at full volume.

With that blackcurrant and lemonade concoction coursing through mind, body and soul, with the forceful yet laidback groove of the song and the seductiveness of Mariska Veres' voice, I feel free of anything that might stop me from being, right now, quite possibly the world's greatest dancer. I shimmy, like Colin Bell, onto the floor.

I bounce on my right foot before switching to the left; rock on both feet while moving my shoulders up and down; coolly move my head from side to side, up and down. Occasionally I mouth some of the lyrics, to let kids from school and different Manchester neighbourhoods know that I am, definitely, where it is totally at.

The Pop Inn is situated above the Co-op on the corner of Yew Tree Avenue and Platt Lane. It operates as a dance class in the week and at weekends we kids go crazy for a few hours on music, dancing, dragon's blood and highballs (cola and milk).

Arthur Conley's 'Funky Street' begins to play and I realise some of these kids attend the dance classes in the week too; as the intro brass is playing, they form some kind of line and all begin doing the same steps. They skip with one foot behind them, which then switches to the other foot. It looks so good that I pick it up in a flash.

Then there's a series of thrown poses; they all know these, and on the next play of the song so will I. They accompany the first verse, which is made up of vocal, brass and drums, the pose changing with each punctuation.

If I thought the feeling of dancing alone was freeing, then dancing together like this is about as liberating as it gets right now.

Or at least that's what I think, until my parents rekindle their need, from my childhood, to get me anything I want. So they buy me a Raleigh Chopper bicycle – and a cat called Tigger.

Tigger goes missing within weeks, and so is replaced by a brown and white mongrel dog I call Butch – much to my mum's chagrin. Butch develops a terrible habit of rubbing himself off on anybody's leg that he can find, so he's constantly scolded by my dad.

I just hoist him into the air when he does it to me, and kind of smile when he lands with a slight whimper. Then I feel bad as his face shows confusion, so I mess with him, rubbing his ears and belly until he's happy again, running around the garden, yapping away.

I come home from school to see my dad holding Butch down with his left hand and right foot, whacking him hard with his belt. Butch looks terrified, more confused than ever, and with each strike of the belt he whimpers hard.

I look on, rooted to the spot as my dad casts me an eye that says, '*I dare you.*'

Within days Butch has gone, disappeared, like Tigger. 'Run away' is what my dad tells me. I can't blame him.

Chapter Twelve

The school is hosting a dance at the local youth club.

I am sporting a brand new Ben Sherman red-and-blue checked shirt and draped in a black Crombie wool overcoat with red silk lining, a three-pointed silk handkerchief in the top pocket and a jewelled stud keeping it in place.

I shuffle and posture my way into the building, hoping the DJ plays songs that will help me show off my skills. I look nervously around. Everyone seems so different out of their school uniforms. A who's-the-coolest competition ensues as us boys stand around, antagonising each other. I decide to act as if I've been here so many times before and tell those guys that I'll see them later. (On my way home, no doubt, with a 'bird' on each arm.)

A couple of girls look away as I approach them, so I make a space for myself to shimmy my way through a couple of songs: 'Band Of Gold' by Freda Payne and 'Young, Gifted And Black' by Bob & Marcia.

Unlike the Pop Inn, there is no formation dancing, no sense of being part of a team. As the night wears on, the only person I'm moving closer to is myself.

The DJ announces all too quickly that this is the last song of the evening. Amidst the sighs, there is also a slightly more electric feel in the air now, as even kids who were nailed to the periphery begin to peel themselves off the walls and walk to a space on the dance floor.

A song begins to play and I'm thinking, '*What?*' A simple piano figure demands that we teens loosely (at first) latch onto each other, so we can better bear witness to the sentiment of the song.

Singer-songwriter Harry Nilsson has taken the song 'Without You', written by Pete Ham and Tom Evans of British rock band Badfinger, and with producer Richard Perry, he unashamedly exploits what was a eureka moment for the writers. Ham had a verse but no chorus and Evans had a chorus without a verse, which they joined together into one song. Now Nilsson slowly squeezes the neck of the contrary emotions apparent in the song's heartbreak, to take it to a whole new dimension.

So here's Harry – voice and piano, revealing to us the source of his brokenness. He refrains from pulling any of the punches he's raining down on himself, setting up a character who's vulnerable, willing to be viewed as a pathetic figure. At the same time, he is deluding himself to believe his position is one of strength.

We coupled-up youth clumsily pull each other closer as it becomes a bit strange and otherworldly. The second verse mocks reality as the bass drops, the strings descend into the ground, and Harry sings:

And I had you there but then I let you go…

Harry now harmonises with himself, adding to the psychodramatic intensity of his longing. The chorus is set up for just what might be an unbearable truth.

Like everyone else on the dance floor, lights arcing from red to blue, I'm in a trance of mystification waiting for the truth to be told.

Two girls, their heads drooped over shorter boys' shoulders, begin to cry. I ask my not-quite-so-significant other why. She tells me, 'Y'know?' I look at her dumbfounded. 'Break-ups… and this song?'

The chorus kicks in as my inner camera pulls out to reveal the everything of everything. The connection between songs and the hidden, human, inner world.

I can't live, if living is without you

No further harmony. Extra pathos to go.

After three minutes and twenty-two seconds, the lights go up and the whole of what just happened is forgotten about. There is an almost triumphant march to another world as we all fade into nothingness. After chips and gravy, there is no chance of getting a snog at the bus stop.

*   *   *

Last week in July and first week in August, we head off to Abbeyford caravan park in Towyn, just outside Rhyl, North Wales. We do this every year for our annual summer holidays. Even my gran comes with us this year, replacing Our Kid.

We are met at the shop by an effervescent lady from Liverpool, who I assume owns this land and all the caravans on it. Her voice is incredible to me, all accentuated vowels and punctuated consonants. She addresses my mum as though they've been friends for years. I find her quite loud and scary.

*   *   *

Settled in, with the beds pulled down and tucked away until nightfall, my dad slips me a fiver to 'go and have a wander'. I head off past several rows of caravans, making sure I'm not prying on anyone – though I'm looking enough to see who's who, or if I recognise anyone from a previous year. Especially if there are any girls my age.

The park opens up by the flowerbeds, near to the shops. It feels like a magnet to me. I don't know whether to engage further with the scary lady's garrulousness or just wander through all the colourful retail.

I scoot past with my head purposefully down, picking up the pace as I mosey on past, but I can't help but look to see if she is there. Thankfully she is serving somebody, but she catches my eye as I throw her a glance, which she sends back, meaning, '*See you later, young man.*'

The pavements on Bryn Road that lead to 'the front', also known as Towyn Road, are tiny. I find myself constantly bobbing and weaving to avoid bumping into anyone. I become more excited as I reach Towyn Road, tun left, pass the pub, the chippy and the cafe, and arrive at my final destination.

The Black Cat amusement arcade.

*   *   *

This is my place of worship. Loud music, slot machine after slot machine, pinball games aplenty. There's even a massive bingo hall, where I often see my parents and my gran as I pass through.

The best thing is that the Black Cat has a 'jukebox booth' – which is exactly what it says. If I'm lucky enough, I can be left alone in that booth, enraptured by my record of choice right now, at full volume: 'Get It On' by T.Rex.

This is what I listen to over and over as I'm pinned to the wall of the booth. I allow it to take me over and in the darkness I imagine myself as a very different person, more powerful than anyone else alive.

The guitar plays, and then drums slam into the intro as a piano runs up (or down) the spine before Marc Bolan sings.

I feel myself changing. My confidence is growing. My usual reasons for keeping my head down are being lifted up and away from me.

The record revolves around and around a blues figure, with punctuated guitar stabs in the high register over a chugging twelve-bar guitar. Brass and backing vocals flavour the arrangement, with strings on the chorus. Each verse builds upon the last with a growing seductiveness.

After the final chorus, a twelve- or thirteen-note guitar solo (depending on how you consider 'bending' notes), adds a kind of yearning before the fadeout, where Bolan gives a verbal echo of Chuck Berry's 'Little Queenie'.

It kind of grounds the listener, but leaves them wanting to get back to getting it on. I play the record again…

Two kids a bit older than me enter the booth as the drums slam in. They begin snogging, right next to me. I watch them and wonder what it must be like for them, with me just standing there. They seem not to be bothered by me at all.

I walk out of the booth, out of the Black Cat and back to the caravan for a cheese and pickle sandwich.

* * *

That night, I wake up with something warm and sticky covering the tops of my legs. I flashback to sitting in class, in form 1S, and us kids laughing our heads off as someone (possibly me) sang Max Romeo's reggae song 'Wet Dream'. I could only imagine at that time what everybody was laughing at. Some were blushing, some were disgusted and some of the girls hid their heads in their desks until the moment had passed.

Every night me go to sleep, me have wet dreams

I feel like a milestone has been reached as I imagine all the girls that are going to lie down and let me *'push it up, push it up'*.

My main worry now, though, is how I'm going to clean myself up without being spotted by my gran, who's lying across from me and happily snoring away. She's having a few dreams of her own, no doubt as dry as they come.

After breakfast I'm asked, 'Where are you off to now, kiddo?' as I down my last bit of bacon. I didn't even hint that I was going anywhere, so I quickly put a plan together that I feel I should have already thought of.

'Might go look around Towyn Bay.'

'That's nice, love,' says my mum as she dries dishes.

I head on out after being told, 'Be back for lunch, as we might go for a drive this afternoon.' I let out a small sigh that suggests it might interfere with my plans, while secretly relieved that we're going to do something, all of us, together.

This time I head out of the caravan in the opposite direction, towards Knightly's Fun Park, across the railway bridge and down to the sea. There are two roads that can be taken, either through the park itself or down Sandbank Road.

I take the park route as, hopefully, when we get back, we'll stroll down Sandbank Road and go to the cakeshop there, the Sandbank Bakery.

After Knightly's, I walk over the railway bridge, enjoy the temporary elevation and then arrive at the walled seafront. I walk a little further, behind the stone wall looking out to sea, before finding somewhere to sit and think – mainly about buying the T.Rex album *Electric Warrior...*

* * *

Back in Withington, my dad has bought a Grundig tape recorder and set it up in the kitchen so that we can tape Alan 'Fluff' Freeman's *Pick Of The Pops*, every Sunday.

This technology is so innovative and, of course, my dad just has to have all the latest gadgets on the marketplace, including the new Polaroid Land Camera and now this recorder-player.

I'm super excited too, figuring out how the machine works in no time.

Each Sunday, the show is divided into four segments: Chart Newcomers (latest climbers); New Releases; an LP Spot; and the weekly Top 10.

This particular week in late August nineteen seventy-two, he plays a new release by a band called Roxy Music. The song is called 'Virginia Plain'.

Out of nowhere, the song slowly fades up and onto the airwaves. A piano plays two chords, eight to the bar, alongside two stretched-out and sustained guitar notes; it throws up an enticing question which is answered after eight bars, when the song slams into existence.

It carves itself out of an older-sounding rock'n'roll terrain by aiming for a new style and sonority altogether. Along the way it references, discards and lays to rest a culture now past – influential no doubt, but also suffocating. There's no chorus, just a four-chord musical reiteration that is kicked around, moulded and sculptured, announced at every turn as being the new now.

Ambitious and carefree, Bryan Ferry sings with a strange affectation that will be imitated by others. But right here and now, with an exaggerated vibrato and an overdramatic Dylanesque turn of phrase, he is unique.

Ferry makes public his goal, announcing the band's arrival by talking about a deal he's taking to Robert E Lee, one of the top music lawyers of the time. He knows that we're *in*. That we're all strapped into our seats and ready for the glam-rock journey of a lifetime.

After two mind-bending verses, an audaciously improvised guitar solo from Phil Manzanera slices expectations in two, supported by Andy Mackay's psychotically wailing saxophone. Rik Kenton's bass reverberates out of space. There's no let-up on the next two verses, just a breakdown that destroys the past by introducing the self-consciously feminised and exotic Eno. It brings his synthesised sequential phrasing to a platform that both perfectly announces his own arrival and the Roxy manifesto.

The tape recording of the song is played over and over, right there in the kitchen, as I ponder the worlds of Marc Bolan and Bryan Ferry.

I catch myself reflected in the kitchen window as light falls. The electric bulbs begin to glow and I wonder why the black kids at Ducie High approach me with an air of caution – sometimes revulsion even. They never really try to connect with me.

But now I realise that in fact it's *me* that keeps *them* at bay. By embracing a white world that isn't particularly interested in or reflective (in a truly mirroring sense) of my outer one, my inner world continues to grow, despite this daily negative affirmation.

Though I can't help but notice this disaccord, I have to embrace it as being exactly who I am.

Chapter Thirteen

We are in the fourth form now. The September sun bounces off the classroom windows as we eye each other up, having been away for six long weeks that seemed to last a lifetime.

The upper school feels like a total graduation, as we've moved across the road from lower school and now huddle together in the enormous playground that sits outside the big L-shaped building. There is also an annexe to the left, which is a common room for the sixth formers.

For the back-to-school party, I've managed to tuck myself into a tight-fitting, denim, flared-trousered jumpsuit. After spending a long time figuring where my knob and balls should be positioned, I decide to dress to my left (your right) and, rather uncomfortably, tuck everything to one side.

My new black-and-cream platform shoes, with stars on the front, finish the look. Though they're not the sparkly silver-and-black ones I've been lusting after, something Marc Bolan would doubtless wear, they're cool and give me extra height. They also hide the weight gain I pass off as my puppy-fat stage, even though, to me, I already look like a fully grown hound.

I stare at the picture of Bolan next to a towering stack of amplification on the cover of *Electric Warrior*, all surrounded by a golden halo. On the song 'Cosmic Dancer', he achingly sings in a language that seems somewhat off-kilter but, as sung by Marc, is beautiful:

What's it like to be a loon?
I liken it to a balloon

After downing thirteen Pernod and blackcurrants the night before, the next day at school I go about my business in my own quiet way. At the same time, I'm being told about what I did last night: how funny I was; how I really went for it; how I fell over.

Now my face contorts into that of somebody who's never even met the person they're talking about, let alone actually *is* him.

But despite the sore ankle I'm enduring after going over on those bloomin' shoes, I still love them. Judging by everybody's attitude towards me today, when the usual limp I carry goes largely unnoticed, I will *deffo* be wearing that outfit again.

*   *   *

Our new English teacher is as cool as you like. Maybe because he is so much younger than the other teachers, he seems like one of us. He asks if, for a change, we would like to go around to his house and take the lesson there, as it will be more relaxed?

The selected five of us glance furtively towards each other as we pile into his car. We arrive at his place in no time, cross the gravel and enter the building. Once inside his flat, we spread ourselves around the living room.

He tells us he'll be 'back in a sec'. Then, when he comes back into the room brandishing a tin, he opens it to reveal a bunch of finely chopped leaves, asking, 'Who knows what this is?' We throw quizzical eyebrows at each other as he smiles, wondering how this relates to an English lesson – or if it does at all.

He then takes out a card packet with thin papers inside it. He takes three of the papers and sticks two of them together lengthways by a sticky bit that runs along the top, adding the third paper across the other two like a building block to solidify the structure.

Then he takes out the leaves and sprinkles them onto the paper, adding a bit of tobacco from a cigarette and rolling the whole thing up. We are transfixed, giving each other nudges with our elbows as he licks the edge of the papers, smiling and looking over his spectacles, nodding his head as if to say, '*This is going to be great.*'

He takes one end and twirls the paper so that nothing falls out. Holding it by the tip like a pen, he observes it, then rips off a piece of card to put in the other end. He admires his handiwork and says, 'For those of you not in the know, this is a 'joint'. Spliff. Hash. Grass. Pot. Bush. Weed. Dope. Shit. Tea. Pot. Reefer. Ganja. Cannabis. Marijuana.'

He lights the joint and inhales the smoke, holding it in his lungs. Just before his head explodes or he chokes to death, he slowly lets the smoke out. He repeats this a couple more times and then we see him relax alright. His body goes all limp and he lets out a little chuckle. Then he begins to pass the bush around.

I copy the way that our English teacher smokes it, feeling my body become powerful and, at the same time, very relaxed. My right hip has been bothering me of late, but even that nagging thought seems to be disappearing along with the pain itself.

He plays some rock music and I feel it enter my every pore and organ. The clarity of the music is unbelievable. I seem to be able to isolate each instrument with ease, as though the musicians were right here in the room – the way that I could after the pre-med injection went into my vein, just before I fell into a deep sleep for my hip operation.

He brings out a bunch of American comics. I get it that this might be the lesson. The first one I pick up has a story about a blues artists' manager, travelling around the Deep South of America, looking for 'authentic' blues musicians. He travels in a limo and is partially hidden behind the car's window as different musicians play to him when he pulls up.

Eventually, he finds the singer who fits the bill. Winding the window down, he tells the singer that his new name is 'Blind Willie Johnson'. Willie says, 'But I ain't blind!' At which point, the manager leans out of his window and, spreading two fingers apart, thrusts them into the eyes of the bluesman. In huge letters, the word '*FOIT!*' – the sound of the fingers entering the bluesman's eyes – is written across the image. 'You are now!' says the manager.

The next story is about a rock star called 'Vince Clit'. I'm just getting into Vince, all slicked-back hair and leather jacket, when we're told, 'That's it.' We're heading back to school.

'Here endeth the lesson,' our English teacher says. 'Make sure you have all your belongings.' But we're all just giggling at everything.

That night, I sleep better than I have in a while, as I recall *FOIT!* and Vince Clit. I also notice that I seem to have lost about two stone in weight.

* * *

I grab a seat upstairs on the school bus as we head on out to Hough End for our games lessons. The sun coruscates through the window as the bus turns into Princess Road by the brewery. It blinds me a little, until the shadow of Joey Gray darkens my view.

'That's my seat.' There's a kind of hush that takes up space in a moment like this.

Everybody knows that Joey Gray is the cock of the school, including me. The 'cock' being the toughest kid, the best fighter. The question on everybody's mind on that bus is '*What the fuck is Adamson going to do about it?*'

My whole life flashes before me as the bus passes Leech's Funeral Service on Princess Road. I think about Elvis' 'It's Now Or Never'; my hip operations; the damn cast; the effort it took for me to walk again; Mark's cock in my mouth.

The other kids look at me as though I've just walked out onstage for the first time. 'Actually, I think you'll find that this seat is mine,' I say, not unlike some pompous aristocrat.

Joey spots an immediate weakness. '*Actually?*' he mocks, throwing me slightly off-centre. I see it as a warning.

I absorb the first blow as I'm able to see it coming, taking it in the chest rather than on the chin. He hasn't hit the bee on my breast pocket, so he can fuck right off. I come back with a right and a left. He dominates me in size but *fuck him*, I beat Tony Martin at Old Moat and he was bigger than this twat.

I catch him in the face and he bites me, which gives me time to hit him again. We've slipped between the seats and he has the better of me at this moment, for sure. Even though my spirit is telling me that I can have him, no problem, I'm quickly realising why he's the cock. He is willing to die for this. Also, with him being white, it's a well-known fact that you don't fuck with 'half-castes' – we are all willing to die in a fight. The odds, then, are even, though my breath seems to leave me while he has me on the ground.

121

Next thing I know is that the bus has come to a halt. Joey Gray has been pulled off me and dragged downstairs by the games teacher.

And so the seat is now, officially, mine.

After the adrenaline has worn off, I feel low as I walk back into school after lunch. Word has got around that I dared to take on the cock of the school. A mixture of fear and respect pervades the air as two of his mates approach me.

One of them pokes me in the chest, challenging me as to how I could even think that was the end of it. Didn't I know there was going to be a price to pay?

The other one keeps saying, 'Yeah.'

All the while, I'm backing up into the playground as everybody else is going to lessons.

While I'm busily destroying the second guy with a look that reflects his total stupidity, the first guy catches me with a right hook. It's on again. Both of them are on me and I'm sinking with each blow.

I land on the ground and know that if I don't do something, I'm gonna get the shit kicked out of me. I look up to where I should be in class. I see the girls looking down at me and remember a move I saw in a wrestling match on *World Of Sport.*

I roll my legs up towards my stomach, as though I'm about to roll into a ball, but instead, I flick my legs into the air from this prone position and manage to hit the first guy in the face, the shock of which sends them both reeling.

The girls have told the teacher, who now screams from the window as they stagger off. I'm drawn into the office of the head, Miss Blackburn, and read the riot act. I am, however, given clemency as she seems to know who I am, who Joey Gray is and, indeed, about the reign of terror acted out by his thug mates.

She tries to instil in me the idea that if I stay on the right path then there's a future for me, a good one. I take it on board, as she seems to have an intricate understanding of exactly where I'm positioned in life right now.

I head back to the class through empty corridors and echoing staircases, listening to the muffled sounds of learning. I knock on the door then silently take my seat. The others are bursting to know what my punishment was, but I act as if nothing has changed for better or worse.

Then I stare out of the window at where they had me on the floor, unsure if I even won.

I feel like I'm developing a whole new set of personalities, but it also feels like I'm in the loneliest place on the planet.

Try as I might to connect with Winston Bryan, Roger Sanford, Keithley Brandy and the Palmers, all of whom are black, they see right through me. See right past me. Or don't even see me at all.

Winston gives me a moment – indeed, he's given me quite a few – and even lets Joey Gray know that it's not a good idea to go there with me again. But I feel a distance in the same way that I feel towards my dad.

I wonder if they all, in fact, see someone with the word 'NEED' beaming from their forehead. If, unconsciously, they know that this need is way, way bigger than any friendship could bear. And so they kick the ball in the other direction.

* * *

Willie Trotter reappears. It's the first time I've seen him since the days of Embden Street School where, in my oversized pram, I first sought his attention. We stand in the school corridor together now.

I can gauge his curiosity about how I now stand strong, firm, kicking a ball with the best of them. I've conquered my weaknesses, while at the same time I carry something of my past physical state that only he can see, yet will never speak about.

There is an instant respect between us, as he also understands that I can see through his insouciant mask. There's a savvy cover-up going on of his own Irish roots, which at the same time are flaunted by his family of hard-edged survivors.

His brother Sammy wears his detachment on his sleeve, to the point of what might seem cool. But he comes across mainly as a loner with a grudge, who one day might either kill or settle into daily religious worship. He is highly vulnerable and, to my mind, slightly unhinged. One moment he is a ball of unexpressed anger and the next full of joy, darting past like a man released. He puts a kind of fear into me that keeps me at a distance.

Their sister Margaret (Maggie) is like a walking, talking, deflecting machine. Each and every sentence is overexaggerated, so that you don't miss a single wide-eyed word she says. (If you ever do, she will pin you to the ground with her disbelief.)

Maggie often gesticulates on the brink of tears, oscillating between a grounded, practical commonsense and hysteria. She always explains everything as though catastrophe is around the corner. Whenever I see her, though, my heart swells.

As for Willie, like me, his carefully constructed guise reveals nothing about the boy inside. His skill at mirroring others makes sure you feel safe in his presence, though, in actuality, there is only one of you there.

He can make you venerate him. His ability to make you believe you are right where you're meant to be is second to none. As is his attention to your detail, except for an occasional furtive glance over his shoulder before he leans into you and drops a juicy nugget about one of the other kids' misfortunes. He takes no prisoners in his observations, bringing tiny elements of both Sammy and Maggie to his game – though he'll deny any connection to either.

In the corridor, doors quickly burst open from a class that has just finished lessons. I then hear one of my classmates say, 'Quick, let's get to the canteen before the niggers do.' I look in the direction of where the remark seemed to come from.

Me and Willie are then frozen in a space only we will understand. It will stay that way forever, as this moment shall never be spoken of again.

* * *

On the way home, I stare across the fields from the bus as it wobbles down Princess Road. I anticipate when its fall and rise will occur, so that when I stand up and eventually make my way downstairs, I won't keel over.

I watch the road we're travelling down from above. The natural sound fades out and a song called 'Split – Part One' by rock band Groundhogs begins to well up on my inner soundtrack.

Groundhogs' sound has a traditional rock leaning, with multi-layered guitars and vocals dominating, but their main influence is the blues. Songwriter/singer/guitarist Tony McPhee meditates on anticipation of a peace that must surely be his at the end of the day.

However, as with me, it does not come. I lose sight of the bus as guitar solos begin to play out in my head, running hard across Hough End fields as Tony sings:

But in place of slumber comes a bolt of fear instead

Chapter Fourteen

Dave Hughes is a mate who lives on Whitchurch Road. He has one brother. Unlike me and Dave, his brother is as thin as a wire. He also has jet-black hair and only one eye, as he lost the other one when somebody threw a dart at him.

He enjoys seeing me and Dave squirm at tales of his job at the hospital – of which he tells us, for example, 'A guy came in with a broken bottle lodged up his arse, he was in fucking agony.'

He also whips out his false eye for a laugh. Compared to his brother, me and Dave are gentlefolk.

The coat of the moment is a sheepskin, or 'sheepy'. Sheepskins are the coat of choice for businessmen who smoke cigars and drive Rolls-Royce Silver Shadows, dodgy dealers who might try to sell you that same car, football managers (and commentators), skinheads and suedeheads.

A luxury coat like this is a staple of the stylish, an eye-catching classic that exudes the idea you are not just a 'somebody' but actually somewhere above the somebody you're trying to be.

They can also cost a small fortune. I pester my parents into buying me one and my parcel arrives in no time. My brand-new sheepskin coat feels very nice. My parents glow with pride that they were able to keep me up to date with the world of high fashion, via the catalogue. Plus they've given me something that lets others know I want for nothing.

I notice, though, that the tan of the pelt looks a little on the orange side. The wool looks just a bit too white, too, which I put down to the newness of the garment. Like a new pair of brogue shoes, once it's broken in it will look absolutely boss.

When me and Dave and a few others meet up to mess about and shoot air pistols, I wear my new sheepskin with delight and dignity.

I pocket my pistol and head off down Longport Avenue, down the passageway and across to Whitchurch Road where a small group gather near Dave's house.

I wait for them to fall at my feet in admiration of just how cool I look. I expect them to bow their heads in shame, even, because they cannot compete with me. To acknowledge therefore, by default, that I am their new leader.

I ask, rather sheepishly, 'What do you reckon to my new sheepy?'

Dave smirks at me and says, 'That's not a sheepy, it's a *cheapy*!'

The others laugh at the shrewdness of his observation but I'm totally crestfallen. My blood begins to boil and my breathing starts to accelerate.

Such is the volume of the laughter that surrounds me, and so foolish do I feel, that I take out my air pistol. I want to shoot him right through his fucking eye,

I don't, though, electing to drop the pistol's aim and shoot him in the kneecap instead. There is a look of horror on his face as he deflates, like Yogi Bear with a pencil stuck in him.

His look says, *'I can't believe you just did that'* – which is the perfect response, as it's exactly how I feel about what he said to me.

I hope one day we can both see the funny side of it all. But for now, all I can think about is how Dave may not be the mate I thought he was – and how to get rid of that coat, without seeming ungrateful to my parents.

* * *

Everybody at Ducie seems to have lost, or is in the process of losing, their virginity. I'm a little bit behind all of them, to say the least.

Here I am, fifteen years old and abso-bloody-lutely no action at all. Meanwhile, my mates are all pairing off left, right and centre, letting me know they've been behind the bike sheds by way of sticking their fingers under my nose and telling me to 'smell that'. 'She's got tits,' they say and wander off, satiating themselves on whoever's vaginal juices might be lingering on their fingers.

My mum says I'm a late developer. That must be why I don't have any pubes yet, pubic hair being *the* symbol of adulthood. It's also the reason I'm quite shy about putting myself out there.

I decide to practise kissing on my upper arm. It's not like I haven't kissed a girl before, but I feel the need to get myself ready for when the full-blown French kissing sessions will start. Then the fingering can begin.

On past school trips I remember trying to kiss Alison Beggs or Karen Hutchkinson, but I ended up headbutting them instead. I did run off with a certain badge of honour after sneaking into Withington's Scala cinema to see a movie called *El Condor*, where naked sex was on display. Obviously, much joy awaits. As my mum likes to tell me, I don't want to be backwards at coming forwards, so I'd better get practising.

I look at my left arm and it appears to be waiting for me to make some kind of move, like it can read my insecurity. It's almost telling me, '*Just jump in and get on with it, for fuck's sake!*'

I lean into my arm, close my eyes, open my mouth and move my neck forwards to connect with the fleshy limb. '*A bit salty?*' asks the voice in my head.

I begin to relax into it. '*This is getting good,*' I tell myself as I pull away from a satisfied (but slightly wet) arm. I also notice that I've given myself a love bite.

Music and the prospect of one day having sex have both become central to my existence. In fact, my previous attempts at French kissing my mum resulted in her throwing me across the room in disgust, not that many years ago.

But the records I listen to seem to connect to my need to prepare for a life of sexual abandon. So, one day, I have the idea of practising having sex on the couch. (No, make that sex *with* the couch.)

I turn on the radio when everyone is out and wait for the moment of arousal. When 'Blockbuster' by The Sweet plays, heralded by the sound of the siren at the beginning, I know that moment has arrived.

The Bowie-like 'Jean Genie' riff kicks in as the band wail like a siren. Their cry is followed by a tale of an everyday predator called Buster, who seems to be all about stealing your girlfriend – and therefore needs to be blocked. The overall sentiment of the song is defeating said Buster.

I think that because the couch is rough, I need to put a plastic bag under the cushion seat so that I can slide my knob right under there. Which I'm now doing. I begin the back-and-forth motion that I witnessed in *El Condor* as lead vocalist Brian Connolly enquires right in my ear as to whether anyone knows the way.

I certainly don't know the way – or at least I didn't then – as I switch between Buster, who seems a pretty cool customer to me, and the guy in fear of what Buster might take from him.

The song's chorus pauses, then echoes on and on as though giving me an injection of pure white light. I become completely at one with myself, with the song, with the moment and with... the sofa?

*   *   *

But fuck the charts.

There is now officially much better music outside the charts and it is literally taking me over.

I still listen to Tony Blackburn's radio show in the morning and then wave my mum off to work, before heading off myself to school. But today I feel a nausea, decide that I'm sick and need to stay off school – if not for the rest of term, then at least for today.

Before too long, the postman arrives with the imports I've ordered from America of two Alice Cooper albums: *Love It To Death* and *Killer*.

Alice Cooper's *Love It To Death* and *Killer* arrive on my doorstep, nineteen seventy-three.

I turn off the radio, crunch on some more toast with that fucking Golly marmalade, slurp some tea and stare at the sleeves for a good few hours. I look at the cardboard packaging and imagine them being packed to send to the UK. To England. To Greater Manchester. To Longport Avenue. To number nine. To me.

I almost don't want to listen to them, thinking that maybe I'll just keep them unplayed, so that the shining black vinyl is never separated from its clinging white inner sleeve.

'Caught In A Dream' is the first track on *Love It To Death*. It says everything I want to say, word for word, expressing my inner world perfectly. The need to escape the everyday; the idea of being entitled to the riches of the world, just because I exist; some kind of pay-off for the toughness of having to keep my feelings in check, when I really just want to tell everybody to fuck off:

> *I'm caught in a dream, so what?*
> *You don't know what I'm going through*

The whole album holds up a bright and shiny mirror that also resonates with an almost shocking darkness I've not heard on record before. I see myself in it, standing outside everything that I understand about the world right now.

After *Love It To Death, Killer* just might be the greatest rock album of all time. The Alice Cooper darkness permeates both albums: death, black magic, apocalypse, madness – all new curiosities that are becoming part of my burgeoning mindset.

Eight songs. Thirty-seven minutes long. Side One: 'Under My Wheels'; 'Be My Lover'; 'Halo Of Flies'; 'Desperado'. Side Two: 'You Drive Me Nervous'; 'Yeah Yeah Yeah'; 'Dead Babies'; 'Killer'.

The sheer energy and power of these two records, how every lyric resonates with me, provides an almost elasticated forcefield I can bounce off. I now have something in my corner when I need to come out fighting. All my darkest fears are given over to a new empowerment, where the darkness I try to hide is magically embraced. I realise that all of it, *the all* of it, is exactly who I am.

Losing my virginity seems now to come a very poor second to learning every nuance of these two albums, committing them to memory: from the lyrics to the sound of the guitars, to Alice's whisky-soaked voice and the strings that are suddenly introduced in 'Halo Of Flies', before it veers off into a King Crimson-esque bout of prog rock. In the hands of producer Bob Ezrin, all is remarkable.

Each track builds on the last, with not a single moment wasted; Ezrin's rule being that every song on the record should be a 'killer'. And each one is. Every song seems to sum up my life.

I float back into the upper school. The funereal organ march from Alice Cooper's 'Killer' plays out beside me like a new best friend. It's a complete soundtrack which I bask in, removing me from reality even as I move into the school playground.

It's as though I've grown a few feet in the night as I flailed away in my sleep. Shedding my skin, I've grown a newer, thicker one. My head is high.

I look at those kids playing football. They stop kicking and let the ball run away with itself, directionless, until it hits the school fencing.

The girls titter to themselves, flushing. Some stare as if seeing me for the first time.

In my view, Willie Trotter and all the others – Dempsey, Robertson, Bryan, Sandiford, Palmer, Brandy, Cole – will now understand the truth about me.

That I am special.

That I am gifted beyond the norm.

That my skits and my skilful impressions of others, plus my gift of memorising everything off the telly are not just something that anyone can do.

They now see that I am something beyond this 'half-caste'.

That I am beyond the limp that I carry.

That I am a bright and shining star – now, henceforth and forever to be held in the highest regard possible.

I'm caught in a dream, so what?

Carol Griffiths also floats through the upper school. She is the only person not to notice that I'm doing exactly the same as I float towards her. She drifts right past me. Losing myself, I hit the wall with a thud.

I slide down the wall as a string orchestra slowly slides from a high to low note. I look like a complete dickhead.

Carol has read the whole situation perfectly and knows that she has me by the short and curlies. In this defining moment, everything is changed forever as far as I'm concerned.

She also believes she is too good for me, largely based on ideas that, once broken down, we both know are absolute bullshit. But for now, this situation will have to be. I'm carefully weighing up the odds before a move can be made. A word uttered. A gesture shaped.

In the meantime, I prepare the necessary ground to devote my life to her. When she casts an eye my way, I move my hand slowly towards my pocket to deflect my limp.

I also make sure that when she sees me with my boys, I'm the one that is the centre of their attention: the funniest guy on the planet, adored by all. That way, she can start ticking the boxes that, in my mind, I've already taken for granted.

I also sweep aside any general societal notions, for example, that 'mixed marriages' don't work. Being Mormons, her family believe that black people shall perish on this earth and only become enriched when they enter the Kingdom of Heaven. But these are just minor obstacles to the progress of something that could be truly wonderful.

As for anybody else, they cannot touch her.

I also note that singing Mormon family sensation The Osmonds are the centre of every schoolgirl's universe. So much so that Carol and her best friend have become devotees of the Osmond faith. Competing with Carol's most recently demented religious conversion is going to be something else to contend with.

I arrive home, trying to figure out how to swerve what simply cannot be bypassed. I search out a copy of The Osmonds' 'Crazy Horses' on tape. I listen to it with intent and intensity, realising it is a stone-cold classic. Even though it feels manufactured and less raw than Alice, there is a concrete groove, a boss chorus and a very cool guitar solo. The brass has a rough-edged pop/soul feel as Donny sings his arse off.

I get it. I get why she would have a moment where she felt she needed to prepare herself for Donny, I really do. But that will not stop me in my quest to be with her forever.

And a day.

* * *

It's Friday night now. My mum tells me she has a new job as manageress of an old people's home in Gorton. We're all going to be living there as the job is 'live-in'.

Starting from Monday.

Chapter Fifteen

As I lie in my tiny bed thinking about Carol, the bedroom door slowly opens. In the dimly lit corridor, standing before me, I see a woman in her eighties, in a see-through nightie. As she quietly bemoans her lot a little puddle of wee forms at her ankles, catching the light.

She now begins to cry as she inches towards me. Then my mum appears, as do a couple of carers from the nightshift, torches waving. The scene is surrealistic, but then they've part blinded me with their lights.

If this wasn't Carisbrooke Old People's Home then I'd be unsure as to whether what just happened was real or the stuff of nightmares. Either way, this situation is not in any way, shape or form an ideal scenario for any teenager, though I have a smidge of compassion for the old bat – I mean, old Doris. As she is being led away, saying, 'I was only looking for the light of the moon. What's so wrong about that?'

Luckily, I've managed to sneak a couple of copies of *Fiesta* and *Mayfair* magazines from my dad's cupboard drawer, to quell the after-effects of such incidents. Which, to be honest, are happening quite often, as is my foraging around my dad's cupboard for the latest editions.

The pay-off is worth the fear of being found out. Now, I can soothe myself back to sleep and, anyway, I can sneak 'em back into his cupboard drawer after he goes to work in the morning. In the meantime, though, I can never (and will never) ponder over why *he* has these magazines in the first place.

So… after a gentle perusal of the seemingly untouchable women of *Mayfair*, it's straight to the 'Readers' Wives' section of *Fiesta*. There is something so exciting about seeing photos of somebody who might just live down the street from me. Pitted against the impossibility of actually getting with somebody who graces those colourful porn pin-up pages, here in black and white is Norma from Doncaster, June from Bristol, Eve from Nottingham in stockings and suspenders and…

That's me. Done.

* * *

Pips is a nightclub in Fennel Street, in the city centre of Manchester, behind the cathedral. Through huge black double-doors and down twenty or so steps are four rooms. Past the admission kiosk, the club splits into two. The upstairs room is on the left, but on the right, past the cloakroom, are stairs down to the 'commercial room'. Past what is known as the 'Roxy room'.

Here, everybody dresses like Bryan Ferry. Most dance like him too, which is simply to lean from left to right with an added gentle sway that exudes the coolest of the cool. With eyes half-closed, wallowing in one's own greatness, lest others don't notice you.

I meet Clint, who has a Sunday job at the *Daily Express*, in that rather large building on Ancoats Street. Clint, even though he is mousy of hair, *is* Bryan Ferry. He embodies every movement and mannerism of the man; his dress sense, like Ferry's, is impeccable. As his dad is the art editor there, he reckons he can get me a job on the *Express* as a touch-up artists' assistant – which he duly does.

The job is from 2pm until 10pm every Sunday. The wage is £3.99. I wait at a 'station' with Clint for photographs to come down a chute from the library; then I take them to the artists and wait for said photos to be touched up (extra details highlighted or added). Then I put them back up the chute to editorial, pin them to copy or walk to the news desk to deliver them by hand.

Here, I also meet Jamie, Ian and Martin. Jamie is the opposite of Clint, more Bowie than Ferry but more feral than Bowie. He blows bubbles from saliva in his mouth as a hint of how cool he is and smells a little off, like he lives a harder life than we do.

Ian is the son of the sub-editor and acts (like his father) as though he owns the place. At first I have to ask if that is actually the case, so convincing is their proprietorial double act. Ian's friend is Martin, a bespectacled, quiet, quick-witted and keenly observational guy known as 'Scat' from his second name, Scattergood.

Once Ian stops blustering, Scat drops lines that tell you he's no foil (to Ian's self-perceived 'rapier wit'). He uses this skill to navigate his way through, so I give him a heads-up nod – to which he nods back in a mimicking, knowing but not *fully* knowing way.

We spend our wages on clothes, more gigs, Belle Vue on a Saturday night, eating burgers at the Great American Disaster and drinking in the bars along Spring Street. I allow myself to point out to Scat that, in most of the bars we go to, I'm the only black person in the room. It takes him aback so he racks up a moment of empathy, speculating on how that must be for me.

Having seen David Bowie play at Manchester Free Trade Hall last year – his last Ziggy Stardust and the Spiders from Mars show before breaking up the band at Hammersmith Odeon, weeks later – gigs, the new currency of youth, are now everything.

It is the norm that week after week the greatest bands in the history of rock music visit Manchester to play the Free Trade Hall, the Apollo (just down the road from me, an easy walk home) or Belle Vue (also down the road from me, in the other direction).

With a mixture of friends I see:

Black Sabbath
Deep Purple
Hawkwind
Groundhogs
The Sensational Alex Harvey Band
Alice Cooper
Focus
Johnny Winter
Iggy and the Stooges
Nazareth
Rick Wakeman
Tangerine Dream

Soft Machine
Wishbone Ash
Robin Trower
Bowie again
Kiss.

Me and Steve Dempsey, another friend from school who, like me, has a passion for music and fashion, travel to the Buxton Festival, arriving on Friday night. We both wear Afghan coats splattered with patchouli oil and think we are the coolest kids on earth. With the site not yet open, we bed down in a ditch. We're really cutting our teeth on the festival circuit. Tomorrow we will be fully fledged festival attendees, coated in mud and with little rest.

Poster for Buxton Music Festival, July nineteen seventy-three.

As if to prove the point, our alarm call is not the ringing of a distant bell in a sleepy Derbyshire clock tower but an awakening by Hells Angels who walk over us, stomping us further into our ditch with each footstep.

After that somewhat harrowing ordeal, we're in. With the as-expected awful festival weather and the Hells Angels dominating the event, word is that several bands aren't going to play – amongst them Groundhogs and Medicine Head, who we were really hoping to see.

Instead, the Sensational Alex Harvey Band will appear later. But first the Edgar Broughton Band take the stage, offering their rousing chant of 'Out Demons Out'.

The sun appears briefly, shining on our addled, trodden-on souls.

The Sensational Alex Harvey Band are a complete revelation. Alex himself, all drunken Scottish swagger and fifties blues influence, wearing a black-and-white hooped t-shirt under a black leather jacket, fronts a band that sound as strange and wonderful as they look.

In particular, guitarist Zal Cleminson wears a bright green leotard and geisha make-up, like a garish combination of The Joker-cum-Riddler from *Batman*. His playing is outrageously brilliant, up there with Glen Buxton and Michael Bruce from Alice Cooper's band.

They jump onto the stage and kick in with a version of The Osmonds' 'Crazy Horses' (for me, no doubt, gluing my future to that of Carol Griffiths just that little bit more). During one song, Alex jumps off the stage and faces up to a Hells Angel who is about to pummel some kid, preventing him from doing so. Then a moody synthesizer sequence pulsates and Zal throws guitar stabs across it. The sound is hypnotic and strange. Alex leans into us and sings 'Faith Healer'. He throws his arms out, holding them there like a demented priest.

Later in the day there's Nazareth, a hard rock band. For some utterly naive reason, on hearing them play I expect them to have flown over from America. I'm shocked to later find out they're actually from Dunfermline in Scotland. But when they play a song called 'Bad Bad Boy' I'm completely sold, wherever the fuck they come from.

Canned Heat – who definitely, at no expense spared, have flown in from America – play raw boogie. Singer Bob 'the Bear' Hite's incredible voice and blues harp stand out as something else; 'On the Road Again' is a complete classic that, sure as hell, will live on long after any of us who are present here.

Then Chuck Berry appears, as do a whole bunch of Hells Angels. Hats off to him, he braves a shortened set by simply getting on with it as the Angels copy his famous duck-walk across the stage. It's pretty evident though that he's shitting himself. He heads for the hills and no encore is forthcoming. As the crowd sends a hail of beer cans towards the stage, the Hells Angels wade in to 'calm things down'.

That's enough for me and Dempsey.

* * *

Back in Manchester, with Scat, I see Wishbone Ash. There is a slight sense that my liking for prog rock is starting to get a bit too much. For the first time, I start to feel a little lost and that music isn't going to (as Don McLean sings in 'American Pie') save my mortal soul.

In fact at the next gig, Soft Machine are so awful that we leave mid-set. Existential angst prevails, our brows furrowed as we walk along Peter Street to the strains of the band.

In some sort of twisted reality it could have been the sound of a string quartet from bygone years, playing from the roof of the overtly grand Midland Hotel facing St Peter's Square. This is the spot where Charles Rolls met Henry Royce in nineteen-hundred and four, when a car was born.

The fact is that I love this steel-framed, red-brick, polished granite and terracotta, Edwardian baroque palace. I raise my head up to admire Charles Trubshaw's brilliant architecture, though it's something I keep very much to myself.

I dream of rooming here at some point in the not-too-distant future, staying in the finest suite with service like I've never experienced before. I can see why Adolf Hitler considered taking it over as the Third Reich's UK headquarters: its opulence and grandiosity loom large.

A limousine slides in front of us, stopping us dead in our tracks. At first I think it's some kind of hold-up. Then we gape in awe as the occupants all jump out at once.

It's Roxy Music.

Phil Manzanera and Eno run past us as sax player Andy Mackay steals my eye. Then I look around and see Scat completely flattened to the ground by a hurrying Bryan Ferry. Unlike The Beatles in the sixties, the hotel won't be turning them away for 'inappropriate dress'.

* * *

Back at Ducie High school, the art teacher, Mr Griffiths (no relation to Carol), notices that I'm paying attention to how composition in drawing, painting and photography is crucial to conveying the aesthetic of the piece; to how the eye works in terms of 'reading' a picture; and that I understand why Mondrian is so brilliant.

His air is one not of encouragement but that of a man used to the imparting of knowledge falling on deaf ears and closed eyes. He woefully expounds on what was clearly once, for him, the exact and exciting element that got him out of bed every morning. A passion that, when presented in a clear and cohesive manner, he believed could be imprinted on young minds seeking artistic direction, with endless possibilities.

Mr Griffiths has lit that kind of fire within me. I want to know more. He is somewhat aware that he's helping my confidence grow, that I might be on to something with my sketches. I might even have a career.

He refuses to believe it, though. All he has seen, over and over again, is a fleeting interest go to waste and turn into a pointless exercise.

When the class finishes, he sees me come-a-running and so he quickly skedaddles downstairs, holding onto the polished wooden cylindrical rail for dear life. I pursue, firing a million questions at him.

Mr Griffiths is the spitting image of film actor Peter Cushing, who appears in horror movies as Dracula's nemesis. I imagine, therefore, that he is off to drive a wooden stake into the heart of Christopher Lee and doesn't have time for my trivial questions about cubism, why Mondrian was pushed to abstraction and who else was a part of the Abstraction-Création group?

The fact that I can draw a bit now earns me a strange respect amongst my peers. I suspect that this ability also keeps me out of trouble. Plus I can freely give it as a gift, as I do when I see that my friend Alan Cole is feeling troubled. To see his face lit up by a simple sketch that I draw of entertainer Tommy Steele is reward in itself.

My portrait of Tommy Steele, drawn for Alan Cole in nineteen seventy-five.

Right now, the collarless shirt reigns supreme. So I suggest that me and Willie Trotter, together with our mates Peter Robertson and Steve Dempsey, need to go into town to the antique market to buy a bunch of them. And I mean right now – this lunchtime. It's an imperative, so that we can all look (word of the moment) 'morse' (as in 'boss', 'cool as ice').

Oris Seniuk takes us in his dad's Morris Minor. On the way back, flying down Lloyd Street, the car skids out of control and flips onto its roof, travelling two hundred feet on the other side of the road before hitting a bus.

But all is quiet. All is calm.

What saved us is that we're packed in as tight as eggs in a box. As girls on the bus begin wailing for our lives, I ask if everyone's okay. There is a pause as the weight of what's just happened begins to sink in.

141

Then Robertson, in true Robertson style, lays out an optimistic future by simply saying, 'Nurses.' The mood brightens immediately as we all envision women in uniforms and stockings.

After our ordeal, we're welcomed back into the schoolyard and treated almost like firefighters. Survivors of what we should never have survived. We walk through the upper school like kings. The reality hits me, though, as Tony Brierley mocks our heroism by trying to inject humour into proceedings, saying he's heard all about what we've been up to and alleging we'd do anything to get out of school.

I judge him for his carefree constant munching on a bag of crisps and overexcited vocal tone. I hate how he insinuates we were trying to get out of lessons, which leads to me letting off a volley of full-blown anger. I watch him wither and look away, unfairly scolded and not for the first time.

As for tonight, American group Kiss are playing at the Free Trade Hall. Despite my parents' protests that I should rest up after today, the adrenaline is shooting through me.

Just thinking about going to the gig is enough to send me out the door in a totally carefree *whoo-whoo!* way that Tony Brierley would appreciate.

The concert is amazing. But later, back at the old folks' home, everything hurts. Both outside and in. I can't unsee the moment the car flipped over. How I believed that everything that had happened up to that very moment was about to be taken away.

The collarless shirts look – as Mike Rawson (the kid who brought the word into school) would say – still 'fucking morse', though.

Chapter Sixteen

Roman Slobodian mesmerises the sixth-form centre by playing Led Zeppelin's song 'Stairway To Heaven' on an acoustic guitar. His cheeks flush beneath his dark hair as his fingers glide over the fretboard, pushing aside what anyone might think about him being overweight and from a very different land.

I queue from nine in the evening at Piccadilly Records for tickets to see Led Zeppelin at Earl's Court. Scat, cool as a cucumber, rocks up at four a.m. and joins me at the front of the queue. He tries not to but he gently mocks me until, tickets secured, we are off to London.

After seeing Led Zep perform for three hours, I decide right there and then I'll learn to play guitar and join a band. But with their giant speakers hanging in chains from the roof, I wonder just how I'm going to get from where I'm standing now onto any kind of stage.

I'm also reminded of my feelings of longing for Carol Griffiths. This now surely is the time to climb that particular stairway to Heaven.

* * *

I've passed my driving test and now have access to my dad's car, so I can drive from Gorton to Didsbury to see Carol. I have to park a few streets away from her house, because if her parents see what colour I am then it'll be over.

But I'll worry about that later as, right now, nothing makes me happier than to see her turn the corner at the end of the street, approach me with that confident anticipation she wears and jump into the passenger seat.

As night falls, she recounts some scene from her day, peppered with 'I mean this' and 'I mean that,' making the world go away as we drive off to Alderley Edge. Her voice tips into a higher register as she speaks, until she bursts out laughing.

Alderley Edge is an extremely affluent village in Cheshire, some fifteen miles south of Manchester. It is steeped in a folklore that many have their own spin on.

Legend has it, locals tell, of a farmer passing by the edge on the way to nearby Macclesfield. As he reached a place called Thieves' Hole, an old man jumped out and startled hm. The old man ogled the white horse the farmer was taking to market and proceeded to offer him next to nothing for it. The farmer told him where to get off, letting him know he'd get more cash at market. The old man said that if the farmer changed his mind, he'd be at the same spot on his return.

The farmer didn't sell the horse and, indeed, the strange old guy was there on his return journey. This time he agreed to sell the horse.

The old man took the farmer and horse to the hillside at a place known as Stormy Point, where he put his hand upon the rocks. Iron gates revealed themselves, which the old man (who the farmer figured must be a wizard) opened. All three then entered a large cavern.

Inside were men and horses, sound asleep. The wizard took some money from an old chest and paid the farmer for his own horse. The farmer, naturally taken aback, asked the wizard what the hell was going on. He was told that all these sleeping warriors and their horses were ready to awaken, to fight any enemy, should England ever be in danger. The wiz then told him to scarper. As he did, he heard the iron gates slam shut behind him.

There are several versions of this legend. Some later variations say the wizard was, in fact, Merlin and the sleeping men were King Arthur and his knights.

Carrying the weight of local folklore like a shield, I park the car on a piece of land known to local lovers. Losing my virginity is almost certainly on the cards now, as night begins to fall on the heavy-petting stage of our relationship. We ease back the seats of my dad's sporty turquoise Datsun 120A and smile at each other. I move the hair from Carol's pretty face and brush her cheek with my thumb.

10cc, a band of genius musicians who hold the number one spot in the charts with 'I'm Not In Love', live just down the road from where we are now. So when the song plays on the radio, a harmonious trinity is formed of 10cc, King Arthur and the Knights of the Round Table, and me and Carol Griffiths.

A Fender Rhodes electric piano plays a gently rocking figure, with a pulsating bass drum reminiscent of a heartbeat. The sound of the electric piano is steeped in echo and reverb, alluding to the feeling of something buried deep in the soul.

Forty-eight voices represent each note of the chromatic scale, made up of tape loops of each band member singing a single note sixteen times, to create an extraordinary choral backing. Then the lead vocal begins:

I'm not in love ...
It's just a silly phase I'm going through

I pinch open two buttons on Carol's blouse and we kiss again. All that practising on my arm is now coming into its own. Carol surrenders herself a little further, allowing me to pop open her skirt which I pull down slowly, glimpsing the translucent flesh of her thighs before returning my gaze to her eyes.

Outside the lurid blue Datsun, some twenty feet away from the car, two men nudge and smirk at each other, pull on black balaclavas and drop to their knees.

A grand piano is introduced, playing a high single-note melody, supported by a continuing swirl in which higher, quieter notes permeate the soundscape as we float into another world. I pull my trousers down.

The two men signal to each other that one should crawl along the floor to the passenger side and one to the driver's side.

Amidst the swirl, an electric bass plays a melody up high, a bridge part but also a departure from where the song seemed to be heading. It then plunges the listener into deeper emotional water as a woman's whispered voice is heard:

(Be quiet... Big boys don't cry.)

Heavy petting indeed, as my hands begin to wander.

The bass, in a world of its own but perfectly in tune with the rest of the song, fades back into the choral mix that's building up for the next verse.

The two men in black slowly crawl along the ground up to the driver's and passenger's side doors of my dad's Datsun.

In the next verse, the electric piano and the heartbeat play again.

Knowing they are invisible to the naked eye, the two men creep closer.

This is it then. Carol gives me the 'go ahead' to go ahead.

The song arrives at a point of resolution. The swirl gives way to clarity.

But something stops me from going further. Carol doubts herself in a moment that I can't fully explain.

The third verse reiterates the meaning of the song as the word 'love' echoes on and on...

I turn around, rolling away from Carol. In the veiled moonlight, I can just about make out the shape of a man's head pressed against the driver's side window. I make a fist and with the side of my hand bang on the window, shouting out.

The penny drops on the fact that we're being spied on by a couple of perverts, who probably stake out this lovers' lane every night, hoping to catch people like me and Carol at it.

Both of us rush to get our clothes back on and pull the seats up. I start the car, throw it into reverse and fly back about thirty feet. Then I stop to gauge how to turn around and get the hell out of here.

This would be a good time for King Arthur and his knights to appear. In the headlights I see that the two men are laying on the ground, within a few feet of one another, in an attempt to disappear into invisibility.

What to do next is very clear to me, as I imagine the car bumping over their bodies. But I look at Carol and something in her eyes says, '*Don't.*'

The electric piano plays out, peppered by the choir who almost play with the countermelody. I reverse further, my headlights shining away from the two men, back onto the road as the song fades. We don't talk any further and the radio is turned off.

We arrive at the old people's home.

146

On the floor of my little room at the back, I lose my virginity to Carol Griffiths.

As I lie alone in my bed the following morning, after Carol leaves, my mum creeps in to take out a couple of cups and plates. I tell her she doesn't have to be quiet as I'm wide awake. Without looking at me she says, 'I know. I've heard you and I've smelled you.'

* * *

I have an interview at Manchester University to study art and have been drawing pretty much non-stop. My new art teacher is Miss Clayton, who walks through the room like Elizabeth Taylor about to go holidaying in Santorini, with her black, *black* hair, wedge shoes and crocheted miniskirt. I learn nothing, my senses all but captivated by her need to be looked at and adored. Both of which I obligingly do.

Come the day, my dad lets me take the Datsun to the interview. I pack my work into a huge green folder and lay it on the backseat. I've factored in a pick-up for Carol to drop her off at school before I head off to the university. No need to tell my dad this as he waves me off and wishes me good luck.

I head to Didsbury, down Barlow Moor Road, and then see Carol in the rear-view mirror. She waves to me and so I decide to do a U-turn, to impress her by swinging the car around so that she can jump in as I smoothly pull up next to her.

Instead, on swinging it around a hundred and eighty degrees, I miscalculate and wrap the front of it almost around a lamppost, leaving a huge dent in the front. Carol's face opens in shock. I turn a ghostly pale too as she jumps in next to me.

After dropping her off near school, I drive to see the other Carol, my sister, at her place of work. She is the manager of another old people's home, in Fallowfield.

My mind is all over the shop as to how this is going to go. I know I've been totally irresponsible. How am I going to explain this to my dad? As far as the interview goes, am I even going to attend? My sister appears in the driveway of the home and says, 'Bloody 'ell, our Barry, what have you done?'

I try to explain my stupidity as an act of nobility. I was delivering Carol Griffiths to where she needed to go, putting that before anything else. My sister immediately sees through this and tells me we have to drive to see my dad at work, to show him what has happened. *Now.*

She calls to let him know about the accident and that we're on the way. On arrival, my dad's standing at the entrance of the dry goods depot he manages, in a light brown uniform coat, with a row of pens in his top pocket. His hands, bunched into fists, rest on each hip as the car, driven by my sister, creeps down the driveway of his workplace.

A little bit of sick pops into my mouth, which I quickly swallow.

My dad shows no anger but a deep disappointment. He explains that I will pay for the cost of the repairs – probably for the rest of my life.

I fail to be accepted by Manchester University. But I apply for Stockport Technical College to study graphic design instead, and I get in with ease.

*   *   *

A deep melancholy has set into the almost barren sixth-form centre. We're all leaving, which nobody seems to want to face up to. Robertson sweeps his hair back from his face as he settles into a cubicle. Janet Wigglesworth comes blaring over. I try to brush her off and look past her, as I have a crush on Janice Boult's *tristesse* manner.

I'm also obsessed with her huge breasts. She drags herself through the centre, held together by a tight light brown jumper, flowing skirt and dowdy platform shoes.

Carol Griffiths knows about my crush, after finding me holding Janice's hand under a cushion at a party. I'm also getting a bit too friendly with a girl known as 'Ironing Board' (so called because she has no breasts at all). At my last art class, I do little else but watch Miss Clayton's tanned legs and miniskirt as she noisily stomps around the room.

Post-sixth form, me, Robertson, his brother Paul, sidekick Mint and Willie Trotter drive to London to see Bowie. It's his nineteen seventy-six Thin White Duke show.

We stay after the concert and go to an all-night party at the London School of Economics. On the way home the next day, the designated driver – me – falls asleep on the motorway but manages to wake just in time to avoid hitting another car.

We make it. We make it home safe and sound, and so school is, indeed, out forever.

* * *

A million tiny lights swirl around me. As an eighteen-year-old, I'm now free to do what I want. So I apply to join a government-funded group that helps children from deprived areas during the summer, by getting them to put on and perform their own circus.

We're led by a girl called Gina. Pied Piper-style, we gather up children and announce ourselves through our own made up song:

We're going to make a circus
We're going to make a circus
We're going to make a circus
The greatest show on earth

Now it's fantastic (It's fantastic)
A thrill a minute (A thrill a minute)
So come along and be in it
Come along and be in it

One of my jobs at the end of the day is that I have to drop off toys and games at a church on Princess Road, at the Moss Side end quite near school. I explain to the stern-faced caretaker what I'm there for. I can feel his eyes on me, like I'm about to steal something. He follows me about, until I turn to ask if he can let me into the room downstairs.

The old man holds my gaze. In the silence of the empty church, I hear echoes as I follow him down: the sound of pint pots clinking; goals being scored; the phrase, 'They think it's all over, well, it is now.'

In a hallowed corridor of the church basement, he turns to face me, smiling a wicked smile. I feel he is asking me to make a choice of some kind.

He smells exactly like my 'cousin' Mark.

I act deliberately, as if the choice I'm about to make is one hundred per cent my own. At this point, I'm completely unaware of Sigmund Freud's concept of the compulsion to repeat trauma.

149

So here I am, on my knees before a man in his sixties who is smiling down at me. Once he's done emptying his balls, he makes a face like an adult helping a child who doesn't like the food that they've just been given.

He says, '*Urgh! Ewww!* Spit it out!' Which I do, all fortitude gone to the fucking dogs.

My eyes never leave the floor as I make my excuses about needing to get home as fast as I can. I dart up the stairs and out to where there is air.

* * *

I see Carol less and less. When I do, she looks as mystified as I feel, like she is in the presence of a ghost. The question hovering on her lips is the one thing she never says: '*Where have you disappeared to?*'

She meets me at the church one day but I can't get her out of the place quick enough. Away from the beaming caretaker, who once manipulatively held both of my hands to explain the way life works.

My mind shakes its head at me, tuts at me, calls me an idiot and tells me over and over that I've royally fucked everything up. Not just with Carol either.

Back at the circus factory, my friend Ricky notices that I've retreated. That I'm wearing the mask of the unapproachable, judgemental, angry young man to keep him away. And so he stays away. I see his disappointment but can do nothing about it.

I don't want to go home anymore, so I ask my sister if I can stay at hers. She lives in exactly the same set-up as my mum's but there is space to think and be alone when I want to.

Her boyfriend David ('Nip' as in 'nip of a lad', because of his diminutive figure) doesn't really want me there. It's understandable. He's vaguely tolerant but I know the look of someone who's putting up with something all too well.

Walking the fields, the soft summer wind teasing, Alice Cooper's song 'Eighteen' sums up everything I'm feeling:

I've got a baby's brain and an old man's heart ...
Don't always know what I'm talking about

That space between being a boy and a man, without any direction, sums me up alright. I just want to run as far as these fucked-up legs will take me, because I have absolutely no idea who I am or what I want.

This confusion feels like I might just explode across these fields, with football and rugby teams running over my remains, unaware that I ever existed.

And after all, why should they be aware?

It's time to make a move...

Chapter Seventeen

The busiest bus route in Britain, the 192 from Manchester City Centre, takes me all the way to Stockport College. Transport for Greater Manchester has designated this roadway, the A6, as a 'quality bus corridor'.

I sit on the top deck as always, surveying the land, the houses and all the shops as we drive through and past Ardwick Green, Longsight, Levenshulme, Stockport City Centre and then finally Stepping Hill, where the grand old college is situated on Wellington Road.

Stockport College is a medium-sized educational institute, providing further and higher education to school leavers, adults and businesses. It was opened in eighteen eighty-nine as Stockport Technical School. Over time, feeder secondary technical schools were established on a series of sites across the borough, such as Pendlebury Hall. Now, I take my place here amongst Adamsons past and present, to carve my name in stone – like the great Daniel Adamson, the prominent civil engineer who resided in the house next to Pendlebury Hall,

We unseasoned graphic art students huddle around each other like lost sheep, for basic introductions and inevitable formalities. ('You go here, you go there,' and so on.) We also want to see who's cool and who isn't, really.

In my year, there's Simon Biggerstaff, who's a kind of English Freewheelin' Franklin-type stoner, who I bond with immediately; diminutive and levelheaded Dave Allen (not the television comic); the

152

wonderfully named Guy Varley, who will no doubt get his own TV show – *Spying Tonight* might be a good title; 'Know-all Nigel', who seems to know everything, or at least professes to.

Then there's Maddy and Jacqui, who I imagine have been inseparable since birth. They both display a generosity of spirit, Maddy being the mumsy type with her feet on the ground, while Jacqui's head is in the clouds. They make the perfect duo. Then comes Mike Brown, who could be a prop forward for Newcastle Rugby Club, all long-permed alpha male, who with one flick of that perm steals Maddy's heart; while Brenda Cherry steals mine in an instant.

Roy Willan is possibly psychotic, while his sidekick 'Bruiser' (who clearly is neither psychotic nor indeed a bruiser – real name Paul Lancaster) stakes the place out. Then there's the very cool Eileen, who dresses to impress but waylays her confidence with every blush and girlish whimper. Smashing through the lot of us is Bridget (the midget, the queen of the blues), all Scottish balls-out 'get tae fuck'. Battered and bruised and disarmingly beautiful with it.

Next door to the college is the largely ignored War Memorial Art Gallery. Across the road from there is the much loved Nelson Tavern, where we spend possibly more time than at the actual college itself. Cider is the new currency of youth.

Students from other years swing by to check out the fresh meat and see what we've got going on, if anything. There's the effervescent Nick Howard, who can't stop talking about how America is the greatest place in the universe, and Julie, the posh redhead from Cheshire. She carries a sidekick with her like a handbag, a scary dark-haired girl who never speaks, just looks up from the ground every now and then. Julie's hardened northern accent belies her status but, as much as she tries to hide it, I taunt her with the Hall & Oates song 'Rich Girl'.

She can rely on her old man's money and, through her laughter, I see that she knows I'm dead right.

The lectures don't hold me as much as the socialising does, whether it's drinking copious amounts of cider at the Nelson or getting stoned with Simon above a chippie in Northenden. Or meeting up with old school cohort Willie Trotter and his errant sidekick, Jimmy Ellis, who delights in telling me that, in my tight white jeans, I look like I have a vagina.

First days at Stockport College. Me and Simon Biggerstaff on the far right with
Ellen Topham and John Topliss, nineteen seventy-six.

If I'm to become the great architect that I want to be, however, I
must tune into my lectures. One is on how to graphically express our
environment using photographs. I borrow a film camera and some
lenses. Inspired to work hard, I begin to take my time here more
seriously as a result.

Nick Howard comes blasting through the door as though he's from
Philadelphia. He's dancing and insists we all go see Kool & The Gang
and hit a nightclub – which indeed we do.

When I meet up with him on another night, out and about, he's
dressed in a full American police uniform. There is no acknowledgment
of this as he scans the streets for crime, telling me of a possible case he's
on.

Later that night, after being ejected from a club because one of us is dressed like a fucking US cop, I return to the old people's home. Looking in the tiny mirror above the sink in my room, I notice my chest is covered in red spots.

I undress further and see that I'm completely covered. I have chicken pox. The spots are everywhere. Most disturbingly, they're under my foreskin and I simply cannot stop scratching myself. I lie on my bed covered in calamine lotion, which my mum applies liberally all over my body, leaving me looking like a spotty ghost.

I spend my days reading Friedrich Nietzsche's poetic philosophical polemic, *Beyond Good And Evil*, at which my dad kisses his teeth and shakes his head whenever he drops by to see how I am.

Then, a week later, I'm alright.

Back to the Nelson Tavern. Julie and her pal tell us all about these jumpsuits they're selling from a design placement they attended the previous summer. We goad them into trying them on for us (which seems like a laugh). When they appear, jaws drop as they reveal their total voluptuousness. Soon the room is filled with students from every year, ogling them as they spill out of these barely zipped-up jumpsuits.

Jumpsuit Julie invites me over for Sunday breakfast at her house, which is the biggest house I've ever seen. She is spattered with freckles and wears massive spectacles in the style of Deirdre Barlow (played by the wonderful Anne Kirkbride) from *Coronation Street*.

After breakfast, she disappears and reappears in baby-doll lingerie. Forget the jumpsuit! She moves closer to me and, as I move the silverware away, leaps into the air. She lands awkwardly on me, in a scene straight out of *Confessions Of A Would-Be Graphic Designer*.

All my pre-teen pondering and subsequent studies of the clitoris really pay off now. I use my fingers on her, working them deftly to apparent pleasing effect as I feel our Julie yielding to my arousal. It affords me no end of encouragement. She stops me for a second and says in that deep, husky northern voice of hers, '*Ooooh*, you know exactly what to do, don't you?'

I turn and wink to my internal camera as both of our heads disappear out of the frame in a sea of moans before the end credits start rolling.

Roy Willan also invites me to his house, not far from college. I'm shocked to find he is obsessed with *Captain Scarlet And The Mysterons*. It belies an outer image of aggressive coolness, where all such attachments to childhood memory ought to be smashed to smithereens.

The other thing I notice is that there are full-length portraits of his mother everywhere in the house. Everywhere.

* * *

The college dance at Stockport Town Hall is in full swing. There's Roy and Bruiser, Mike Brown, Maddy and Simon, and most of the students from our course.

We are all performing various mating rituals through dance. One of the girls, Astrid, tall and blonde, who works locally as an au pair, makes it known to me that I'm in with a very slight chance.

I head to the bar, where an argument is taking place. Some guy is having a go at Roy Willan. Roy's eyes are almost on fire with indignation. He is dressed as Captain Scarlet but now becomes Captain Black.

As the other guy and a few of his mates wade into him, it is a call to arms to myself and our newly formed friends from college. But then Roy shocks me even further by picking up a glass ashtray and enthusiastically smashing it into the other guy's face.

Silence ensues. That's the end of that then.

On the bus home, I walk upstairs to see a gang of sixteen-year-olds taking drugs via hypodermic needles.

After reading *The Book Of Life* and learning all about heroin addiction, I'm not shocked by this. I tell them to be careful as the driver might be on to them. He was looking at the mirror that reflects the upstairs view and groaning out loud when I got onto the bus.

The bus does stop. The driver's stomping footsteps alert everyone. He walks around, looking between the seats, but they have hidden the drugs and other paraphernalia. When his check is done, the main guy, who seems a little older, nods in my direction. I watch him shoot up, then flick his hair out of his eyes while coolly looking from the bus window into the distance.

* * *

A new energy is starting to surge through every bone in my body. Somewhere inside me, I hear a faint ticking of existence; it gives me the idea that I just might belong to something in this world. Something that isn't dependent on status, colour, parenthood or anything else except a new kind of music. The idea that somehow I might be a part of its creation.

It began with Alice Cooper back in Ducie High School, where the liberation of nonconformity became, for the first time, a source of unlimited power. But here, now, in my own backyard, so to speak, it's as though the volume has been turned up. Now there really is a call to arms.

The Sex Pistols hail from London; they are the initiators of a new kind of music known by the nation as 'punk rock'. They are Glen Matlock on bass, Johnny Rotten on lead vocals, Steve Jones on guitar and Paul Cook on the drums Their music is raucous, full of attitude, balls and honesty. They are currently captivating and appalling the whole country in equal measure, with their abrasive sound and what is seen as an all-out attack on everyday social conformity. Their single, 'Anarchy In The UK', is released on November twenty-sixth, nineteen seventy-six, and becomes a new anthem for disaffected youth, myself included.

The seven-inch record runs out of its groove, with guitar feedback blasting through the speakers of the Alba (now in my bedroom) and throughout the old people's home.

My dad lurches up from leaning on the bedroom wall. 'Is dat what all de fuss is about?' His thick patois has never left him.

I look at him, exasperated, as though the most important record to be released in my entire lifetime has completely fallen on deaf ears.

'Better get on with it then,' he says and simply leaves the room. I roll my head back and, like England, begin to dream. Dream of something other than where I am now.

As punk rock begins to bludgeon the nation, I buy copies of the 'New Rose' by The Damned and 'White Riot' by The Clash, bringing them into college to play on the common-room record player. I hurriedly take The Clash's single out of its sleeve, drop the arm onto the vinyl and hike up the volume. After a rousing '1-2-3-4', the song wallops the senses as guitar chords, drums and bass smash into existence, commentating on the recent Notting Hill riots in London and wishing for similar action by the white working class. We can only imagine what it was like to be there but totally get what Joe Strummer is singing about. The energy of the song sums up anger towards the system perfectly.

As the record is ripping the common room in two, the fire alarm is sounded. Believing that the volume is what has triggered the alarm, I jump up and take it off – to much laughter from the others. My mutinous display of 'anarchy' has very quickly turned into an overblown sense of responsibility and guilt.

The Damned bring something equally fierce, the sound of the record outweighing what folk used to call 'heavy rock'. It's a new brutalism, with everything at full tilt all of the time – and then some more. Rat Scabies' drums are like nothing ever heard on record before. Then, the dense sound of the guitars and the vocal performance give the song the feeling of something altogether unhinged.

It begins with vampiric singer Dave Vanian quoting The Shangri-Las' 'Leader Of The Pack' followed by the most merciless drumbeat to launch the song, unrestrained tribal tom-toms – minus the tribe. It sounds another kind of alarm, before the most messed-up guitar sound crashes in and joins the mayhem. This part ends with a blast of four beats on the kit and Vanian giving a rock'n'roll scream, before the band flail into what is essentially an intro extension. This is usually reserved for less immediate genres, but it only sets up expectations further, which are delivered as the manic vocal begins.

These records are becoming like food, air and water to me. For the first time in my life, I get that I am right where I'm supposed to be.

Chapter Eighteen

The sleeve of Buzzcock's EP *Spiral Scratch*, nineteen seventy-seven.

It is nineteen seventy-seven. On the way to college, I stop at the Stockport shopping centre to buy an EP I've been reading about.

I ask the long-haired hippie at the record-shop counter if he has a copy of *Spiral Scratch* by Buzzcocks. The guy smiles and tells me I have good taste. Once I get past him not looking 'punk' enough to be an authority on such matters, he waxes lyrical about the record and impresses me with his knowledge, introducing himself as Paul Morley.

The record itself is beyond a revelation. The songs are fast, gnarly and repetitive.

Singer Howard Devoto spits out a new currency of complex intelligence across four tracks, lasting nine minutes and thirty-one seconds. His words are daring, original, unique, more Beckett than Bowie, his sense of meaning-through-drama reaching far beyond punk's generic rage.

My life is about to move into a place I've never allowed it to. I begin to see things quite differently. I start to poke up my head just a little higher, seeing new possibilities in my own existence.

Especially after seeing Buzzcocks and experiencing a moment with Pete Shelley, two doors down from me at the bar. He puts down his pint and lurches up to take the stage, some fifty feet away, then picks up a guitar that is sawn in half so that the top of its body is completely missing. The rest of the band then amble onto the stage and begin to play.

No ceremony. Nothing special about the occasion, but then everything is special about it. The exceptionality of the gig has the rug pulled from under it, so that its head lands with a thud on the everyday humdrum of life. Devoto knows this. The band do, too.

It wasn't that long ago that I was seeing Led Zeppelin and the idea of wanting to be in a band seemed impossible. Maybe not anymore...

During the song 'Breakdown', Devoto is wired by static electricity. He fizzes:

> If I seem a little jittery I can't restrain myself
> I'm falling into fancy fragments can't contain myself

I realise that the genius of Devoto lies in the dramatics of what he spits out. The ideas in lines like

> I wander loaded as a crowd, a nowhere wolf of pain

play on classical prose and destroy it by making it burst with newness, without any regard to morality whatsoever.

John Maher's ferocity and skill on the drumkit is lean and precise; that Pete Shelley on guitar and Steve Diggle on bass manage to keep up with him beggars belief. The overall effect of Devoto and the band is one of urgency, a totally inspiring call to do *something*.

If, like me, you feel that frustration and boredom, a voiceless parade of defeat and disappointment, lurk beneath each viaduct and hang around every street corner, then, like me, you will recognise the need to take a brand-new course of action by destroying all that has gone before.

I sit in my room at the old people's home, knowing that it's time I moved out, moved forward, moved into my own skin and listened to the whispers of wisdom now screaming at me from the Sex Pistols, Devoto, The Damned and The Clash.

* * *

At the invitation of Dave Allen and Simon, I leave home and move into a shared house in Darley Avenue, Gately. It's on the other side of Stockport to Manchester, left of Cheadle, below the M60 and onto the A650.

House at Darley Avenue. Photo by Simon Biggerstaff.

Maddy and Jacqui also live there, which means Mike Brown (called 'Brapper' due to his tremendous farting ability, he's always up for lighting a fart and torching a whole room) stays there too. As does little Debbie, who is pregnant.

Every night is a party, much to the vexation of Maddy. We drink cider, get stoned and play loud music. Willie and Jimmy swing by; Jimmy summons up an audience by playing Leonard Cohen songs in the garden. Brapper Brown invites his rugby club over; we all take magic mushrooms and they crash out in Maddy's room, leaving me to liven things up in the morning by blasting out the Sex Pistols' 'God Save The Queen'. Maddy explodes while me and Simon think it's hilarious.

Then there's Eileen, who drops by often, her infectious smile lighting up the place. She stays with me, all hardened and coquettish at the same time, keeping me at a distance.

Debbie turns me on to Do-Dos, a strange kind of tiny brown amphetamine pill. No sleep for a few days or so when taking them, it's as though a match has been lit inside my head. The worst effect of Do-Dos is that the drug shrinks my knob to nothing.

On day two of not sleeping, my dad very kindly offers to drop by and lay a new carpet. (So he can see how I'm living, no doubt.) But the Do-Dos feed into my guilt at not wanting him there. 'Can't he hurry up already?'

Now that the gang have met him, and now that I finally trust them, I'm able to perform skits involving conversations with my dad. They highlight his ruing of me and my imaginary comebacks to him to great comedic effect.

I feel a tremendous warmth towards Maddy, Jacqui, Mike 'Brapsody in' Brown, Debbie, Eileen, Dave and Simon. Acceptance from them sees me growing into myself and worrying less about my place in the world. They give me the courage to move to wherever I now see fit in life, regardless of race or status or anything else that haunts my hidden inner world.

The first year of college draws to a close and, with the long summer ahead, I decide to take a labouring job at an electronics factory called Wylex in Sharston Road, near Wythenshawe.

* * *

162

The job is simple: 'Pick up that pile of stuff from over there and put it somewhere else.' On other days cardboard boxes need to be made up, so the job becomes: 'Fold the cardboard and staple them together, operating the machine by foot, then pile them up over there, son.'

Life is made a whole lot easier when Paul Evans, a red-headed guy my age, starts working there too. Paul has an existential humour about him that brings absurdity to each moment. He will suddenly say, 'Red sky at night, shepherd's cottage on fire.' Or, to the song 'Black Is Black' by Los Bravos, he will sing:

Black is black, I want my foreskin back

Add to which my ear for impersonating various characters on the shopfloor and we're able to get through the day by taking everybody apart and putting situations back together – in an alternate 'punk' manner. A simple offer from one of the workers – 'Do you want lime juice or orange juice?' – will be as though written by Shelagh Delaney, while the mockery that follows is straight out of *A Taste Of Honey*.

Or the cast of *Coronation Street* will be learning their lines for the next scene after lunch, when Eddie, an older labourer, asks us if we want to go to the 'wanking pit' with him. 'Er, no. Not really. (Bloody cheek of it.)'

I arrive early each morning, before everybody else, to watch the rituals unfold in the exact same way each day. The first guy comes in and says, 'Morning!' to a bunch of machinists who have not even arrived yet, calling their names out loud. He waits for each of their responses before he moves on to the next person, which has me frozen at the end of the shopfloor in case he thinks that I think he's mad. So I pretend to be invisible.

Then Paul arrives, cutting through the charade. The others arrive too, and over our shoulder, the banter begins… 'I told you not to do that, you fucking Yorkshire melt!'

Here comes Eddie sniffing around, so we make out like we haven't got any idle hands left for him. He winks at us. 'See you in the wanking pit at lunchtime?' Paul makes a face that says, '*No, you fucking will not, mate,*' and off we go, shoving a pile of rubble from one end of the factory to the other.

My plan is to save and go abroad for a bit, to see the world. So getting that slim brown envelope on a Friday means everything. I even get Willie a job there.

* * *

I stand at the bus stop and look across as the most extraordinary girl arrives at the stop opposite. If ever reckless eyeballing was a crime, you could string me up from the nearest tree. She puts me in mind of the song 'Long Legged Woman Dressed In Black' by Mungo Jerry – more so over the years that follow, as every time I make a move she'll tell me no.

I gaze at a kind of beauty that was never meant for me. I miss several buses to Gatley until the girl, who I believe works at a factory called Sonex, climbs on board the bus bound for Cheadle.

As it glides away, taking her with it, my beating heart and other sounds of reality bring me back to now. I am all a-fluster, as my obsession with her begins to consume my every waking hour from this very moment.

Back at the house, Maddy is slaving away in the kitchen. I come downstairs and pass a couple in the front room, sitting on the couch. I don't know them, so I smile politely.

In the kitchen, I ask our Maddy who her friends are. Through her black fringe, which she blows out of the way of the heat rising from the stove, she casts a quizzical eye at me. 'There's no couple on the couch!' she informs me.

I go back to the front room and it's as she said. It leads into an enquiry about past tenants – a couple who lived at the house and died from a possible overdose.

Weeks later, me and Simon visit the White Hart Tavern in Cheadle. Lo and behold, there's the girl from the bus stop. 'Sonex', the girl I've been telling everyone about, is sat right there with her mate.

This is too much for me. It might testify to the possibility of some kind of god working miracles in my life, if I were to believe in such an idea. Not that I do. But after a few pints, I work up the courage to ask Simon to go over to Sonex and tell her I fancy her.

I feel his eye-rolling hesitance but, at the same time, his enjoyment of the intrigue. This could all go very wrong (or right) and I'm squirming so much that he takes up the challenge.

As though he were approaching her to ask her out on a date himself, his head drops, allowing his long hair to give him camouflage. I can only just about make out his face from a side-view, putting words to his lips from afar by how he shapes the vowels of his soft Hertfordshire accent.

She looks over. Shit.

He returns, holding all his power in a slightly crooked smile. I'm used to Simon's clowning around, but he'd better be dead serious now. He sits, says nothing and picks up his pint. Trying not to lose my cool, I stare at him. It's obvious that I'm dying to know what she said.

'And?'

He places the pint glass slowly down on the table. 'Yeah… she likes you.'

*   *   *

I'm in Withington Village and I bump into Dave Hughes, who's on my list of people to catch up with. Last time we met I told him I wanted to get a bass, as there was a guy who played the flute at Stockport College who had an electronic mouthpiece, like Ian Anderson of Jethro Tull. Since the sudden emergence of punk, though, the idea of playing with him has gone out the window.

We get to Dave's and go upstairs to a room which is nothing short of a musical warehouse, full of guitars, a bass and drumkit. My skills on the guitar stop at just about being able to get through 'Smoke On The Water' by Deep Purple. But my fascination with guitars, basses, in fact any musical instrument, sees me act like I'm in the presence of very rare things of beauty.

As I'm busy picking up each instrument, I come across a bass with two strings missing. It's a Gibson-style Cherry Red, short scale. An Avon SG, forty-five quid new out of the catalogue, Dave tells me.

'You can have that if you want. Might need sorting out, not sure it works.'

This is fantastic. I feel a surge of purpose and I can't quite believe Dave is doing this for me. I head off back to Gatley, well chuffed.

That weekend, me and Will Trotter go into town to get a few bits and bobs and buy the other two strings from Johnny Roadhouse Music. We then go to Virgin Records, to browse punk records, where I see an advert.

Howard Devoto seeks other musicians to perform and record fast and slow music, punk mentality not essential. Come woodwind, brass or fire.

To make sense of this moment, I have to resort to the dictionary:

epiphany: noun
A sudden intuitive perception or insight into the reality or essential meaning of something, usually initiated by some simple, homely, or commonplace occurrence or experience.

'I think I'm gonna call this number,' I say to Will, showing him the advert.

He looks at me with a certain incredulity. We both know that guys like us are not meant to succeed or go further than the inverted trajectory of a bunch of limited beliefs imposed on us by our parents and society.

'Why not? You have nothing to lose,' he says, pushing past the stereotype.

I note down the number, heart beating like a soldier going to war.

I tell Maddy and Jacqui and Dave Allen and Simon and Sonex about the advert and they all cajole me to 'go for it'. But my own limited self-belief, the conviction that I am nothing and everybody else is *something*, is the loudest secret that I keep about myself. These secrets grow in the dark, promising to consume me should I try and escape them.

'I'm not sure anymore. Maybe it's not Howard Devoto? Maybe it's not even real?'

I see their faces drop, as though I've reached some kind of finishing line only to cease running at the last second without crossing it. There is a mixture of disappointment and the understanding that I might need a push here, without being able to ask for it.

Simon threatens to call the number himself. He knows it will see me act on this impending uncoolness, to save myself from ridicule. The ploy enables me to push all darkness aside and make the call.

You can hear a pin drop.

Indeed, it *is* Howard Devoto and the advert is real. He tells me to come to Lower Broughton Road tomorrow, Sunday.

We sit with eyes widened.

166

After several cans of cider and quite a few spliffs, the partying is over. I glide upstairs and carefully put the other two strings on Dave's bass.

I take a couple of Do-Dos. As my knob shrinks and my brain fizzes, I lay the neck of the bass on the bedhead. The framework becomes like a giant amplifier now. I feel the vibration of the whole instrument quake through my body.

The open E string, the lowest note on the instrument, almost scoops my insides out when I pluck it with the heavy-gauge plectrum I bought with the extra strings, or, I use thumb and finger to get an even more subsonic tone from the instrument.

I half expect Angela Lansbury to walk in, as though it's a scene from *Bedknobs And Broomsticks*; the bed will suddenly lift off to the tune of 'Portobello Road':

Portobello Road
Portobello Road
You'll be dancing like a ballerina
Squirming like a toad

That open E continues to offer a world of self-expression as the dawn's early light illuminates Darley Avenue.

On no sleep whatsoever, I get dressed and look in the mirror and here a voice in my head say, 'Best of luck, sunshine.' I smile in the mirror and then exhale sharply.

I make my way to Salford via numerous buses, hope in my heart, bass guitar in my hand.

Chapter Nineteen

On the way to Howard's house, I play a game of 'I would' to distract me from the matter in hand. The new matter in hand consists of looking at women and asking myself whether I would shag them or not. Various subcategories emerge as the game goes on. As in:

'I would.'

'I definitely would.'

'I probably would.'

'Maybe I would?' (Which is slightly different to 'probably'.)

'Not sure if I would.'

'No, I would not.'

This game takes me all the way to Lower Broughton Road where, upon arrival, I take a deep breath and say to myself, '*Sonex? I definitely would.*'

Howard opens the door. I hope he doesn't see the enormity of my gulp as I take in his alien-like hairdo and bright blue cardigan, with mismatching striped trousers. Normally, I'd liken this style of dress to Andy Pandy. However, I view him in another way altogether because, after all, he is Howard Devoto. With my overblown sense of cool put firmly in its place, I reverently bow my head before the great man and enter the front door.

We walk past the front room and stairs, and continue down a never-ending corridor that ends up at the back room, adjacent to the kitchen. He disappears and reappears with cups of tea, telling me about John

McGeoch, an art student finishing his degree in London, who will be back to play lead guitar in a few months.

There is an H&H amplifier staring at me as Howard pulls out Pete Shelley's Starway guitar, the one that was sawn in half and played at the Buzzocks gig.

As I hook up my bass to the amp, using a curly cable I bought at Johnny Roadhouse, I recall Dave Hughes saying, 'It might not work.' I realise that it also might not. I turn up the volume, relieved that there is a swell of low-end sound.

Howard purses his lips in an act of maximum concentration, then plays a six-note riff which hangs in outer space. I realise I'm way out of my depth, but then I see his foot bouncing slightly on the floor in a four beat. I remember how, last night, that big, beautiful bottom E-note bounced me on the bed and flew me into the motherly arms of Angela Lansbury.

I begin to play that single note over and over, on and on, as if it were a Motown beat. I also play it off the beat, bouncing off an invisible heartbeat. Howard extends the riff but I keep on going, asserting the moment. He smiles, beginning the lyric, then shows me the chords to the chorus. He sings 'The Light Pours Out Of Me'.

Howard then plays another riff ('*Or is this one a lick?*' I ask myself). Thirteen notes played over four bars. I marvel at the complexity but realise that a single note, representing the rhythm, needs to underpin each chord. Howard now pumps out the rhythm, sure not to make a single mistake. I play the root note of each chord and throw in a lick from 'Born To Be Wild' at the turnaround, which slides in easily. Howard seems worlds away, lost in the chords he's playing, but manages a nod through closed eyes.

He lights a cigarette and holds it between second and third finger, which draws attention to the act itself and allows the smoke to fill up his reddening cheeks, puffing them up like Dizzy Gillespie about to blow a note. As he lets the smoke go, some of it drifts into his eye and he comes undone for a moment. The attention he draws to such an unsophisticated piece of everydayness makes him seem more human and less alien. He talks to me about drummer Martin Jackson, deflecting the moment.

We are finished and I begin packing up. Howard, on seeing that I'm curious to know how things are going, cannot quite maintain his aloof position of 'If it sounds respectable and not embarrassing, then maybe we can move forward'. He lets me know, cheeks reddening even more, that he can see us getting on and that, musically, there could be something happening.

I cannot wait to tell the others. I call Dave from a phone box and tell him my teenage dreams are starting to come true…

'Why, have you just got laid?' he says. We laugh like fuck as I tell him my good news before jumping on the bus back home. I know full well what Dave has done for me by simply saying, 'You can have that.'

* * *

It's cider, spliffs, Do-Dos and more cider as the summer of nineteen seventy-seven becomes pivotal for me. All I have to do now is tell my parents, who are expecting me to return to college after the summer to resume my second year of three.

My mum is beside herself as she stares out of the front-room window. 'Barry, please tell me this is not bloody happening.'

This is said as my dad is looking at me, hoping I can back up what I've just told them about leaving college to become a musician. Given that I don't play an instrument to any level of acceptability, they are not convinced. At all.

I call Sonex, who gets her dad, a policeman, to drop her off at the White Hart Hotel. I think that I'll be condemned for being black and hanging around his daughter, but he seems quite cheery. She seems to take it all in her stride, knowing how much he adores and trusts her.

We go back to Darley Avenue and I make a move on her. She very gently keeps me at bay. She is able to see what I cannot: that my need is far greater than the situation calls for. Deep down I know she is right. 'No point in rushing things,' I lie to both of us.

In the house, somebody (usually Jacqui) is always singing 'The 59th Street Bridge Song' (also known as 'Feelin' Groovy') by Simon & Garfunkel, which acts like a pacifier for a wanton teen such as myself.

I glimpse Sonex's black bra, noticing the flowery edging on the straps. Her lips are like soft pillows as she struggles to retain her boundaries, enforced in our tender tug of war. I cannot for a single moment push my agenda onto her, even though I think that I should and that it might make me more of a man in her eyes. (If, indeed, that is the problem.)

No. I can see that she wants me as much as I want her, but something – maybe the timing, I don't know – keeps us on a steady edge of unrequited communion, which both of us are reticent to move beyond.

I see Sonex out in the wee small hours. She bows her head ever so slightly and says, 'Thank you for having me, even though you didn't.' She laughs, but then so do I.

I think to myself that I really have something to reel her in with now, as she wriggles off my line into a sea of distance. Her every moment of absence stokes further that fire of constant desire within me.

I head back to have a cheese sandwich with Branston pickle, wondering if there is any Vimto in the house.

* * *

Next day, Simon answers the phone as the receiver practically jumps out of its cradle. His eyes are wide as he passes the phone to me. I steel myself for bad news.

'It's Howard, for you.'

He jumps around like Marcel Marceau, miming his attempts at trying to contain his excitement at having spoken to royalty.

I compose myself as though being given top-secret information in an episode of *The Avengers* or *The Man From U.N.C.L.E.*, noting down the message about getting together with Howard and Martin to 'see how it goes'.

'I'll see you there, Howard.'

On later occasions, Simon will bring confirmation of 'what time tea is being served' at Howard's – which, of course, is code for when we are to have our top-secret meetings.

* * *

On entering Martin Jackson's bedroom, all I see is a wallpaper of drums.

Howard and I plug into Buzzcocks' borrowed amps; they are a kind of hangover to the short but blistering time the band were together. Martin hits the drums so hard that I feel for the neighbours. Then I start pumping the bass and forget about them, as we expand on the ideas we've gone through at Howard's.

Martin rolls out patterns across the toms with hands a-blur, then gives 'The Light Pours Out Of Me' its signature introduction, which I slide into like a knife into butter. We know something is right there and then but cannot wait for John to return.

Rehearsals start in earnest at graphic artist and fellow musician Paul Roberts' basement in Ellesmere Road, Chorlton. The walls are padded and covered in denim. It is known as the 'denim dungeon'.

I meet Bob Dickinson, who sets up a keyboard. I make room for what appears to be his shyness as he sets about making himself quite invisible. I offer him empathy in the form of various facial expressions, conveying that I know what it is to be that shy and to feel that different.

Then John McGeoch comes steamrolling through the room, looking in one direction and walking in the other. He trips himself up in the clumsiest of ways. I decide straight away that I like this guy.

We practise all day for five days a week during August, a time during which Bob plays the spellbinding intro to 'Motorcade'. McGeoch's ideas and solos draw the spotlight to him. Watching him work drops my jaw, inspiring me to push myself as far as he does. 'Motorcade', 'Shot By Both Sides', 'Suddenly We Are Eating Sandwiches', 'The Light Pours Out of Me' and the dirge-like 'Burst' all confirm that the reason I made that call is unfolding right before my eyes.

*   *   *

We make a demo tape of songs at Pennine Studios in Oldham. I keep my copy of the finished cassette tape glued to the palm of my hand, except to play the songs to the Darley Avenue gang and Sonex. Maybe she will now move closer.

As we sit in the car park at the White Hart, listening to the demos, Howard is in London doing our bidding. I eagerly tell Sonex that he has called and said, 'Things are happening, and they are happening now.'

I press 'play' to hear 'Shot by Both Sides' again and then the second track, 'Suddenly We are Eating Sandwiches', putting an arm around her. Sonex nods her head from side to side, betraying the darkness her clothing is meant to express as the bees busily buzz around us. She smiles at me.

*   *   *

Back at rehearsals, John McGeoch sees me with my old-fashioned brass tuning pipes. He comes over to me on a tea break and shows me how to tune up by first establishing the bottom note, which is an E. He plays the note on the keyboard and tells me to hold my finger gently on the string at the twelfth fret and play what he calls a harmonic. He then goes on to point out the way the note is vibrating and moves the machine head at the top of the guitar ever so slightly, until the vibration stops and the note just rings.

'Now,' he says, 'that's bang in tune, so to get the others in tune, you do this...'

He then puts a finger on the E-string at the fifth fret and plays the harmonic, then does the same on the A-string (the next string up), this time on the seventh fret, creating the same note. The note on the A-string is vibrating until, again, he turns the machine head at the top of the bass until the vibration stops.

'Your turn now: do the same with the D- and the G-string,' which I do. We both smile at the results. He then says, 'I'll show you how to play any chord on the piano using three fingers at some point.'

Rehearsal begins again. The newest song, 'Motorcade', just blows me away: from Bob's brilliantly suspenseful and haunting keyboard figure to Jacko's sense of atmosphere as he swells the cymbals and then comments via the tom-toms. Then there's John, stamping his trademark sound and bristling with ideas, as Howard says.

The song is the greatest and strangest thing I've heard. I merely follow the chords on the intro, but once the backbeat kicks in, I feel compelled to fit myself into the picture by swinging the bottom end of the song and then playing almost lead lines, where I see fit.

This completely goes against the grain of how bass players 'should be': anonymous, flared jeans, long hair covering their eyes. Not looking like those prog-rock guys, I'm having none of that. I take my cues from the playing of Bootsy Collins, Larry Graham who plays bass with Sly & the Family Stone, Motown session bass player extraordinaire James Jamerson and Alice Cooper's original bassist, Dennis Dunaway (who admittedly had long prog-rock hair). '*Be different, be yourself, be free,*' is the message my bass heroes are sending me now.

It only leaves Howard to sing in his remarkably idiosyncratic, uncompromising style. He does not disappoint.

I believe all that I read now
Night has come off the corner
Shadows flicker sweet and tame
Dancing like crazy mourners

As the song unfolds at an almost groovy tempo in opposition to Howard's taut, angular lyric, in the third verse he changes the delivery of the words, which gives me the chance to play more lazily against this altered style.

The decision is made to speed the song up in steps, while John begins one of his mesmerising solos. Howard is electrified; the band are on fire. John plays like a demon, Bob finds another line to begin the new part with, and I throw in a sped-up punk-jazz line that bops across the chords as Howard sings:

Here comes the motorcade
Moving so slow and hard
Like a snake in a closet
Holding the sway in the boulevard

The song reaches a frenzied, delirious cadence. John takes off again, dissonant and furious, ending the section with an incredible three sequences of eight arpeggiated notes. We take it for granted but, really, we know it's absolutely astonishing. Howard repeats the last verse and Bob comes back to his second figure, before we jump-cut ourselves and start the beginning again. Everyone takes a beautiful breath, full of a tension we just don't want to let go of.

In the back of his car
Into the null and void he shoots
The man at the centre of the motorcade
Has learnt to tie his boots

John takes another blinding solo. Bob reinstates the second figure to join it all up.

In the boulevard, the motorcade holds sway

174

The band signal the ending by repeating this part several times, bringing it home in an almost classical songwriting sense. As the song has defied any of the usual forms up until now, it provides an extraordinarily satisfying conclusion, after five minutes and forty-four seconds, which seems to last forever.

So… we have these unbelievably great songs. We have a guitarist who just might be the best in the world right now. And we are fronted by Howard Devoto.

It's hard to explain to Simon, Sonex, Maddy and Jacqui, Dave Allen, Willie and Brapper Brown what this feeling, standing on the edge of greatness, looks and feels like. But they already know. They can see it and hear it in the way I'm reporting daily events. I can feel them wanting it to happen. Wanting it to happen to me.

* * *

After playing one-and-a-half gigs, we sign to Virgin Records. Boarding an InterCity train from Piccadilly station to Euston, my excitement is barely containable. I have to work hard to rein in my piss-taking joviality, which I can see is getting on Howard's nerves.

Tea and sandwiches are needed at the halfway mark, so I head towards the buffet section, passing through several carriages. As I do, the feeling of being part of a group falls away from me.

I reach the food carriage, fitted out to accommodate a queue. Towards the end there is a serving hatch of sorts, where I hear voices fussing about where the sugar is. As I reach my destination, the fat man from the estate behind the old people's home turns to ask me if there is something I would like.

More precisely, he asks, 'Do you see anything that you fancy?'

The life is now sucked out of me.

His eyes light up at as I observe his top lip, slightly reddened from a close shave and covered in microbeads of sweat. His hair is greased back with Brylcreem. '*You could smell him from a bloody mile away,*' as my mum would say.

His baldness is not really masked at all by sweptback lines of oiled hair. His stomach bulges way over his trousers, beneath his tucked-in white shirt, and his neck is swollen from a fastened collar. His bow tie almost strangles him.

A wave of bile comes into my throat and my knees start knocking. My jocular sense of humour leaves me at a rate of knots.

I go about my business pretending to have never, ever seen the sweaty fat man who serves food and drink on the train from Manchester Piccadilly to London Euston before.

I never went to his stinky flat. '*It wasn't me,*' is what I tell myself.

He didn't seduce me on the bus home, seeing that I was vulnerable after being nearly beaten up by the black bouncer at the Ranch – who wanted to punish me for some reason.

The need to get out of the food carriage is greater than the need to get away from him was on that very night. After I'd let him take whatever he wanted from me.

I took no joy from any of it. I take no joy from it now, as I arrive back with the lads carrying sandwiches, crisps and drinks I don't remember paying for.

* * *

Vernon Yard, home of Virgin Records in Notting Hill, is our final destination. As we turn sharply off Portobello Road, the street sign puts me in mind of *Bedknobs And Broomsticks*. I've come back to myself, feeling that I'm back in the gang. The incident on the train is far behind me.

Simon Draper, the head of Virgin Records and the proxy face of Richard Branson, appears in a beige shirt and speaks very posh, as if out of an episode of *Whicker's World*. He shakes my hand. His right-arm man, Bruno, is a South African with a beaming smile and affability I warm to instantly.

Our manager, Andrew Graham-Stewart, takes us to a Thai restaurant in Notting Hill to celebrate the signing. I've never eaten Thai food before and have to ask Howard what he thinks would be a good choice. He recommends a gado gado salad. So I add some chicken satay after hearing somebody else say how good it is. 'Peanut sauce with everything' just might become my favourite dish from now on.

Chapter Twenty

After our half-gig at the Electric Circus comprising three songs – 'Shot By Both Sides', 'The Light Pours Out Of Me' and Captain Beefheart's 'I Love You, You Big Dummy' – and our first official gig at Rafters, where we performed nine, we now have a bigger gig at the Queen Elizabeth Hall, Belle Vue. The event is hailed as Punk Comes to Belle Vue, which runs over three days, organised and filmed for the TV show *So It Goes* by TV presenter Tony Wilson.

My dad and my sister come to the show to 'see what you've been up to'. During our performance it's easy to spot them in the crowd: they're the only black people there. I hope they're okay but I have to concentrate on freeing myself up, not dropping notes, performing like an old hand rather than a newcomer.

We play 'Motorcade' and the audience doesn't know quite what it's being hit with. Howard is all make-up and staring eyes, which he uses to his advantage as he plays hide, seek and confront with them, jumping in and out of the shadows to deliver body blow after uppercut after right cross. We have them.

The Clash are the headliners, supported by Siouxsie and the Banshees. The night after we play, me, Willie Trotter and our mate Jimmy Ellis go to see The Clash perform. After the show, Clash guitarist Mick Jones comes over to me at the bar and asks if I'm Barry Adamson. Willie presses his elbow hard against mine to mark a '*What the fuck, is this really happening?*' moment.

I say, 'Yeah. Mick Jones, right? Great show.'

He goes on to tell me how great the bass playing is on 'The Light Pours Out Of Me', reminding him of Motown.

'Do you wanna drink?' I ask.

'Double whisky and Coke, Bal,' he says, watching me gulp the request down.

Mick tells me there's an after-show party and invites us all to it. Trotter and Ellis are beside themselves. I just act as though this is my life now, so we'd all better get used to it. (At the same time I'm thinking exactly the same way they are: '*It's Mick Jones from The Clash... he said my playing was great... he had me for a double whisky... it cost me a fortune...* ')

Soon after the Belle Vue show, the band is summoned to affirm what Howard has decided on already: that Bob Dickinson should leave with immediate effect. I'm a little taken aback. Yes, I get that he is quite reserved and needs crib sheets on stage, coming from a quite different, more classical background.

But Howard says, 'He's gotta go.' And so, go he does.

I take absolutely no pleasure from Bob's obvious pain.

* * *

John McGeoch invites me to live in a shared house with him and girlfriend Janet in Whalley Range. I move into Thirty-Five Mayfield Road and take up space in a large room on the first floor, which has a tiny kitchen and communal toilet outside to the right.

The bay window in the lounge looks out onto the street. I set up a stereo and speakers on a cabinet beneath the window. Malcom Garrett, an artist friend of John's who's working with us, kindly gives me some 'pink punk portraits' he's painted on black plastic bags. I put them up on the walls, which are painted black.

My mum and dad come over and are horrified. My mum says to my dad, 'Oh, Barry, what has he done now?'

We have a cup of tea and I put on the album, *The Idiot* by Iggy Pop. My mum is quite alarmed at the start of the song 'Mass Production', where a wash of synths begins with white noise that eventually turns into a series of bass fall-offs. She gets up and looks out of the window to the skies, as though World War III is about to commence. I reassure her by telling her it's only the noise on the record – eventually.

* * *

It's December of nineteen seventy-seven, and the first single, 'Shot By Both Sides', is recorded at Ridge Farm, residential recording studios in Rusper on the Surrey/Sussex border. The producer is Mick Glossop, who arranged the recordings of the Belle Vue gigs. Me and McGeoch rename him 'Glossy' (as in 'Glossy Magazines').

The recording is simple enough and we feel almost more 'punk' without the keyboards. One night, after getting pissed as farts at the local pub, we come back and record 'Suddenly We Are Eating Sandwiches' as a punk song. The title now becomes 'My Mind Ain't So Open', with a fresh set of lyrics from Howard replacing verbatim quotes from Samuel Beckett.

Martin Jackson, all wannabe spiky hair and safety pins, is as happy as a pig in shit with this frenetic punk workout. He takes offence, though, at me and John referring to him as 'Jocko Homo': a subversion of both 'Jacko' and the Devo song.

It's the 'homo' bit that's taken as offensive. But it only serves to ramp up the piss-taking even further, to the point that his name now becomes 'Jocular Homoculor'. McGeoch pisses himself with laughter.

'Shot By Both Sides', a special moment for all concerned, is released in January nineteen seventy-eight. I set my alarm for three in the morning but can hardly sleep. So, I get stoned on red Lebanese hash and wait for the alarm to go off, before driving to Piccadilly Station in my mum's old Hillman Imp. I meet the train that carries the first boxes of the finished article.

I enter the station at dawn amidst a cloud of cold breath pushed out by passengers and workers alike. Then I see the boxes on the platform, check them out with the guard and take them back to the car.

Back at Mayfield Road I open one of the boxes ever so slowly, smelling the freshly cut sleeves and staring at Malcom Garrett's design. It's based on the eighteen eighty-six work *La Chimère regarda avec effroi toutes choses* ('The Chimera looked at all things in awe') by symbolist artist Odilon Redon. Seeing the sleeve in its total glory, my heart swells like never before.

The *NME* says, 'Magazine are the most convincing post punk band so far. The true inheritors of the mantle of the original Roxy Music,' while *Rolling Stone* refers to the record as 'The best rock'n'roll single of the year.'

And so we hit the road, Jack.

Enter new keyboard player, Dave Formula, who sets up in the rehearsal room in a way that John and myself refer to as 'Keyboard City'. He brings something new to the table, for sure, and I love that funk-soul Hammond organ style he has going on.

But while one of my guilty pleasures is listening over and over to Rick Wakeman's *The Six Wives Of Henry VIII*, I'm unsure about the wobbling synthesizer lines spilling out everywhere. Plus I'm so image-conscious, to the point of it being a distraction, that I question Dave's 'punk authenticity', and even his age, to begin with.

But after a few conversations with him, I see that he's completely out of his mind and can spin a yarn like no other man can. He's as funny as fuck and so he's okay by me… at least for now.

MAGAZINE

24 January
100 CLUB, London
25 January
SANDPIPERS, Nottingham
26 January
RAFTERS, Manchester
27 January
ERICS, Liverpool
30 January
NASHVILLE, London
31 January
BARBARELLAS, Birmingham
1 February
F CLUB, Leeds

Nineteen seventy-eight tour flyer. Artwork by Linder.

The tour begins in London, at the 100 Club on Oxford Street. For sure, we are so scared that we're 'bricking it', but we know what we have to do. The London gig feels like a rite of passage, but we generate a theory that, because London is the all-knowing big city, any slightly less than feverish reception we might receive can be attributed to the 'London Cool'. This means that whenever we play London we must never, ever buy into the almost detached attitude which is instilled into the audience, putting any negative reception aside and playing our hearts out regardless.

We stand our ground with Howard. It won't be long until he's called 'the most important man alive' by the *NME*, but he's being an awkward bugger in not allowing anybody to get into the show for free – even those who work at the record company. Simon Draper is more than a little miffed as he queues halfway down Oxford Street, with the rest of, as I hear a crew member say, the 'Billy Bunters' (punters).

The London Cool unnerves all of us, whether we admit it or not, forcing us to try a little too hard. It's a state in which it almost seems like we're acting rather than being in the moment, launching blood-pumping attack after blood-pumping attack. An air of self-

My drawing of Dave Formula at the 100 Club.

consciousness creeps into the performance, largely unbeknownst to the audience who are swept along by a certain amount of shadow-play and hype. But there are moments when we get over ourselves, remember who we are and let the audience have what they've been reading about.

Not everybody buys into our dazzling grandiosity, though. Some of the reviews lean on Howard's reticent, cantankerous attitude towards the press, a kind of 'catch me if you dare' as he flits between displays of fierceness, adroit acumen and a dumbing down of the supposed 'superior being' he is often presented as.

He flirts with deliberate obtuseness and perversity. We know this and, for now, wouldn't want our main man to play it any other way. However, *Sounds* decides to stick the boot in with the headline 'Animated Egghead fails to impress'.

'Fuck them,' says McGeech (my pet name for McGeoch). The two of us begin to adopt a regal air wherever we go. If somebody recognises us, we say even before they ask, 'Yes, we are…' and inhale their stale air through our noses. We then burst out laughing once they're out of view.

Howard carefully explains to me that you have to be very selective about things like whether you want to be just your average working musician or a living, breathing celebrity. This is something I'm still pondering as I make my way to London, on our second invitation, to play 'Shot By Both Sides' on *Top Of The Pops*. When I leave my parents, all of us are beaming as we know this is the door opening. All Magazine have to do now is simply walk through it.

I head off for the train, nervous about who might serving at the food counter. But when the man with the microbeads of sweat and the ability to suck my energy down his drain is nowhere to be seen, I can let go and be myself again.

I make my way to the underground to head for west London. A man seems to be having trouble with a heavy bag. I sense a chance to help. But as I get nearer to him he looks around and calls out to a guard.

'Darkie?' Then again. 'Darkie, over here! Help me.'

The guard comes over and helps this tweed-jacketed twat off the train. The guard then turns to me with a perplexed look, which changes into a wink, and says, 'I didn't want to tell 'im. Me not a darkie: me black.' Then he laughs his arse off.

I meet up with McGooch (my other pet name for him) and we go shopping for clothes in Kensington Market. To celebrate, I decide to buy a pair of horse-riding boots which I figure will offset my afro with aplomb. A tweed jacket will set the look off perfectly in my role as jackbooted darkie, lord of the manor.

In the canteen, the whole cast of the sci-fi show *Blake's 7* are on a break. This only adds to the surreal nature of not performing the song live but recording a version and miming to it, as we have to now.

The lights begin to dim on Howard's mood. A darkness creeps over him like a stained blanket, where feelings are now definitely facts as far as he's concerned. There's a wrestling match between his overblown ego and a modicum of humility, as he struggles to separate himself from what he is being asked to do now – which in his mind is to humiliate himself in front of the eyes of the world.

I bop around during our performance, as though it's my first and last time to play on a show that nourished me for most of my teenage and pre-teen life. A gateway to the stars.

And here's Howard, seemingly fucking things up by delivering a performance that is so un-Howard like. As though he is saying a massive 'NO' to everyone and every fake value that goes into the making of a performance that is, in effect, just a promotional tool.

I think to myself, '*Just play the game, H.*' However, there is only one game in town and the man at the centre of it all, the man who can choose between coffee and tea, is having none of it.

'*My bat, my ball, my rules*' is what seems to emanate from him.

Howard stands rooted to the spot, the 'X' he was told by the floor manager to stand on, and delivers a purposefully lacklustre performance. It's then that I realise he knows *exactly* what he is doing. '*How punk is that,*' I reason to myself, '*to turn a by-now punk cliché, boredom, into a piece of performance art?*' Genius.

But I watch the record slide back down the charts and disappear below the near-top forty position it occupied last week. The door begins to close on an opportunity that you would think is a no-brainer, even for such a massive brain as Howard's.

I conclude that maybe he doesn't want this, or he is playing a much longer game. As a novice, newcomer, neophyte, whatever you want to call me, I'm possibly not equipped with the perception to make a judgement call on what happened on *Top Of The Pops*.

Howard has his reasons and maybe the world isn't ready for what we have to offer. Otherwise, our song would have gone further up the charts, in the same way those of other punk and post-punk bands flourished after nationwide exposure.

*   *   *

Rehearsals and writing for the first album are enjoying the push-and-pull of Dave in the band, breeding healthy competition between him and John for sonic space. Then there's me on songs like 'Definitive Gaze', jumping to the front and making myself heard above the rest of the band. I do this by playing a figure so high up the neck of the bass that the melody seems to poke out and dismantle the wall of synthesizers that dominate the sound. In my conceit, I view the way that I'm putting my parts together as ground-breaking.

It's the same with 'The Great Beautician In The Sky'. I don't necessarily have to force it, but I know I'm on to something that both serves the song and takes the listener somewhere else within its framework. This action sets both myself and the listener free. I'm quite confident that I'm on to something really great as the smoke from the joint I'm smoking floats around my head.

A chord sequence and melody I've been working on merits showing to the others. The melody is a melancholy figure to be sung over two chords; when repeated, it creates a kind of hidden sorrow. I begin to hear another part to it, adding another chord and another melody before coming back to the two-chord pattern.

It will become the intro and middle section of 'Parade', with Dave adding another melody that takes over from the sombre beginning and adds a colder, more complex component that suits Howard well. McGooch takes the piss by singing the old Frank Ifield song, 'I Remember You'. The first three notes of the piano motif are almost the same as when Frank used to sing, '*I re-memb…*', then you can sing, '*I remember you*' along to the next five notes. I try to make light of it by singing 'Irie Member You' with a Jamaican inflection, to disarm him and to take the song's power back. McGooch knows he has me by the short and curlies, though.

*   *   *

184

We relocate to Ridge Farm again, for the follow-up single 'Touch And Go' and its B-side, 'Goldfinger'. Aside from making the album, I feel the urge to go and mess about with all the equipment that's set up. I come up with ideas which are themes and explorations of something else other than Magazine; it's a moot point as to whether that something else will ever happen.

I record twenty-minute tracks with titles like 'The Man In The Hat' and, as I don't mind missing out on sleep, I seem to power through, sometimes day and night. As though such fortuity will not present itself again anytime soon. I also smoke copious amounts of dope, the drug creating a particular confidence for me to hide behind. At the same time, it acts to open up and heighten my senses. Or so I believe.

With the album recorded and another short tour under our belts, the feeling that we are about to 'make the big time' returns. I feel assured that Howard's manipulations and gameplaying with the press are a mere carving-out of his personality; he's shoving it into the face of the world when the world isn't necessarily looking, creating a *cause célèbre* for himself. This, I'm sure, will lead us to greatness. The album is the battering ram that will open any door closed to us. Of that I am also sure.

I see now that the fame that eluded us, by way of *Top Of The Pops*, can come to us in a way which fits much better with Howard's way. We continue being cited as one of the best bands out there, with myself coming in as seventh best bass player in the nineteen seventy-eight *NME* poll – above Paul Simenon of The Clash, who I've idolised since 'White Riot' back in college.

I approach my twentieth birthday in a better place than I've ever been before. As my mum says, 'You have the rest of your life to look forward to.'

Chapter Twenty-One

Linder is an artist. She is also Howard's girlfriend.

When Linder speaks, her eyes dart to the floor and then back onto you. Her face flushes ever so slightly. Her voice then lowers slightly, as though woozy with some kind of borrowed power, as she pushes her point.

Her arms gesticulate in front of her when she gets lubricious in a quite idiosyncratic way. Her vivacious and voracious laugh takes the whole room by surprise.

She will thrust forwards a concern for you when you seem troubled, oscillating between Liverpudlian ne'er-do-well and somebody embodying a different class altogether. Nobility, perhaps? This mixture of personalities presents a dizzying charm and attractiveness.

What I was once learning at Stockport College feels like something from the Victorian era, compared to Linder's artistic luminosity and how I see the world now.

She is four years older than me and the pedestal that I'm putting her on might just break my back. I've spent sleepless nights carving and refining it, making it ready for her to take my hand and climb up onto.

Linder glides across the room in her navy-blue work overalls, feet turned slightly inward. Both the overalls, and her sullen, quite awkward, stroll, fail to disguise her potent, portentous sexuality. Her eyes and lips shift my focal point as I hang on to her every word.

I become the willing student and hope to offer my own kind of fascination. But in reality I see myself as a lowly competitor to Howard, whose currency (as we already know) is intelligence. Who am I? This mixed-race kid coming in practically from high school, walking onto a far bigger stage than I've ever known. While I enthuse about art and intellect, I really wouldn't know my Dostoyevsky from my Huysmans. (*Or would I?* – as McGeoch often jokes with me.)

* * *

With the release of *Real Life*, our first album, we are well on our way to literally touring non-stop, from the beginning of July to the middle of December. I embrace the lifestyle with gusto, offering my hotel room as the assigned after-show party room, where copious amounts of booze and dope are consumed (especially by me).

Martin Jackson becomes very pissed off, though; he leaves at the end of the summer after a show at the Lyceum in London, where Howard had a lookalike, singer Andy Corrigan from The Mekons, come onstage before him and mime to the first song.

Neither is Wacko Jacko having any of Dave Formula's wibbly-wobbly way with 'those bloody keyboards'. As for 'Parade': 'Well, it's bloody tea-room music.'

Now I'm pissed off by that remark about my one and only moment of songwriting and soul-bearing for the band thus far. But on reflection, I think 'tea-room music' would be a rather astute observation, if it hadn't been so laden with distaste. I hear those opening bars and see white china cups gently colliding with their saucers as the camera softly tracks a waitress at her table. (Maybe Frank Ifield could drop in for a cuppa?)

Paul Spencer takes Martin Jackson's place for a while. We do not hit it off at all, with him reacting to my judging the length of his hair by sneering and joking about my relationship with John. (In later years he'll confess that he felt me to be insecure, with a dependency on John, as though I needed his approval throughout this time.)

A tour of Germany with Patti Smith is our first supporting tour and first time overseas, in September nineteen seventy-eight. It's laced with excitement as, after a couple of initial shows that begin on a grey deserted Tuesday night in Düsseldorf, we make our way across the oppressed eastern sector and head for Berlin. A parade of little green cars, all looking the same, pepper the road as we load up on cheap, green-labelled vodka from service stations and eat sausages floating in pea soup.

On arrival in Berlin, it's as though the floodgates to another world have opened. There seems to be one very cool party going on, all the time. There is a frustration throughout the camp, however, as we are relegated to less-than-important by Smith and her crew. At the same time, one of ours discloses he is having an affair with her.

I find the whole thing absolutely intriguing, as there is often not much else to do except wait forever for Patti Smith to soundcheck. I opt to be go-between, more out of curiosity than anything else. For this, I am rewarded with plectrums stamped with the words 'Rock N Roll Nigger'.

Rock N Roll Nigger plectrum, awarded by Patti Smith.

Back in dear old Blighty, me and McGurcher (yes, you know him by now) sit Paul Spencer down at a trendy coiffeur so that his bloody beige bales of straw can be given the chop. Then he can represent us in a more befitting manner, as we are to appear on *The Old Grey Whistle Test*.

While I'm there, dying for a piss during a filming break, I find a backstage toilet to relieve myself. I'm alone, but then I hear the door open and footsteps getting closer. Standing at the adjacent urinal, I sense an enormous presence.

I look down to my left and see what looks like a size-fifteen Converse basketball shoe. I make my way up the threadbare pair of jeans and see a leather jacket. Heading right up to the sky, I stare into the face of Joey Ramone.

'How ya doin', kid?' he says to me and smiles. He guesses from my blown-away expression that I know every word to the first Ramones album. I'm completely in awe of the man and will cherish this moment for the rest of my life.

Shortly after his locks are shorn, drummer Spencer is also given the chop. We don't have that long to find another one, but enough to take just a little breather before the next jaunt.

＊　　＊　　＊

Howard has business in London.

I get together with Linder, at Lower Broughton Road, and we end up going to Rafters to see some bands. Just generally going out on the town.

The night, though, seems to laboriously drag on. Same old scene, as Bryan Ferry will later croon. In fact we talk about Roxy Music most of the time tonight. Linder wears a trouser suit and bow tie, not unlike Lulu when she performed Bowie's 'The Man Who Sold The World'.

We communicate as friends, observing each other naturally, but then Linder asks me If I want to go back to the house she shares with Howard. To which I say yes.

The sticky mood immediately lightens. I note more than a hint of wickedness in her eyes, and an image of Anne Bancroft and Dustin Hoffman in *The Graduate* springs to mind: '*Are you trying to seduce me, Mrs Robinson?*' No doubt it's an attempt on my side to deny my part in what's happening, to ease all boundaries into touch.

On arrival at Lower Broughton Road, we enter the front door but do not walk down the long corridor to the room where I auditioned before. (Where I was earlier this evening, in fact.) Instead, we go directly to the front room. Linder's work is everywhere on the black-painted walls.

I realise that I'm about to have sex with my boss's girlfriend. Her eyes dart to the floor then back up to me. I draw her bow tie through her shirt collar before peeling her out of her men's suit, in an almost studiedly homoerotic manner.

The next morning, I feel a strange tenderness between us that I know she feels too.

As my taxi approaches home, in the aptly named Whalley Range, a sober dawn creeps over me. I enter my room and load up the bong I bought the other day and light it up, bubbles bursting with each inhale of the finest Moroccan hash. In the quiet of an exhaled breath, I hear my mum's voice say quite clearly, '*Oh, Barry, what have you done now? You stupid, bloody idiot.*'

*   *   *

After the slum clearances of the sixties, Manchester's inner-city district of Hulme saw a radical departure from the usual 'two up-two down' social housing of previous decades. A futuristic vision of deck accessed flats, maisonettes and huge brutalist 'crescents' had promised to bring comfortable living, combined with large open areas of green space to its newly housed residents, less than a mile from the city centre.

However, this idyllic utopia never materialised in working class Manchester, and in 1978, the social housing scheme was blasted by the then chair of Manchester City Council's Housing Committee, who described the re-development of Hulme as an absolute disaster. 'It shouldn't have been planned and it shouldn't have been built,' he claimed.

The four main crescents that dominated Hulme – Robert Adam, John Nash, Charles Barry and William Kent were named after the main architects for Georgian Bath, from which the crescent designs drew inspiration. This second version of Hulme was planned, and it was built – and whilst there were many problems and difficult times for residents, there were also memorable ones too. During its turbulent lifespan a diverse and tight-knit community made Hulme a place like no other.

A positive outlet against the troubled backdrop was the Factory night at The Russell Club. Situated on Royce Road it was launched by Factory's Alan Erasmus and Tony Wilson with the help of local promoter Alan Wise. The name Factory was used [in] homage to the New York club of the same and was Tony's vision of a Warhol-esque set up in Manchester. The Factory night attracted numerous touring bands to the area and many upcoming post punk bands passed through its doors... The Fall, The Passage, Ultravox, Wire, Pere Ubu, Ludus and

190

Penetration, while 1979 saw visits from Gang of Four, Crass, Stiff Little Fingers, The Cure, Cabaret Voltaire, Skids, Throbbing Gristle, The Human League, Mekons, Pink Military, The Raincoats, Simple Minds, The Cramps, Teardrop Explodes, Echo and the Bunnymen, B-52s, Joy Division and Magazine.

Paul Wright

The Factory at the Russell Club. Photo by Ros Daniels.

One afternoon on a day off, I shoot up to the Russell Club to see 'International Reggae Superstar' Tapper Zukie soundcheck for a gig later that evening. I stand by the mixing desk chatting to Factory co-owner Alan Erasmus, as what look like a pair of wardrobes are carried in. They are assembled on stage and the bass player plugs into an amp which is connected to these humongous speakers.

The sound is joyously deafening as they work through the songs 'MPLA', 'Pick Up The Rockers' and 'Go De Natty'. My stereo at Mayfield Road, where I've listened to the *MPLA* album a thousand times, now seems like the sound of my Sony Walkman compared to the blast I'm hearing now. With the soundcheck over and everyone ready for the show, I'm about to leave when I see Tapper himself walking over to the mixing desk. The mix engineer asks him if everything is okay with the sound, to which he says, 'Turn up de bass.'

Friday nights upstairs at the Russell, everyone I know or will soon get to know passes through. The club also supplies the necessary soundtrack to where we are right now, through a mixture of live music and heavy dub sounds.

A band called A Certain Ratio play this one night. They are four teenagers. Two guitars, bass and a singer who is absolutely spellbinding beyond his years. They wear khaki shorts and come off like a solemn Hitler Youth group.

They also play a song called 'Crippled Child', a slow dirge without any drums or percussion. Bass player Jez Kerr and guitarists Peter Terrell and Martin Moscrop push and pull at the listener's senses through an array of swirling sounds as singer Simon Topping's woeful, sonorous voice cuts through, sharp and low, hooking you into the story. The lyric details the narrator's hopes for a perfect future, complete with a home of his own and a wife with green eyes. However, at the birth of their first child, he sees that the baby's '*legs are bent*', declaring, '*You've given me the wrong child.*'

To my ears, this is as brilliant as it gets right now. Not only do I relate in the most absurd way to the lyric via my own story, but the sonic expression hooks me into a musical future. ACR play an array of similar songs, each with a singular strength about them, with such uplifting titles as 'Genotype Phenotype', 'Faceless', 'Choir', 'I Fail' and 'Strain'.

Joy Division also often play at the Factory. I pop backstage to say hello. Ian Curtis is such a brilliant and affable man, with an intensity that burns through his eyes.

He is dripping in sweat post-show but open to having a chat. As he talks to me about how he thought it went, he removes his shirt and I notice how his torso is covered entirely in fine half-inch cuts. On his chest, his arms and his back.

I say nothing, but it's as though he is showing me the depths of his intensity as he looks at me to measure my reaction. This moment puts an image in my mind that I will never be able to let go of.

Chapter Twenty-Two

Linder comes over to Mayfield Road. How we dance! 'Flash Light' by Funkadelic takes us both away.

I cannot get enough of her: boyish, shy and simpering in that boilersuit of hers. Here she comes again…

Or Kate, another girl I'm seeing at the same time, who, almost elflike, dances away from herself and into my bed, leaving that same self behind in an intense and beautiful manner.

Or Penny, a girl I meet at Pips while watching The Pop Group. (Singer Mark Stewart asks me if I'm there to film the band, when I introduce myself to him.) Penny always looks at me with a desperation that begs me not to tell her to fuck off because she stinks of another man's spunk. I never do and she gives herself to me all the more.

These peculiar pleasures take place in the darkened setting of my room, intensified (as per M Huysmans) by inner recollections of bygone troubles. The smell of hell, with Penny's steely gaze constantly upon me, provides a rush of thrilling contempt as I open her legs as wide as they can go.

Eventually I work out who her stinky other lover is. Then I quietly tell her to fuck off, as the sense of competition has me flailing over hot coals of endless comparison.

* * *

Back in Magazine land, I do wonder whether, in this era of post-'free love', Howard actually knows about me and Linder. Do they have some kind of an arrangement?

I know this betrays my working-class simplicity, where 'doing the right and just thing' is its own reward and must surely take precedence over a decadence I now seem to be embracing. So let the conflict begin…

Howard's words prod at my confusion with a blunt knife that will eventually sear my skin. Almost everything he says seems to reflect how I just can't let go of what I have going on with Linder.

A part of me wants to confess all and beg Howard's forgiveness. I become, at times, a walking receptacle of fears and phobias. But the weed that I'm smoking more and more has my back; it enables me to forget any sanctimoniously moral ethics that might cause me to attack myself.

So I let it go and look forward to the next time Linder bathes me in endless affirmation. Our relationship gains importance to me, where others have died of natural causes. I hope it's not just the forbidden nature of it, that something pure is firing the engine of my constant desire for her that extends beyond even the physical or cerebral.

Linder takes Polaroid photographs of me wearing make-up and female clothes. She firmly pushes to make me see the feminine that she's always telling me dwells inside the masculine.

Truth be told, under her guidance I'm somewhat keen to explore it myself. The Polaroids are not too far away from the shots used on the back sleeve of Magazine single 'Touch And Go'. But we take the idea much further privately.

* * *

Work begins on a song called 'TV Baby'. It's a real hoot to Howard, for some reason. He bounces around the rehearsal room as though he's on something. I haven't seen him drunk, or on some kind of high like this, for some time.

I can't help but see my playing dress-up with Linder as information that he might be holding, using it to secure a power over me. Either that or I'm serving up my power to him on a metaphorical plate, seeing things that simply don't exist.

The single 'Give Me Everything', coupled with 'I Love You, You Big Dummy', is released. The record sees drummer John Doyle enter the fray. Solid as a rock, he hits 'em as hard as fuck and lives just down the road from my mum's old people's home.

His rock-funk style suits the songs really well. I'm able to pull out a bass-line feature on 'Give Me Everything'. Formula finds a slice of old-school Hammond to layer on the top while Howard snaps:

There will be rooms
Where we shouldn't meet
Times I wanna screw you up
And leave you in the street
You know everybody
You don't know a thing
You watch me in you
I know what you're really seeing

We have played Beefheart's 'Dummy' since the beginning of the band. I rejoice in releasing it, giving it life on record, pushing the song to its limit. Howard's vocal is one tremendous fulmination from start to finish, my favourite-ever vocal performance of his.

To constantly put that much energy into the lines takes something extraordinary. The characters he pulls out of himself along the way are

Sleeve to 'Give Me Everything'. Image by Odilon Redon,
design by Sir Malcolm Garrett.

195

as great a feat as the vocal itself. You feel the band feeding off those characters as we flail our way through an exorcism of sorts.

John Doyle sets the pace with a ferocity that melds the rest of us into a tight unit, the definitive Magazine line-up. You can hear it in the introduction before we lay that stone-cold riff and build a foundation that is, at that moment, totally unshakable.

* * *

Howard and Linder breeze on over to Mayfield Road. '*It's nice to see them socialising,*' I reason with myself. I wonder, though, if this is the moment when they hold hands at a distance and tell me what a complete idiot I am. Didn't I realise how I was underestimating the sheer buffoonery of my own choices?

I also wonder whether, if I'd pushed myself more and gone to university, I might have been sophisticated enough to handle this better. '*Lord bless us and save us,*' as my mum now says in my head.

Linder knows every nook and cranny of my L-shaped room, making herself at home immediately. Howard sits at my desk and casts a curious eye over how I exercise my equally curious but weaker intellect, no doubt marking my copy of James Baldwin's novel, *Another Country*.

The new Kraftwerk album, *The Man Machine*, plays.

After I've rattled around the kitchen, with Linder buzzing around me like a drunken fly, I ask, in an attempt to try and placate her, if she wants a chair to sit on. After laying herself out on my bed, she playfully replies, 'We never sit on chairs when there is a chance to use the beds.'

After awkward frivolities, at the end of the evening I wave them goodnight. I see the glint in Linder's eye as she glances over Howard's shoulder. They walk off into the night, her laughter echoing on and on.

I close the front door and run back upstairs to my room. I still see them both sat there for a moment, until the image fades and I really am alone.

I lie on the bed that I've made for myself and breathe Linder in. As I'm no stranger to humping the soft furnishings, I imagine her giving (only to me) everything as I ride her shadow.

* * *

Nineteen seventy-nine. The *Secondhand Daylight* album is well underway.

Colin ('Thirsty') Thurston is at the controls, after a possible deal with John Barry as producer failed to see the light of day. Thirsty brings a Tony Visconti/Bowie-like sound to the table and impresses by sending the drums (and everything else) through a piece of kit known as an H910 Harmonizer. I can hear traces of Iggy Pop's *The Idiot* leaking through whatever is touched by this amazing effect. It's a beautiful, joyous sound.

We are entering the full-on period of Magazine at its finest; to my mind, this is a unique and exceptional batch of new songs. Working at Good Earth Studios in London is just magnificent. I am inspired by each track to explore new territories and give my all.

Besides, Howard's giving up on exclusively being the writer just a little, signalling possibilities of (some) equality in the group. I co-write three of the nine songs: the first is 'Rhythm Of Cruelty' with John McG, for which he shows me the main riff at Mayfield Road and I add an extra three-chord bridge. This is the first single, preceding the release of an album which will contain further dimensions of time and space.

We are recording 'Back To Nature' in a live setting but the sound of the bass just isn't cutting it. Thirsty suggests something other than my Rickenbacker or Gibson EB3. He pulls out a Fender Precision after we agree on the need for a harder sound, somewhere in the realm of The Stranglers' great bass player, Jean-Jacques Burnel.

I manage to get a clank out of the instrument, before the cliché 'plays like a dream' springs to mind. I'm invigorated by walking the scale of the neck. With my Boss Chorus SE C11 pedal at my feet, I feel like a master of my craft. The song allows me to be as utterly dexterous as I feel, even though I'm only just one feature, as everything about it is so, so strong.

I'm not sleeping or eating much. On a jaunt to Oxford Street with Dave, I keel over. He saves the day by dragging me to McDonald's, getting a burger and Coke inside me. Then it's back to the studio.

In my bones, I feel 'Permafrost' is the song that will propel us into a rarefied stratosphere that will see us at the top of everybody's game. I've hooked the song with a nod to Serge Gainsbourg's 'Melody Nelson' by bending the high notes, the way that the amazing Herbie Flowers does on that very song. It provides a suitably hallucinatory mood, along with a kind of frozen loucheness that gets nods of approval from all directions.

The guitar solo is a moment beyond all others as John McGeoch kicks in some feedback, hovering over the song with menace. John Doyle's jaw drops to the floor, mine too, as he continues down his avenue of perplexity. As he begins to peak, Thirsty kicks in the harmonizer while John bends and blends his guitar strings into a wonderful and scintillating nausea ahead of the last chorus.

* * *

Huddled up to myself at Mayfield Road, I am leafing through *The Outsider* by Colin Wilson when there is a shout up the stairs.

'Barry, it's Howard for you.'

I make my way down to the ground floor, where a bare-chested flatmate, Roger, holds the handle of the wall phone. I nod, 'Thanks, Dodger,' as he saunters away, scratching his pale skin.

My mind records a still of me on the phone, just listening. I prop it back into its cradle as the sound of my gulp fills my head.

Howard will be over shortly. Time to take a hit from the bong.

He arrives on time. After well-mannered formalities I lead him upstairs, so that he can lead me to the slaughterhouse.

Howard sits at my desk and throws an admiring glance towards the Wilson book. He then lights a cigarette, holding it between his second and third finger as usual. His cheeks redden and a large vein pulsates above his left eye.

Silence.

My heart sinks into my chest and travels ever downwards until it hits the floor. It slides sideways until it leaps into Howard's hands, so that he can throw it at the wall behind my bed. The bed where Linder makes a man of me, every time.

I ready myself for a sesquipedalian outburst of denunciation. He then says, quite orderly and without fluster, 'I know about you and Linder.'

The silence is as loud as the H-bomb that H has just dropped.

In the moment I can't help but feel penitent. For some reason, though, I refuse (or more likely am unable) to give voice to my feeling of shame.

Upon realising the words have got stuck in my throat, rather than stick a knife in to free them up, Howard says, 'It's okay, though. We've split up and are going our separate ways.'

198

His eyes greet mine now. He seems to be wondering why I'm not jubilant about the enormous gift he has just given me.

True, there's a relief sailing around my body like a sped-up cruise ship. But this is too easy, as though my role in the band outweighs the frivolity of all things lovey-dovey.

Or maybe it's something else?

Howard stands and makes to leave. I'm all over the shop. He bats away my awkward form of self-recrimination.

Looking at the floor, he then produces from his inside jacket pocket a Polaroid photo. It's of me in full make-up and a rather fetching woman's corset.

Still red-cheeked, he says, 'I think this belongs to you.'

And leaves.

* * *

Linder moves into Mayfield Road.

She takes a room upstairs and sets up a studio, popping down every now and then to have me. We are not *together*, from what I can tell, and nothing is said about it. We merely share a certain kind of fruit, as it appears I've finally entered the land of 'free love'. Certainly, I am free to love whoever. '*So go on then*,' I tell myself.

CUT TO:

An array of bursting bubbles in the bong with an image of me running around the world, suitcase in my hand. I hold on to my hat, carrying labels from countries and cities which are underscored by music reminiscent of The Swingle Singers. The sound of an upright bass, walking at double speed, brings in the singers who blend choral and jazz styles effortlessly. I skip through France and on to Germany, soaring up into the clouds with the bubbles popping all around me.

FADE OUT.

I travel to Amsterdam to see the lovely Bettie, another artist I met at a show there. I take with me some of the strongest hash I've ever smoked in my life, from Malawi in East Africa via Didsbury in Manchester, and the whole journey feels like one big strange dream.

Bettie is sweet, gentle and more than a tad vulnerable at times. However, she teaches me the Dutch word 'lekker', meaning 'yummy', by way of sticking her finger up my bum and then putting it under my nose.

She also plays the sax with two other guys in an offbeat jazz trio. Over the weekend, they come over and we all hang out. I have to go pee and, on the way back, see one of the guys in her bedroom, pocketing a pair of her panties with a wry smile across his chops.

My mind is a blur, unsure as to whether they are lovers. Should I just get out of town on the next ferry? Or maybe kick the living shit out of him?

I smoke a joint, preferring to bring it up later with Bettie, who is mortified. I say that I'm just popping to the shop for some milk, then head back to the UK without a word.

It will be some time before I make amends to her for being a spineless, uncaring, egotistical twat. I will let her scream at me in the street and I will take it – before buying her a new bike, which will be stolen within days.

I am also learning that there is nothing quite like the smell of your own shit. So you'd better learn to accept it, brothers and sisters.

*　*　*

One morning, Linder knocks on my door. Upon opening it I see her down on her knees, saying that she cannot see. She is frantic with blindness, and as I've just woken up, I'm not sure if this is real. I'm also so shocked that I have no idea what to do.

I call my mum, hoping her years as a district nurse will shine through and she'll know exactly what's wrong. She tells me, 'Get her to bloody casualty, now!'

Various tests later. It's the afternoon and Linder is seeing clearly again. I don't know exactly why it happened and we don't talk about it, preferring to make out with each other in the privacy of a private hospital room.

Both of us are relieved that she didn't begin bleeding from her eyes and wasn't going through some bizarre religious conversion, ordained by some strange deity that she doesn't even subscribe to.

Then, a decision of sorts to move to London meets with various responses. Formula, by way of a tipoff from somebody at Virgin, gets us into a flat in Devonshire Mews West, Marylebone.

I travel alone on the train, dodging the food cart. Upon arrival in London, I feel a familiarity with the underground starting to take hold as I make my way into its bowels.

The tube train arrives and I stand before the doors. As they open, my way is blocked by a huge man in a dogtooth-checked, three-piece suit. He stands in a way that says, '*My movements on and off this train are the only ones that shall be considered.*'

Looking up into the face of Enoch Powell, I hear my dad tell me about the 'Rivers of Blood' speech and how he probably wouldn't want to get in the way of such a man. Before Enoch just about walks through me, I begrudgingly move to one side.

Devonshire Mews West resembles an olde worlde slice of England. A cobbled street, almost northern in appearance, is lined by a strange enclave of tiny houses. You can hear the sounds of a bygone era, the horseshoe clatter on the cobbles, perhaps carrying noblewomen to Regent's Park.

Inside the terraced mews house, our landlady lives amidst an array of chintz. She may just be the poshest person I've ever met. In keeping with the old world she inhabits, she insists on calling me 'Barrington'. It doesn't sound Jamaican in any sense, just a remnant from an older age, like her house itself.

But she has a boyfriend of mixed race, like me. I'm hoping this similarity is the way to instant bonding with a stranger, as I smile knowingly at him. He is totally without wit or empathy, though, giving me a look along the lines of Enoch.

I enjoy the empty Marylebone weekends, when tourists disappear and the streets are quiet. I take a paper and amble to the park.

On returning, I see that our good landlady has bruises about her face and arms. Her lover gives me a venomous look that asks if there is something I would like to say. Her battered eyes beg me to say nothing.

* * *

A party is held in Notting Hill, at John McGeoch's friend Lydia's house off Portobello Road. It's a late Saturday afternoon, still light. I'm in the kitchen, getting a beer, when I hear shouting. Somebody runs past me and shouts, '*GATECRASHERS!*'

I run to the front of the house to see John fending off several louts, determined to fight their way into the party. McGeoch defends Lydia's domain with honour, compelling me to join him.

I manage to confront a couple of them, drawing on a rare rage, but as the second is sent running I see a third, armed with what I quickly assess is a piece of scaffolding.

He swings furiously at me. I instinctively turn my back. The scaffolding catches me square on the spine, the adrenaline muting the immediate pain.

Fracas over. There's a lot of panting and checking to see if all are okay; I ask Siouxsie (of the Banshees) how my back looks. Lifting my shirt, I see her wince.

I turn to the bathroom mirror and see a chunk of flesh missing. The near future promises a stay in hospital, with an operation to decompress my discs and fit a small clamp so that my back stays stable.

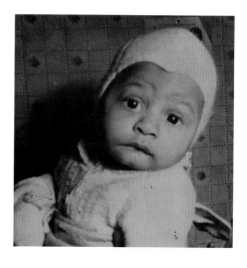

◀ Hand-coloured photo of my mum and dad's wedding, nineteen forty-eight.

▲ Me by my dad, nineteen fifty-nine.

▲ With Our Kid at home, Eighty-Eight Upper Medlock Street, Manchester, early sixties.

With my ▶ mum, nineteen sixty-five.

Our annual summer ▶
holiday destination.
The Black Cat
Amusement Arcade,
Towyn, North Wales,
early seventies.

Holidays in
town with my
mum, dad and
step-gran in the
seventies.
▼

EMPIRE POOL, WEMBLEY

M.A.M./John Smith Entertainments/
Earley Associates presents

DAVID BOWIE

ON STAGE

SATURDAY, 8 MAY, 1976
at 8 p.m.

SOUTH GRAND TIER

£2.75

TO BE RETAINED. See conditions on back

MAY
8

ENTER AT
SOUTH DOOR
ENTRANCE

77

ROW
D

SEAT
130

Peter Robertson, me and Pete's mate Mint in London for the Bowie gig. Photo by Will Trotter.

With Howard Devoto during a demo recording session at Penine Studio, Manchester, nineteen seventy-seven. Photo by Kevin Cummins.

A trip to London the year we left school to see Bowie at Wembley, nineteen seventy-six. Thanks, Peter Robertson.

▲
With Nick Cave in Amsterdam,
mid-eighties. Photo by Danny de Jong.

Wedding day, November
nineteen eighty-three.
With my dad.

With Our Kid. ▶

With Caitlin
and Will Trotter.
▼

Right and below ▶
Nick Cave and the Bad Seeds in Athens, nineteen eighty-four. Photos by Teo Papadopoulos, owner of Berlin Bar Thessaloniki.

Me and
Celia.
▼

▲
By the Thames,
nineteen
eighty-six.
Photo by Celia
Johnstone.

◀ A vintage
memory
of holidays
in Wales
with my
dad, early
seventies.

A broken jaw ▶
after a Bad
Seeds concert,
nineteen
eighty-seven.

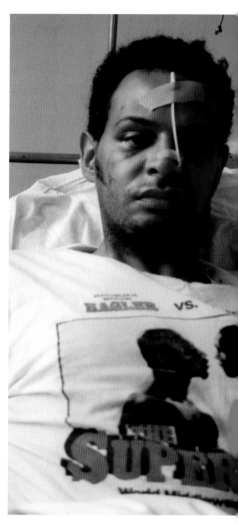

▲
Photo session
with Celia
Johnstone,
mid-eighties.

◀ On the
houseboat
with Bella the
cat, Cheyne
Walk, London,
nineteen
eighty-eight.

Chapter Twenty-Three

Touring for 'Rhythm Of Cruelty' and *Secondhand Daylight* begins in February ninety seventy-nine. Our biggest, most ambitious tour yet, it will last pretty much all year, covering the UK and Europe, and for the first time will also take in America and Canada.

I'm excited beyond belief about being spat on some more. After the European leg, I'll also turn twenty-one and get the keys to whatever kingdom I'm allowed into. This is a major tour, as they say, playing major venues and the fever runs high. Actually, I'm really excited.

Simple Minds will support us on the UK leg. They are a great bunch of lads who sound a bit like us. They probably won't go that far but good luck to them, I say.

We set off for Malvern Winter Gardens for our first show. When we get to Leicester De Montford Hall, Simple Minds earn themselves more praise than ever. As the show is invaded by the National Front, they effectively save us from getting a right kicking.

The NF wade in from the far right, kicking and punching people in the audience. Howard leaps off the stage to wade right into the heart of the crowd as I whip my bass off, ready to use it as a weapon. Several NF members try to rush the stage as several members of Simple Minds and their crew wrestle them back. The side-stage becomes a blur, out of which one of the enemy slips through, before I whack him. The crew get Howard the hell out of there, order is restored and the show carries on.

Towards the end of the UK leg, there's a special addition to the show at the Theatre Royal, Drury Lane. We have 'dancing suits' fly across the stage during 'I Love You, You Big Dummy'. This is achieved by a complicated system of pulleys and winches hanging from the ceiling, which whiz the suits back and forth and around us.

The success of the show and the tour spurs me on past disappointing reviews of the album which, truth be told, leave me somewhat gutted. But seeing how the shows are breaking house records, it becomes the perfect antidote to any of the negativity spewing from the press. It gives the band the necessary incentive to push on through Europe.

No longer a newcomer, a fledgling, the time feels right to ply my trade much farther afield. We've all set our sights on conquering the world, starting with the USA.

While there's violence constantly around me in the mews flat, with the looming threat that it could so easily happen to me, I quietly prepare myself for what I see as the journey of a lifetime. I do this by sewing shoulder pads into my favourite pale blue jacket, emulating a design by Thierry Mugler. He calls it the 'Superman look': I feel like anything but, as my landlady's psychopathic boyfriend smirks and asks me why the fuck I'm doing what I'm doing.

He mimics my responses in an effeminate manner, to humiliate me like the bouncer at the Ranch did not that long ago. In the same way as that guy, he thrives on intimidation, oppression, disrespect, direct putdowns, and, of course, in-your-face mockery.

I see it as a way to break a person (in this case me) down, which is what he's been doing to our landlady. I hear her scream and then watch him come downstairs, flexing his muscles and laughing.

I'm determined now not to waver from the vision I have of myself, which includes looking as cool as a fuck at all times. So I take an empty suitcase to America and fill it with the coolest clothes I can find, wearing them on the tour.

* * *

The flight to America is showing the John Travolta/Olivia Newton John film *Grease*. I don't particularly like it, but I really like the songs: the playing, in particular, and their singalong nature.

However, I wouldn't be caught dead singing along to 'Summer Nights' (especially attempting that high note at the end) or 'You're The One That I Want'. No. Best to stay aloof, even to ask, 'What is this that we're watching?', while lighting up a Rothmans cigarette and downing another beer.

The title song 'Grease', though, *is* the word; it does have groove and meaning. Frankie Valli, the man whose voice holds the song together, always had a top-quality arrangement around him. I'm a huge fan of his Four Seasons, their song 'The Night' being an inspirational tour de force of writing, arranging and performing.

Arriving in New York, I step onto the runway and I'm hit by another tour de force, the humidity. I can't believe how hot and wet the air feels. It's a relief to go inside and feel the ice-cold blast of the air conditioning.

I'm struck by how much the Big Apple is exactly like the television detective show *Kojak*. The cops have guns, the taxis are indeed yellow, and I am in a state of constant awe as we head into town.

At the Iroquois hotel on West Forty-Fourth Street, amidst the hustle and bustle, I see Iggy Pop in the bar, supremely holding court.

I head out for a wander. A small crowd gathers across the street as a kid performs incredible dancing skills on a piece of cardboard, while another plays records on two decks and makes scratching noises by dragging the record under the needle. The beat is immense, as the bass from 'Good Times' by Chic grooves along to a song I later find out is called 'Rapper's Delight'. This mix of taking one song and putting it on top of another, plus scratching the record in time, is mind-blowingly revolutionary.

I walk a few blocks down from the Iroquois and as I turn into Forty-Second Street, a gang of black youths come running past me. One of them shouts at me to come on. I pick up the pace and run with them down an alleyway. Another one of them asks me, 'Did you see it?' I look at him, slightly flummoxed. 'See what?' 'Fucking great big fat rat, man,' he shoots back at me. 'No.'

He holds my gaze for a while. We stop running. 'Stick out your hand.'

I do and the guy turns my hand over. I make a gentle fist; he then dumps cocaine powder into the fleshy part between finger and thumb.

'Go ahead,' he says. I snort the coke and feel myself lift off, just as somebody yells, 'There it is!'

The gang starts running again. I follow them back onto the street but become seduced by the lights, the hookers, the XXX cinemas, the seediness of Forty-Second Street – known also as 'the Deuce'. I fall mesmerisingly under the spell of this open and scary wound, where I feel strangely at home.

Following my nose, I slip into nearby Bryant Park where I wind up buying five joints for five dollars. I'm so unaware of the dangers, having no idea of the shocking crime rate here, as I slip into a packed porn cinema where mainly men – though some women – openly masturbate and give each other head as the film plays. My Englishness surpasses everything else as I realise that, while this is all very eye-opening, I'm completely and utterly out of my depth.

Within minutes of arriving I leave, shadowed by an overbearing image of a blonde woman being fucked by a black man, moaning and groaning (like the rest of the cinemagoers) for all her worth. I glance back to notice how her pale blue eyeshadow matches her negligee. Nice. The black guy stares back at me as he's coming.

I bolt out of the door and onto the street. Back to all the comforting funk and junk.

I'm in another time zone altogether when I start back to the hotel. Back in my room, I smoke the joints – only three of which are actual weed, the others being paper, but I smoke them anyway.

As I begin to pass out, I become aware of a new attraction to a deeper darkness that is growing inside of me. I begin to nod my head as I recall Herbie Flowers' bass part from Lou Reed's 'Walk On The Wild Side', playing two parts in one, sliding up the upright double bass and down at the same time. This *is* the sound of NYC, baby...

* * *

Rehearsals begin after a hearty eggs-over-easy, bacon, home fries and toast, with grape jello and as much coffee as I can drink. I note that the waitress says to me and Doyley, 'Oh, only two of you eating today?' It's familiarity that sends me back to the same restaurant every day while in New York.

In fact, the very next day the same waitress points at me and says, 'Eggs-over-easy, bacon, home fries and toast, with grape jello and as much coffee as you can drink?' It takes me a while to work out this is the standard breakfast. It's quite easy to remember, but right now I'm as naively impressed as I want to be.

Frank, the moustached wrestling crewman, hooks up a U-Haul trailer for the gear. After initial shows at the Hot Club in Philadelphia and the Bayou in Washington, DC, we steel ourselves to wow New York City. Word is that we already bring a certain hipness we've carried from the UK, like other British bands before us.

This viewpoint is endorsed by the continual validation of our new manager, Raf Edmunds. Raf is hip, slick and cool. He's not afraid to play the fool, though he also acts like the guy who knows it all and has seen it all.

Because he has.

Raf hangs with us guys and gets involved in the after-show 'extracurricular activity'. But he's also there for Howard, who doesn't. He bonds the band further, almost becoming a sixth member, mentor and father figure at the same time. His dress is sharp and he's always on the money, which is his job.

* * *

Raf is right about word spreading across the Atlantic, as the very lovely promoter Ruth Polsky has booked us to play a couple of shows at Hurrah on West Sixty-Seventh Street. They are sold out.

The Lounge Lizards play with us at Hurrah. They are a 'No Wave' avant-garde jazz outfit. The sax player, John Lurie, kills it on classical good looks alone. '*These guys are seriously hip,*' I think to myself as we perform to an audience that makes the London Cool look awkward. I wonder if we look awkward too. Or maybe that's cool?

However, when some twelve rows from the front I see Andy Warhol, watching us with an intensity, I can't wait to tell the folks back home that one of the greatest artists in the world was right there tonight, at our show.

We move through America at a frenzied pace. Hip and naive. East to west. North to south. Through Canada, stopping for a tourist trip at Niagara Falls. It's as hot as hell in Texas. Then we move on to…

The famous Whisky a Go Go, in LA. We play three nights there. On the last night, I get a hold of some Quaaludes and drop a couple. Seems like no big deal.

So after about ten minutes, I approach three black girls who are standing near the dressing-room doorway. The room is huge. I make my way over to them, hoping to lose my 'never slept with a black girl' virginity.

Then my legs buckle as the 'ludes kick in. As I get there the girls turn away from me, rightly observing, 'He can't even walk.'

Jello Biafra of the Dead Kennedys invites us to a party. I see Jack Nicholson at breakfast next to the Tropicana hotel, where we're staying.

But then there's an incident in Minneapolis, where I steal a girl right from under Dave Formula's nose. Boy, is he pissed off at me!

She is mid-twenties, dark-haired and sharp as anything. Once I get to work, using every charm in the book, I can see she prefers me to him and so I make my move.

On the way to the hotel, she says she just has to make a stop at her friend's house to pick something up. We're all in the van, so we pull in and I go with her to this apartment. She tells me on the way that she has to score some coke and it won't take long. She looks at me as if to say, '*Are you in?*'

'I'm totally in,' I respond. 'I have a fifty in my pocket.'

She knocks on the door. A black man with no shirt and a gun shoved down the front of his trousers opens up the door. He stares at me and tells us both to 'get the fuck inside'.

Once inside, I see two guys, one white and one black, playing chess. The white guy plays with the white pieces and the black guy plays with the black, like a set-up from some movie. The carpet is of a thick white shagpile throughout. The two men don't look up or break concentration as we walk through the room.

The guy who answered the door tells me to sit at a small kitchen table where another man is already sitting in front of weighing scales and a mountain of cocaine. He is dividing it up into small plastic bags.

The guy with the gun stands next to me, his huge belly almost in my face. He loads a small pipe with hash. 'Smoke it,' he says, which in a very English way I decline. He then shoves the thing in my mouth, smashing my front tooth.

The effect of the hash is immediate. He leans into me and says, 'Do you see what I got on my back?'

I look over his shoulder. 'No, sir, I do not.'

I think that my deference will make this guy see I'm no threat to him whatsoever.

'You don't see the dorsal fin that I've got on my back?'

I feel like I have this now, so I offer, 'Oh yeah. I see it. A dorsal fin.'

He stares at me in total disbelief. 'What?' As he looks around the room, the others smile.

'Ain't no dorsal fin on my back!'

'Sorry, yes, sir. My mistake,' I say, still looking for a way to get out of this.

He eyes the bandana I'm wearing around my neck, like I'm some kind of fucking cowboy. 'Where you from?' He squints at me, maybe expecting Delaware or someplace like that.

I tell him: 'The UK.'

He furrows his brow. My answer has clearly gone way over his head, but he tries not to let it show.

'What choo want?' he asks.

The girl steps in and asks for fifty dollars' worth of cocaine. I take the note from my pocket. Slowly. He takes it from me, screws it up and tosses it onto the floor.

'Your fifty dollars ain't worth shit.'

The girl winks at me knowingly. She then puts on the most convincing piece of theatre I've seen this side of Broadway.

Flinging herself on Gun Guy, she begins crying her little heart out. He in turn picks up his cue, apologising profusely to his 'little mama'. He tells her to wipe away her tears. 'It's all gone be okay, baby.'

The guy who is bagging up the coke hasn't stopped smiling throughout this whole debacle. He slides a bag my way and winks at me.

I take the coke and we leave, with Gun Guy still apologising to the girl.

We get back to the van. Howard tells me we were taking so long that he came up to the apartment to see where we were. He almost knocked at the door but decided not to. '*Jesus H!*' I think to myself.

Back at the hotel, the girl gives me the coke and I begin, with shaky hand, to chop it up. But she stops me, taking two hypodermic syringes from her purse.

'I do it this way.'

I pause for about a week before answering. She looks far from what I'd imagine somebody who shoots up coke to look like. 'Sounds good to me.' I gulp down my misgivings before they slap me around the face.

She ties up my arm and injects me with cocaine. Images of the last hour's events fly off into the night.

I remember floating around the hospital. I remember laughter and good times.

We are fucking like rabid dogs. Music swirls around my head from somewhere as the scene fades into the night...

*   *   *

A few days later, Dave asks me about that night. I tell him everything and he goes mad. Mad like your dad would.

He asks me to promise I will never do that again. I don't know whether he means stealing the girl or shooting drugs, but he gives me such a severe bollocking that I feel bad on both counts.

John McGeoch, me and Dave Formula, broken down in Sheffield, Texas, USA.
Photo by John Doyle.

After the last show of thirty-three, ending in Vancouver, it's decided we'll drive back to NYC right across America. It's a trip which will take three days and two nights. We load up the car and I make sure there's enough pot to last the journey.

Along the way we pick up hitchhikers and drop them off. I fear for one girl, who seems like she's on the run from someone or something. When asked any questions, she says nothing. We drop her off but I want to go back and make sure she's okay.

We drive through Cheyenne, shop around for cowboy boots and visit Yellowstone Park, unofficial home of Yogi Bear. Further along the road, we break down in the middle of the night and the middle of nowhere.

We have very little to drink and the only entertainment is a party of insects, who bop around endlessly. Raf is reaching out through the CB radio in an unconvincing American accent, something I mercilessly take the piss out of. He does, however, get us help.

We get back on the road again. We'll return safely to the UK to start work on the next album.

Chapter Twenty-Four

I stay briefly at the Pembridge Hotel, on Pembridge Gardens, Notting Hill, leaving Manchester behind more and more. The two brothers who own the place are fans of the band and want in on the scene, so to speak. They let me stay there for a few weeks in a huge room. From there, looking out of the window, I can see the house where Jimi Hendrix died.

The on-the-road antics continue off the road now. A party is held in my room one weekend and the whole dance troupe from the Kenny Everett TV show, Hot Gossip, turn up. I play down my desires as the girls enjoy their own attractiveness. And rightly so. They're flirty and fun.

I become friends with a couple of permanent fixtures at the hotel, upcoming black American actor Ray Shell and his friend, 'Deep Joan' – so called by me for her intensity when speaking about the everyday. I also bump into Sonex from the good old days of Manchester, on the street near Portobello Road underground station. So I invite her back to the hotel.

We go to bed in the middle of the afternoon, which feels so right it cannot be wrong. I remember how she thanked me for having her, even though I didn't. She doesn't have to repeat herself now, but we play out the same heavy petting scenario as before, getting close to a consummation of sorts without going any further.

I say goodbye, but not for the last time. I whisper her name to myself as she leaves, light up a spliff and stare out across the square as she walks into the distance.

* * *

Work begins on the album that will become *The Correct Use Of Soap*.

Howard is on holiday in America, so we jam the life out of ideas and collectively come up with some great stuff for him to add his words to. This is a new way of doing things but it seems to be working, despite my core idea that bands as a democracy *don't* work. There has to be a leader, or two, even though like anybody else I strive for equality.

I therefore sense relief when Howard returns and adds some brilliant songs, particularly 'You Never Knew Me'. Order is restored.

I'm devastated, though, that on returning to Summa studios, where we rehearse, I find my upright bass is broken in two.

How this happened, I don't know. Chris, the studio owner, offers without hesitation to have it fixed. Luckily, there is a carpenter who works across the way who can glue the neck back onto the body and clamp it together.

The Townhouse mobile studio is parked up. I think nothing of playing as loud as I can, in a room across the courtyard to the rehearsal studio. During the recording of 'Philadelphia', I'm pumping away at full throttle as the door flies open. A very irate gentleman is screaming at me. I don't want to lose the groove but manage to slip one ear out of the headphone, to hear him shout, 'Do you mind? That fucking bass is frying us up there!'

I cast a face of empathy in order to get to the end of the take, before copious apologies. But it's time for me to get funky. I present a bass line, three notes thumbed then the third note pulled an octave up before thumbing the lower note again.

The songs on this album are not of the rocky darkness that emanated from *Secondhand Daylight*, but more reflective of a widening worldview. The swagger of 'Because You're Frightened' is there for all to feel, as it is in 'Model Worker'. 'I Want To Burn Again' is breathtakingly beautiful. 'I'm A Party' swings in a way we've never allowed ourselves to before, while the version we play of Sly & the Family Stone's 'Thank You (Falletinme Be Mice Elf Agin)' feels like I've been given the very keys to the kingdom that has been eluding me. As for 'A Song From Under The Floorboards', we believe we definitely have a hit on our hands.

So why am I not happy? Why do I feel a terrible discontent? Why am I irritable all the time? Why do I feel like some bizarre internal rot is beginning to take place?

Out of step with the others in the group, Barry Adamson has reservations about their third album, maintaining that the production sounds dated.
                                    Helen Chase, *Magazine: The Biography*

Mal and his pal Dougie let me stay at theirs on Baron's Court Road, opposite West Kensington tube station. Mal is Magazine's full-time roadie, whose arms, chest and legs match his massive generosity. I call him 'Mold Man', as he is always talking about his 'old man' in a heavy Scottish accident. He laughs out loud, like a child almost.

Doubt him, though, and watch him lean his force into you, to question what you're saying. Once tempered and understood, he will sweep his hair back from his eyes as if to say, *'For fuck's sake,'* before walking away to take a shower. Dougie, as Mal would say, is just Dougie. I sense a sly old (young) fox. A bone buried somewhere.

I lie awake, tugging hard on a spliff. I think and think and think, wrestling with a bout of figure-it-out-ism. I muse:

What is clever and interesting about the rot is that it begins to settle in quite insidiously and somewhat unexpectedly. One day you are fine; connected, productive, with a total sense of purpose. The next day you wake up and there is a vulture at the end of the bed, staring at you. It says in an accusatory way, 'What time do you call this, you lazy fucking bastard?' Alarmed but equally bemused, you try to reason with this huge dark thing. 'Excuse me, Mr Vulture, don't be so bloody rude. It's six a.m. and I have nothing to prove to your good self.' The Vulture comes back with, 'You know I'm going to kill you, right?' You think to yourself, 'Actually I'm quite happy, so you can fuck right off with that death shit too.' Then you realise you've just had a dialogue with something that doesn't actually exist. It's not like you can turn up at rehearsals and say you've spent the morning being put down by a vulture. Best 'act as if'. Act as if you're on the same page as everyone else. Act as if nothing has changed since the previous album; that it does not pain you that your differences with the others are now highlighted for all to see. Or at least that's what you imagine as they go about their business with a jovial lightness of spirit. Above all, you must keep quiet. Even though the sage, the seer, the all-seeing (naked) eye that protrudes from the centre of your forehead perceives the truth. And then maybe... just maybe... The Vulture will leave you alone if you don't mention that the rot is setting in. Even though you suspect that the same Vulture is paying weekly visits to Howard and is almost certainly sitting daily on the bedpost of John McGeoch.

214

CHAPTER TWENTY-FOUR

The late, great John McGeoch.

The first half of nineteen-eighty sees us pushing on, promoting the new album on the radio, then on the road, both ahead of its May release.

At Maida Vale Studios, on the seventh of January, we record several songs from *The Correct Use Of Soap* for a John Peel session and flex our muscles in the usual way. During a break I go to find a sandwich and lose myself along several corridors where I stumble upon rooms full of orchestral instruments: a sea of tympani and harps and at the end of another corridor, an array of strange and wonderful noises emanating from behind a door labelled Central Control.

* * *

The Vulture is currently nowhere to be seen and inspiration beckons. However, the bomb will drop in July.

After flirting with the New Romantic studio group Visage, 'Double-Date Dave' (who is flirting with both camps) and myself (less so) will taste the instant gratification of single sales going through the roof in

Germany. John's perfidious ambitions finally divorce him from the Magazine marriage for his second love, Siouxsie and the Banshees.

A spotlight to call his own and a bigger audience just might give him the thing he feels is lacking, chasing his tail around rehearsals, writing, recording, the road – the endless circuit of disenchantment. While it's true that most marriages have to be navigated around the seemingly endless nature of routine, it also has to be accepted at some stage.

And so now a midday gloom hangs heavy over Lots Road, London SW10. We need to regroup at Summa rehearsal studio to process our loss, in order to move forwards. Our assemblage is funereal, however…

Howard pushes his grief to the side as though it were a meal he's no longer interested in, letting it grow cold until it's seemingly only fit for the bin. Dave goes into scatterbrain mode, finally drunk on his confused yet somehow reassuring verbal meanderings of old. But he's glitching his system in the process, diverting himself onto an entirely different course.

'D for Doyle' betrays his disappointment by pretending to be the kid who couldn't care less. Like the playmate who, when killed in a game of cowboys and Indians, gets up and announces that, as sheriff, he can't die and so gets back on his imaginary horse.

And me?

Well, rather than any introspection, I observe the others from way up on high, with the fastidious eye of The Vulture. I cast my Asperger's aspersions aside and suck on my sorrow, hiding behind a wall of something I don't understand.

I decide that the only way forward is to pledge allegiance to the boss, who furthers my disenchantment by expressing himself in a very plain English.

Howard glances up briefly from his notebook and says, 'Well, we'd better get someone else in then.'

As if by magic, enter Robin Simon. Robin was in a much earlier version of Ultravox and definitely has his guitar sounds down.

But the 'magic' has been really tiresome and uninspiring. Guitarist after guitarist wonders why we are on our knees. Bad feelings slowly bleed through the process of finding somebody to fit a bill that cannot be filled.

We again 'act as if' and play the UK and Europe. As if nothing has changed in terms of the audience, the experience, us. By going through this motion, it is hoped that changes for the better will take place. That we and everybody else will see that this is just the natural progression of the band. Act as if this is so and it will become so, being the logic.

Dave, Robin Simon, Doyley, me and Howard. Photo by Ebet Roberts/Getty.

*   *   *

The next tour of America begins in Washington DC on August the fifth, nineteen-eighty, and offers a much needed lift. Robin has been doing such a brilliant impersonation of John McGeoch that we can forget him for now. The anger over his betrayal can be diffused, but not the grief. That will continue to surface and prick away at the very skin of the beast, until it erupts.

We fly instead of drive on this tour, so no more breaking down in the dead of night in deserted towns. At the Santa Monica Civic we're filmed as part of *Urgh! A Music War*, showcasing an array of bands on the so-called 'new wave' scene. I'm enthralled to be at the side of the stage watching Pere Ubu, who to my eyes and ears are totally beyond anyone else and quite brilliant with it. Singer David Thomas is a revelation.

217

Then we fly to New Zealand. I can't help but feel like Auckland might be twinned with a small town in the north of England. The gig is wrecked by skinheads who clearly think this is the way to be 'punk', so we are driven around to sightsee. The greenery calms my nerves, and the shops, the 'corner dairies', displace my sense of where I actually am.

Visiting Australia for the first time is like being born again. No wonder they call it God's country. This sense of rebirth fills me with fearless possibility, in the same way that naivety eases danger out of the way. The pursuit of happiness can begin again.

We play nine shows in Sydney and six in Melbourne, as well as Adelaide, Canberra and Brisbane. Sydney offers a 'no worries' lifestyle, as the sun blazes off Bondi beach and says, '*We've been waiting for you – what took you so bloody long, mate?*' I expect to bump into Alan Whicker at any moment.

I fucking love it here. Once I hear somebody say, 'You fuckin' beauty,' then I know this is where I want to spend the rest of my life. I don my stage look of suit but no jacket and a boss pair of cufflinks I've bought in an 'op shop' (secondhand store) to celebrate my newfound, absolute love of the place.

After the first show in Sydney, however, we miss the plane to Adelaide, so our tour manager, Kathy Acquaviva, the woman with the coolest name and the sharpest dress, hires a seven-seater plane to fly across Australia. None of us will ever experience this again.

In Melbourne, I notice something of a feeling akin to being in Manchester. The locals seem like the people back home – a raggedy-ass gang who all know each other and live out of each other's pockets. Boys who flirt with limitless danger and girls who flirt harder, in ripped tights and glossy red lips. They are untouchable, broken and defiant. All of them dress like Eton messes with (as John Cooper Clarke likes to say) 'teasy-weasy', high, lacquered hair.

At the Crystal Ballroom in Melbourne, their answer to the Russell Club in Manchester, I meet Leigh. All black spiky hair, massive lips and a peculiar squint.

Back at the hotel the next day, I notice The Vulture, motionless on the end of the bed. I'm waiting for Leigh to come back from an errand that I agreed she really should run, on the basis of my reasoning why Charlie Parker, Miles Davis and John Coltrane were able to play above and beyond the call of duty.

The Vulture pipes up: 'I had high hopes for you, son. Thing is, you cannot, no matter how hard you try, avoid the rot. I told you before.'

At the eighth hour of waiting, there is a banging at the door. I open it up and Leigh brushes past me like the heat have been on her tail all the way back here. But within moments...

The heroin is poured into a spoon and lemon juice (or maybe vinegar) is added to break the drug down, as well as a measured dose of water from a syringe. The spoon is heated from underneath by a flame from a lighter (or maybe a match) until the mixture liquifies. A small cotton bud is dropped into this mixture, so that when the syringe sucks up the smack, impurities will be lessened. The drug is now ready to be injected into my arm.

And when it is, I float back to the UK. To Manchester. To Pendlebury Children's Hospital.

I am bathed in white light, levitating about six feet above my bed. The plaster cast that covers my body from chest to ankle begins cracking and then splits into two, moving away from me. I open my eyes as the sounds of the Beach Boys' 'Good Vibrations' play out infinitely, while I ever so gently lower myself towards the bed.

The ward is crammed with everybody I know. My parents are crying as others survey the scene, somewhat concerned. I see Mark from the pub in Oldham, who rolls his eyes as a light shines from the top of my head and illuminates the darkened ward. 'Good Vibrations' is now sung *a cappella* by everybody in the hospital as snow begins to fall. They gently sway with lamps as my parents are led away. My dad has an arm around my mum, bowing his head towards her to whisper assurances as she continues to weep.

Leigh is tapping me on the shoulder.

'Bazza?' I open my eyes and think to ask if she was at the hospital, or was it just me? But I gently scratch my face instead.

She asks me if I've heard of the Boys Next Door, before deliriously telling me how they've changed their name to the Birthday Party. I start scratching like a monkey all over and narrow my eyes. I'm having trouble tuning into her because I'm so busy tuning into myself: into how extraordinary I feel; into how every bone in my body feels like it should have done for all of my life.

'Listen to this,' she says as I start to nod off again. The song she plays me is called 'Mr Clarinet'.

A distorted organ calls the other instruments forwards, bringing them in line like toy soldiers by setting the pace and the tone. The drums and bass drop in, marching alongside meanly and precisely, the bass in particular making drunken slurs.

The organ then plays a lofty, bombastic melody to announce the singer, who seems to be shouting to be heard through a sea of tears. During the line '*You make me laugh and then cry...*,' I notice that he uses an aristocratically English inflection on the word 'laugh'.

There's also a brilliantly disgusted funkiness about the song. It is hidden but it gripes along, and the bass player's drunken loucheness is a joy to my ears. He pins down every fourth beat and quite naturally deflects the rhythm by throwing in syncopated notes which also support the lyric. He then releases a melody underpinning the lofty organ part, which becomes the chorus. The effect is staggeringly wonderful.

I have heard the future.

* * *

Back in the UK, we start to pull a new album together.

On arrival at the rehearsal room, I notice that Robin appears more agitated than usual. He seems nervous and withdrawn. Gone is the man who knowingly says, '*Soup de jour?* That's my favourite soup, that one.'

We push ideas around and it is as though Robin has been replaced by an android. To pepper the unreality, I wait for Emma Peel from *The Avengers* to jump out and karate chop Robin, the words '*Soup du jour!*' bellowed out as a repeated glitch as his eyes roll around their sockets.

Steed toys with the head of his umbrella as he now tells Howard, 'Well, we couldn't have him crawling back home to Ma now, could we?' He then drops his bowler at a rakish angle onto his head as the soundtrack (already playing a light orchestral waltz) plays two plucked notes to end the sequence, Howard's head exploding while he angrily looks at me beneath not one, but two, quizzical eyebrows.

Instead, it seems like tumbleweed is drifting through Summa as the discomfort mounts. Robin has frozen, and nothing can be said or done to unfreeze him, save him making his leaving statement.

I offer to take his final brown envelope (pay packet) to his house at the end of the tube line, in Dollis Hill. The house is empty, as though Robin, his beautiful American girlfriend and the woman I assume to be her sister are about to jump on a plane. Either that or they've just moved in and have yet to buy any furniture. I hand him the envelope and feel mentally ushered out of the door. '*Clearly there's furniture to be bought,*' I surmise.

At least we can ride on the wings of our live album, *Play*, where Formula without McGeoch but with Simon cook up a storm over Melbourne Festival Hall. But as the year closes, where the fuck do we go from here?

Leigh keeps threatening to come over. I wish she would, as I do miss her so.

*   *   *

'*I wouldn't bloody stand for that,*' whispers my mum internally as Howard's old student friend and new guitarist Ben Mandelson looks at me less than favourably when I offer him the joint I'm smoking. Rather than accept the traditional peace pipe, his attitude has already offended me before he's played a single note.

But Howard seems confident that, rather than filling anyone's boots, Ben will take the group in another direction. That or maybe Howard's actually using him as part of a greater plan.

I wonder about this as the drug fills my lungs and my mind. The Vulture sits on top of my amp, filing its talons and glancing at me in an '*I think you might be on to something*' way.

Leigh comes over from Australia and stays with me at Baron's Court, introducing me to other Australians who all seem to live together in a squat on Wandsworth Road. They hover around me 'like flies on shit, mate,' as though *I'm* the one who's just arrived from the other side of the world. Their curiosity makes me feel akin to the new kid in a production of *Oliver!* But I don't consider myself part of the furniture as, like Robin Simon, they don't have any.

We return home and the needle goes in again. The dots are now joining up since I last saw Leigh in Australia. I move towards her, relaxed and ready to carry things further. She tells me, 'Urgh, no thanks. I can't bloody stand flesh.'

Shortly after this, the Birthday Party arrive. They swing by Baron's Court and devour all the food I've bought. The singer, Nick Cave, doesn't say much, just looks at me, constantly eyeing me up. They play the Venue in Victoria to about twelve people. Within a couple of weeks, though, the queue at the very same venue is around the block.

New guitarist Ben's playing has a North African leaning. He also plays the violin. If we make another album and then tour again, we can get some money from the record company.

But is that what this is about? Is this what bringing in a mate who doesn't speak our musical language means? Sitting back and counting the cash while Summa burns, with us in it?

Howard pouts and punches out four chords on the guitar, over and over. The Vulture looks at me and says, '*Don't look at me.*'

As the needle goes in again, I arrive at rehearsal out of my mind: on cloud nine, not giving a toss. Which is evident when John Doyle appears, having gone over on his ankle and possibly broken it.

All empathy begins to leave me in favour of seizing the *Schadenfreude* moment. I now find it hilarious that he won't be able to use that foot on the bass drum pedal. The others look on, incredulous.

The album's songs leave me somewhat cold. I relate to 'This Poison', though, believing everything (including this part of the lyric) to now be about me.

Now put me down upon the lawn
Right here – next to my favourite tree
I'm being foolish can't you tell?
They all look just the same to me

I took a little poison
I took it carefully
It built for me a house on fire
This poison takes after me

'*Not everything's about you,*' offers my mum, in my head, to which I reply, '*Unless it is.*'

Ray Shell from the Pembridge Hotel comes into the studio and sings back-up with me as we parody The Supremes on 'About The Weather'. We spread the joy where none is forthcoming. Ben, amazingly, tells producer John Brand, that we don't like his work and scapegoats him into submission. (Puppetry by Howard, perhaps?)

'Let's bring in Martin Hannett' is the answer to the question tickling the edge of my lips. Martin reworks and revises, and I'm not keen, but, as John McGeoch used to say, 'We are Magazine.'

*   *   *

Album done. I visit Howard at a flat in Walworth Road, South London, and he seems as flat as a pancake. I ask him if he has any ideas about what to call the record. His girlfriend is changing her top in the room next door and I can see her reflection in the mirror behind his head. I avert my gaze. Lessons have been learned on that score.

'Don't know,' he moodily answers. I then ask him what the album is about, and he says, 'Magic, murder and the weather.'

The light behind Howard fades, pouring out of neither of us. His smile broadens.

Chapter Twenty-Five

WE the undersigned formerly all members of the Group known as "Magazine"
agree as follows:-
1. With effect from 27th May   1981 our partnership as the Group"Magazine"
shall be dissolved.
2. The total value of the equipment owned by the partnership shall be treated

Section of the contract dissolving the group Magazine.

In the summer of nineteen eighty-one, my mum stands staring out the
window of Carisbrooke Old People's Home in silence.

My dad sits at a nearby table, busying himself making lists in his
impeccable handwriting, occasionally muttering a self-congratulatory
ah-hum for a job well done.

In the bedroom, I rifle through my art folder. It's a handy reminder
of my recent past, a marker of just how far I've come in a few years.

I walk across the corridor and enter the sitting room where my
parents are. I take the seat on the far left, sitting in the place where I
told my parents I was prematurely leaving college to join a band. Now
I'm here to tell them the band is no more.

I steady myself and take a deep breath to form the words, readying
to shoot them out.

'I've been sacked,' my mum says. My dad is still paying no attention
to her, writing away as though removed in space and time.

'Sacked?' I ask. She does not move from her fixed position of staring out the window.

'Yes', she says. 'Sacked for mental cruelty.'

My mind runs over the possible ways she might have enacted this 'cruelty'.

'We have to move,' she says.

'*Where to?*' I wonder to myself

'Whalley Range,' my mum says, as though reading my mind and pre-emptively shutting my gaping mouth.

My dad corrects a mistake on the page and mutters, 'I'll show them this time.' It turns out that he's being racially abused by a co-worker. In his own way of addressing the situation, he is writing a letter to the 'head of department', stating what has been happening. Not only is he this man's superior, he wants him reprimanded and to receive a public apology from said offender.

This is clearly not the right time to add my own bad news. I tell them I'll come and see them once they've settled into their new address at Whalley Range, and head back to London.

I make the obligatory stop at Our Kid's place in School Lane, Didsbury. She is now married to Nip and they have a small child, a daughter, Lisa, who is as cute as a button. Nip casts an eye over me like he can see through my act of normality. Like he knows that I know that he knows that I'm a bad seed. He's not wrong.

*   *   *

Back in London, the Birthday Party invite me to the studio where they're recording new songs 'Release The Bats' and 'Blast Off'. The seventeen-year-old engineer, Nick Launay, seems to be conjuring sounds out of the instruments and the mixing desk which I've never heard before.

He talks me through how the drums are 'compressed to fuck' and has me take note of how everything is right on the edge of how far it's possible to push things, which is exactly what the band are doing. I've never heard a more joyous racket in my life.

*   *   *

Leigh advises that I bring a coat with me when I come to Australia to see her. 'It can get pretty cold in Melbourne, it being in a valley,' she tells me.

When I arrive at dawn, once I'm outside in the cool Melbourne morning I take my coat off.

Leigh's friend, Leah, is the first person I meet when we get to the apartment at Glenhuntly Road. They have been friends since the dawn of time and are happy just saying 'Aloe Vera' over and over, cracking each other up. They remind me of every girlfriends' double-act I've met through the ages. I leave them to talk about me while I take a bath, knowing that is exactly what they'll do.

In the early morning the sunlight is a reversal of where I've just come from. The warm water gives me an odd feeling of womblike safety. My mind flashes back to the Room.

Everything is upside down here, and now so am I. I reflect on how everything has worked out up until now. I reassure myself that it will again, despite there being no more Magazine.

When I'm done bathing and getting dressed, Leigh says, 'Come on, let's go.' I grab my coat but she tells me I probably won't need it.

After a day in Melbourne, op-shopping, we drive to Ballarat, in the Central Highlands of Victoria, one hundred and fifteen-point-nine kilometres from Melbourne. The drive takes us an hour and a half. Leigh asks me, 'Wanna go skinny dipping?' Leah feigns a kind of embarrassment as I say, 'Sure.'

We drive through the night until Leah swerves the car off the road and pulls up, overlooking a small lake. With the lights on, the water glows as we peel off and jump in.

Something shifts from me. The worries of recent times, which have seen me push against the wind as I walk, now dissolve as we whoop and holler. I note the echo as time stops in the present and trouble drifts away in the cool, shimmering water.

We visit Leigh's mum back in Melbourne. She is a short woman with short-cut red hair and rules the roost, casually putting Leigh and her sister Karen in their place by colouring outside the lines. She is quite free and without boundaries in talking about sex, for example. She creases me up when she describes a man who can't get it up by saying, 'You can't put a marshmallow in a money box.'

Leigh responds with a total eye-rolling cringe, plus a hint of admiration. Then she leaves the room and heads to the outside toilet, or the 'dunny' as I've heard people say.

(The scene reminds me of the time I bought the Alice Cooper album *School's Out*, in nineteen seventy-two. Dave Hughes came over so that we could listen to it together. I opened the packaging and, on seeing the record encased in a pair of girl's knickers, my mum hauled herself across the room to say, 'I'll have those.' Dave folded into himself to cover up his response. He later described a look of disgust that engulfed my whole being.)

*   *   *

Back home, things are hotting up. I receive a telegram from Willie Trotter.

He lets me know that it's all kicking off in Moss Side. It transpires that the riots started at Moss Side police station and then spread to the surrounding areas over the next few nights. A serious lack of employment prospects brought about by the early eighties recession and the underlying racial tensions between abusive cops and black youths

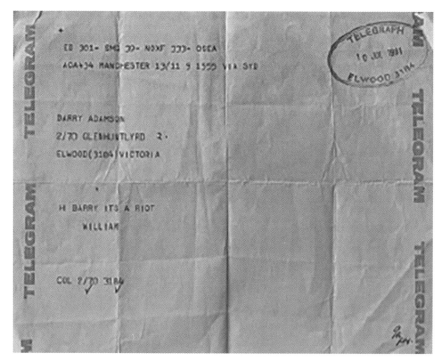

Telegram from Willie Trotter.

seem to have lit the fuse. Around a thousand kids surrounded the police station, smashing all the windows and setting police cars on fire. Police equipped themselves with riot gear after one officer was shot through the leg with a crossbow bolt. The riots lasted for forty-eight hours, with burnin' and a-lootin' of shops down Claremont Road, Princess Road and surrounding areas.

The riots ended on the night of the eleventh of July, when Chief Constable James Anderton ordered his officers to advance and clear the streets in a massive show of force. Anderton had used the previous two days to gather enough officers trained and equipped in public-order tactics. A mobile taskforce of five hundred and sixty in fifty transit vans and Land Rovers had been assembled in local police stations around the area.

As part of the planned dispersal operation, Anderton authorised the use of vehicle-based rapid dispersal tactics, previously only used by the Royal Ulster Constabulary and the British Army in Northern Ireland. These involved vehicles containing 'snatch squads' driven at high speed into groups of rioters, with officers leaping out to make arrests. Over two hours, a hundred and fifty people were arrested with no police injuries reported.

* * *

Far away in Melbourne, I take a trip out one night with Leigh's sister, Karen, to get myself stoned. On the way back, we see one side of a house in flames. On hearing screaming kids, we enter by the front door. We get two young girls out into the front garden, one must be about six and the other one four. The four-year-old attempts to run back into the house, saying that her hamster is in there. I grab her just as the kitchen, which is off to the left, bursts into flames. We wait for the cops and the fire brigade to come, tell our story and go home, so that I can get on with what we went out to do in the first place.

The next night, I drift into a local bar and order a beer. The scene is straight out of a movie, as the barmaid pulls a drink and without looking at me says, 'Quite the hero, they tell me?'

This prompts me to read from a script that my shy and introverted character has no option but to stick to. 'Oh… you mean the fire? It was nothing.'

The barmaid then tells me my drinks are on the house for the rest of the night. With her face slightly lowered, she gives me a look that can only be interpreted one way.

Meanwhile, I can only imagine what is happening back in the Moss.

* * *

Back in Baron's Court, days after returning from Australia, I'm listening to Talking Heads – in particular, the bass playing of Tina Weymouth. I smoke a joint and tune into the albums *Fear Of Music* and their new one, *Remain In Light,* knowing I can expect greatness.

The song 'Cities' kicks in. Before the lyric even begins, Tina is refraining and riffing the melody that becomes the chorus, ahead of us getting there. She plays high. Like me. The part is beautiful and when the verse arrives, Tina grooves on a new line and repeats it so that David Byrne can take centre-stage, with a lyric that describes London as a small, dark city.

When the chorus catches up to her, it all makes sense psychologically. The sheer coolness of her whole approach takes me back to seeing her play 'Psycho Killer' on *The Old Grey Whistle Test,* drawing my ears and eyes right into the TV screen.

At one of the nightly parties that don't seem to differentiate between being on the road and days off, where getting slaughtered is the order of the day, Nick Cave tells me Lydia Lunch lives around the corner. He suggests I should go around and see her, after I rave about her *Queen Of Siam* album.

Indeed, she does live in a flat which is only a stone's throw away. I visit her for a cup of tea, and when I see her, my chest and neck tighten as she floods my senses with a feeling I've not yet experienced. I garble my words and show a total lack of personality, such is her own intensity. She might just swallow me whole as she draws me into her sphere of influence.

I realise, though, that her performance might not be just for me. That maybe we are not alone, as the wardrobe door creaks ever so slightly, more than once.

I take my leave and go buy Bounty and Twix bars, to calm me down.

* * *

I get back home and smoke a joint, pulling out my prized copy of Hubert Selby Jr's novel, *Last Exit To Brooklyn* – given to me by Gerry, a friend of Leigh. This book is like a mentor to me, if you will. It portrays a world beyond mine, yet something is identifiable about it. It affirms the tough and tender vulnerability of the human condition with each and every one of the stories portrayed therein.

The brutal existence described by Selby is something that resonates with me. His largely untutored writing style feels more 'punk' than anything I've ever read in my life. It devalues any currency of intellect by coming totally from the soul, albeit a once broken one that is sharply adept in its observation and commentary on other broken souls.

I meet with John Doyle and Dave Formula. We decide to put a group together where we play what we want to play and split everything the same way. So we put out an ad for a singer. We go back into Summa for the duration and it all feels a little too familiar as singers come and go. Until… in walks Pamela.

All American, with a pop sensibility and almost operatic voice, she fits the bill perfectly. So we begin to look for a name: Dave has the idea to call us I Am A Camera while I want us to be called The Primal Scream.

On my way to rehearsal, on the Fulham Palace Road, I'm stopped and searched under the 'Sus' (suspected person) laws. My inner world crumbles as I realise I'm carrying heroin and a 1ml diabetic syringe. I carry these along with a teaspoon in my spectacles case.

They ask me what I'm doing here; I tell them. They seem unconcerned with my answer. The two cops begin their search and pull various articles out of my pockets: keys, chewing gum, plectrums. Then they take out the spectacles case, which they lay on the bonnet of a nearby car along with everything else and carry on their search. They joke with each other, seeing the power that they have over me.

'Right,' they say, handing me back the specs case, 'have a good day, sir.' I stand motionless for a while as the two coppers laugh before leaving the scene. I finally break into the sweat I've been holding back for the last ten minutes.

I get to the rehearsal room and head straight for the bathroom. I observe that I am a man of shaky hand, something I've had trouble accepting in others; now I must acknowledge it in myself.

We play around a jazz theme. It seems to suit our identity and suggests the coolness that we're trying to convey. The problem is, for me, that Pamela is obsessed with some guy who seems to feature in most of her songs, making us in a sense her backing band.

As long as she concentrates on him, she forgoes any (largely unspoken) commitment to singing about subjects the rest of us can relate to. As long as Dave, me and John offer nothing in the department of ideas ourselves, we have to go along with what feels like a triangulation between Pamela, us and someone who goes by the name of Johnny.

Our combined efforts break down soon after we make a demo. (I'd pushed for getting Adrian Sherwood involved but, while he's just fantastic, dub we are not.) Dave seems to become very familiar with Pamela all of a sudden, so we do publicity shots without him. Then the whole thing is over before you know it.

With Leigh, I decide to move out of Baron's Court to get a place of our own, to begin something that just might be for the long haul. We find a small one-bedroom flat around the corner in West Kensington, on the other side to Lydia.

But I need money for the deposit. I need money for drugs. I need money full stop.

I hit my parents up for the deposit on the flat and use it to buy drugs... then I get the money together for the deposit by doing session work. The deceit does not go unnoticed by The Vulture, who whispers in my ear, '*Let the games begin, dear boy.*'

One of the Australian girls I met at the squat comes over to our new place, which is largely decorated in white with a fair-sized living room and a small kitchen bathroom. The girl is all smiley and complimentary about how we're living.

Leigh begins to put on make-up for the first time in a while, her huge lips as bright a hue of red as I've ever seen. The two girls go off into the night together, to Shepherd's Bush market or someplace.

Afterwards, I take Leigh aside and ask, 'What the fuck is going on?' Even though I already know, she talks past me as she sees the penny drop. I push for confirmation of what I fear.

'Just leave it, Bazza,' she says. 'I know what I'm doing and I'm sorry how that affects you, but this is the way it's happening.'

As the girls leave, my heart sinks to the floor.

I pick up a pair of scissors and drive them into my forearm. I stare at the wound, quite removed, as though I have no idea how it got there in the first place. Or, most importantly, who put it there. The Vulture nods in approval.

Not many nights later, Leigh leaves for Australia. For good.

I wake up the next day with a complete start. A single tear burns like acid, escaping the corner of my eye and slowly rolling down my cheek.

I'm sad, and I am also getting really sick.

As the heroin leaves my system, I experience for the first time what can only be described as the horrors. A panic ensues as I begin to sweat and shake. There is nothing else, even Leigh leaving, on my mind right now other than to reverse this situation.

I call Leigh's friend from the night of the scissors, who knows exactly where I'm at. Laughing down the phone, she's only too happy to help me out.

Chapter Twenty-Six

I start to see more and more of the Birthday Party. On one such social occasion I meet Caitlin, who lives with bass player Tracy Pew, when I take my double bass over to their flat in Tooting. Tracy wants to learn to play stand-up bass and so I gladly lend him mine.

A few of the band are there too, so I join the party and try to impress by messing about on the upright, playing along to *West Side Story* and putting on a one-man show. It's obvious that I'm not accomplished on the instrument, but the way I handle it, with some comedic self-deprecating moments, gives me an edge. Especially up close, with an instrument nobody has stood next to before.

The band leave for a two-month tour of Australia, but Caitlin stays in the UK. She lets me know, gradually, that Tracy has a new girl, Kate. So maybe I'd like to try filling the big fella's boots?

While the band are in Australia, Tracy is arrested for drunk driving. For this offence and several others – including the theft of a sewing machine, rice and frankfurter sausages – he is sentenced to nine months in HM Prison Pentridge. He serves only two and a half, but this means the band need to cancel shows in New Zealand, California and Germany.

When the band arrive back in the UK without Tracy, they also ask me to fill the big fella's boots. I set to work learning the songs as quickly as I can. There will be one rehearsal only. I hope I can get the job done and bring something of my own to the table. I admit to no one that I find the task absolutely daunting.

I'm back at Dougie and Mal's in Baron's Court. Caitlin comes to visit me between work shifts. After she leaves, I reach for the vials of morphine in my sock draw.

At rehearsal, the simple fact that singer Nick Cave, guitarist Mick Harvey, lead guitarist Rowland Howard and drummer Phill Calvert tower over me, all coming in at around six foot three or four, is more than enough to fill me with dread. As the day moves on, Mick, eyes widened slightly, states that 'At least we know Barry is better than the rest of us.' A statement I want him to retract immediately, so as not to fan the flames of a fire I might not be able to put out.

The first show at the Venue in Victoria goes well enough.

Add to this the fact that bassist Tracy Pew is back home doing time on a labour farm, and that his temporary replacement – the great Barry Adamson – had only been through one rehearsal, and things weren't altogether looking bright.

But any fears that may have existed within the capacity audience were promptly allayed by a volley of intense and hectic songs which reduced most of the spectators to speechlessness. Adamson, moreover, was clearly in complete control.

On Friday night, the group revisited their surreal junkyard of forms and images with a higher intoxication than ever. They may choose to be 'buried neck high in British snow', but the songs they bring back from the antipodes boil the coldest native hearts. That forlorn and shimmering ballad 'She's Hit', already aired on several occasions before their Christmas departure, has taken on added starkness and splendour, perfectly brought out on this occasion by Adamson's languorous, acoustic-sounding bass.

Barney Hoskyns, *New Musical Express*, March 1982

The shows, in general, seem wild and crazy to me, complete with fire-breathing hyper-fan Bob 'Bingo' Bingham, who drinks petrol and then floods the stage with flame. There's also an incident with Caitlin that sees me at a hospital in Fulham all night, after the Hammersmith Palais show.

At the hospital, once she's stable, I head for the bathroom to finish the shot I never got off on backstage. I catch myself in the bathroom mirror afterwards, then quickly pretend I haven't. I know that I've placed getting high before the welfare of my loved one. Thus begins the creation of a subpersonality that is nothing more than a self-centred child.

* * *

I play with the band on a TV show called *Riverside*, where we perform 'Dead Joe' and 'Big Jesus Trash Can', before they resume work on their *Junkyard* album at Matrix Studios in Fulham. I'm also called in to play on a couple of tracks, 'Kiss Me Black' and 'Dead Joe'.

At the session, Rowland is in a bad mood and tells me, 'This is what it's like when Nick decides that he is not your friend anymore.' He seems very isolated from the others. I don't fully understand the dynamics so I don't get involved, though I feel for Rowland. I go to see him and note the abject poverty that surrounds him – save for a trouser press. He is one stylish man, that's for sure.

He asks me to work with him, Mick Harvey, Lydia Lunch and his girlfriend, Genevieve McGuckin, on a version of a Lee Hazlewood song, 'Some Velvet Morning'. I'm only too happy to. Not only do I love that song, it's a chance to bring in my double bass for the session – though this time it's no *West Side Story* routine.

I play my last gig with the Birthday Party before Harry Howard steps in to replace me. But Nick is becoming more of a friend, mainly through us goofing around, so I can't really imagine what Rowland is talking about *re* their broken friendship.

I'm bonding with all of the band. Nights are spent around mine, just like I used to throw a party every night on the road in my room. It carries on now, tonight and every night, with most of the Birthday Party and the people from the squat dropping by.

The first two Suicide albums are played most nights. The song 'Harlem', from the second album, is a favourite of Nick's. I'm all about the first album, particularly 'Girl', 'Frankie Teardrop', 'Cheree' and 'Ghost Rider'. Though I do like the songs on the second album: 'Diamonds, Fur Coat, Champagne', 'Fast Money Music' and 'Touch Me', while Caitlin has a soft spot for 'Sweetheart'.

I slip into a dream and tell myself that one day I'll do a version of 'Girl'. Singer Alan Vega will write a letter to me, telling me what a great version he thinks it is, that the parts I've added are of note. Then, in a separate paragraph right after his thoughts about the instrumentation, he'll say, '*Adamson, man, what a voice, you have.*'

I laugh out loud. Nick shouts to put on 'Harlem' again.

* * *

I regularly go to see Heather, a dealer (not art or antiques) in Chelsea, and it's always an arduous affair. Think of Lou Reed's song 'I'm Waiting For The Man,' but in this case 'the man' is a beautiful woman from New Zealand:

Heather scores off this jaundice-faced prison thug and then sells the stuff on to the likes of me. After waiting hours for him, because he also deals to a rich and famous guitarist who lives nearby, he finally arrives with his two cronies. He turns to Heather and says, 'I need to talk to you... lose the coon.'

* * *

I take a trip up the motorway to see my mum and dad's new flat. My mum sweetly shows me a tiny bedroom off to the side. 'If ever you want to come home, love, there's always a room for you here.'

I thank her, pecking her on the cheek, noting how her skin is ageing and getting softer. I nod to my dad, whose head is buried in a newspaper, before fleeing back to London.

I stop at Sandbach services on the M6, stride to the toilets and shoot myself up. On the motorway back, I'm driving in the first lane then appear to be in the third, completely unsure of how I got there. This happens several times before I slip into an involuntary 'nod' of the heroin user's kind. I wake up on hearing the tyres rubbing frantically against the central reservation.

The Vulture opens one eye and says, '*Oh, this is just wonderful.*'

I arrive home, noting that my death-by-stupidity trial is now over, and smoke a joint.

Visage are selling singles by the bucketload. The song 'Fade To Grey' charts around Europe, becoming a top ten hit in the UK, top five in five countries and number one in Germany and Switzerland. As part of the group, I'm invited to fly over to Germany to pick up a prestigious platinum disc for sales in excess of hundreds of thousands of units.

On the day of travel, though, I'm late getting up and have to rush out of the flat to the airport. At the check-in I realise I've forgotten my passport. Although I'm allowed to get on the plane, on arrival in Germany I'm not allowed into the country. Instead, I'm turned around like a naughty schoolkid and have to board the same plane that I arrived on, to fly straight back to England. Even the cabin crew are the same.

I find out later that the gentleman's agreement we all shook hands on is not financially forthcoming enough to include me. At all.

I feel I've been not just shot but sucked in, chewed up, spat out and stepped on by both sides. As the needle goes in again, it takes all the fight from me as I slip into another stupor.

I use more drugs and sleep with Heather and another dealer, Shonia in White City, while Caitlin is in Australia. Humility and accountability are getting farther and farther away from me with each dumb move. Not much later in the month, I forget to meet Caitlin at the airport, believing she's arriving at six in the evening rather than six in the morning. There is hell to pay.

Then, John Doyle kindly offers to let Caitlin and myself move into his place in Rotherhithe. This feels like a breath of much needed fresh air. A chance to rest and reset.

Caitlin now works at a cinema in Camden that sells the best ice cream ever, according to John, so he and his wife Linda go up there to see her. Often. There is harmony between us for a while, but the toxicity starts creeping in again despite the change in habitat. We argue and fight. One day, mid-argument, I slam on the brakes in the car in frustration, almost sending her through the windscreen.

We watch the runners in the London Marathon from the flat as they tear around en masse, directly below us in the early days of spring. That breath of fresh air dissolves in the overpowering stench of runners' sweat. After they pass, a strange effect ensues, as if the road is constantly moving backwards.

Only a few months after meeting Caitlin, on a balmy evening in August when stomping feet and reeking bodies still pepper the Rotherhithe nights, she tells me she is pregnant. Baby makes three now.

'I couldn't be happier,' I announce to all and sundry.

The Vulture tells me, '*Cut the bullshit, just do a fucking runner and leave the rest to me.*' It mocks me with the refrain of Visage's 'Fade To Grey'.

Will Trotter. Photo by me.

I get a letter from my dad. He tells me that where women are concerned, you have to do the right thing by them. I should stand by Caitlin in her decision to have the baby, no matter what. I agree with him.

Our Kid always talks about Christmas in the sense that, to her, the word means 'Christ the master'. I want to emphasise the importance bestowed on our baby girl when she arrives, so I push for the name Christina – the 'Christ in her'.

I live on a thread of hope. I hope this is the right thing to do. I hope that we can make it. I hope that I can get clean and therefore live some kind of normal life. Whatever 'normal' is. I guess I mean a life that isn't ultimately governed by using heroin, merely surviving each day with only pain and fear to look forward to tomorrow.

And so we move back to Manchester. Back to Moss Side. We stay at Will Trotter's place in Roseberry Street until we can get a place of our own.

Caitlin is relentless in going up against bureaucracy, just as Will is unrelenting in his friendship with me. She will beat the crap out of all who stand in her way, metaphorically speaking, until we get a small two-bedroom house in nearby Wheeldon Street.

I've already secured a gold-coloured Ford Zodiac, so my priorities are well in order: it's for the sudden dash to the hospital when the baby's due. One of Will's posh mates notes that my car is a 'very spacious mobile'; I note in turn that this guy is a 'complete twat'. (Though it will be a few years until Will's wedding, when the same knobhead will tell me, 'It's good to see you bringing a bit of colour to the dance floor.')

We start to move in with the help of Will's dad, a man who has the words 'hard work' etched throughout his whole frame. I've never seen him out of work mode, as with my own dad; they're both men of an admirable era.

Several local kids run around outside as we head back to Will's for the evening. The next day, we go back to find a small window open, the place robbed and a huge human turd in the middle of the sitting-room floor. My dad comes over to help us clean up as we're still staring in disbelief.

Returning from the Co-op.

Caitlin announces that some of her favourite jewellery has gone. The kids outside smile knowingly as my dad and Will's, in a rare immigrant-to-immigrant conference, discuss the state of play. They are two giants dominating the doorframe.

* * *

Now we're moved in, my mum and sister come over. My mum runs a finger along the windowsill, looks at the dust and gives Caitlin the stink-eye. They fail to connect, whereas my sister at least tries to welcome her to the neighbourhood, asking her lots of questions – albeit while looking slightly down her nose.

But the struggle within – using drugs/not using drugs – continues. Before I know it, I have a network of different people in the nearby crescents in Hulme to go and score from, or use with.

This makes using as easy as picking up a bag of sugar from the Co-op. Which is often what I say I'm doing.

Chapter Twenty-Seven

Cover of Pete Shelley's single 'Telephone Operator'.

Pete Shelley has invited me to play on his solo album, which he will write and record at Martin Rushent's Genelec Studios in Reading. Martin was the tape operator on T.Rex's *Electric Warrior* album. Just his presence on that record was enough for me to not question getting involved. It means being away from home for weeks at a time, sure, but I see it also as a chance to clean up my act in preparation for the fast-approaching future.

241

I've known Pete since joining Magazine and also through Francis Cookson and Eric Random, who are in a band with him called the Tiller Boys. I play bass with them sometimes, on songs like 'A Mogadon Is A Mogadon' and 'Funky As Fuck' – both classics, by the way.

Socially, I see Pete at parties around town. We have a blast together at Tony Wilson's place out in the wilds, between the red and white twin roses Lancashire and Yorkshire. At this all-nighter, high on acid, me and Pete laugh ourselves stupid over some splashes of paint on a tiny badge, which we perceive to be dogs wearing burglars' masks and black-and-white striped jumpers. We laugh at this for (approximately) four hours.

At around seven in the morning, Tony drops Pete back to Manchester. Me and Will are left with Tony's wife Lindsey holding court – dancing seductively, somewhat light of clothing, and singing along to one of her own songs, 'Everything Is Opposite'.

Tony arrives back with a look of '*What the fuck's going on here?*' as shadows dance outside, behind the curtains. We stare in their direction. Photographers now surround the windows. The paranoia from the acid underlines fears that we'll be plastered across the *Manchester Evening News* tomorrow, after trying to explain ourselves to both Tony Wilson and the drugs squad.

Then Tony announces that the ex-manager of Manchester United, Tommy Docherty, must be in trouble again. He was famously sacked a few years back for running off with the club's physiotherapist. Tommy lives next door and the press are swarming.

* * *

So I say yes to the job with Pete. Most of the time it's him, me and Martin Rushent producing. A guy called Jim Russell is the assistant, clearly an affable chap who's hungry to learn everything he can about production.

It's always the same on occasions like these, though, if you use heroin. Hope fades quickly in the face of need. An awful chasm of unacceptable, indescribable, inappropriate *need*. Out comes the mask over a friendly dinner, the learned gestures, while my insides begin to scream. I think, '*In four days, this part will be over,*' and then, without the heroin in my system, I'll be able to function better than before, but... I can't stand myself enough to walk the earth a free man.

242

Back at the hotel, Pete Shelley is writing songs. I allow any subdued homosexuality in me to shift from latent to blatant, by making Pete the object of my need for something outside myself. Something to take the pain away.

He knows that I don't, in the conventional sense, fancy him. He also knows that I look at him through the eyes of gentle envy, focusing on what might be negative character traits so as to report them mockingly to others. It's a glaring negative trait of my own.

I offer him the chance to seize it all back in one go. To take revenge, to undermine my will and my power, in one fell swoop. Right now. He agrees to the terms in an '*if that's what you want*' kind of way and my downfall is complete.

There is no joy. No fun. No good time. And, of course, the whole surrendering to what I don't really need leaves me needing a fix, more than ever.

It's amazing that the record is getting made, as there is now so much tension in the studio. But still, it is.

Jim picks us up from the hotel and seems baffled by the deflated mood. I'm hurting from heroin withdrawal. Raf Edmunds swings by and, God love him, tries to help me with courses of vitamins. Francis turns up too and runs me to London one afternoon, so that I can score to take the edge off.

Luckily, Martin has a thing for Beaujolais, which arrives by the crateload and provides a means to detach myself from the need to be out of it, from the nagging of The Vulture.

All by eleven o'clock in the morning. Cheers!

'Telephone Operator' is clearly the LP's hit single. At least that is the hope that permeates the studio. It also makes me think, '*Shit, I must call Caitlin.*'

> *Telephone operator*
> *Why can't I see you later?*
> *Tell me is it wine*
> *That makes things so fine*
> *Or is it 'cos you're mine?*

I play with the band that Pete puts together to promote the record, but I do myself no favours whatsoever. Me and The Vulture watch the

243

keyboard player devour chocolate Minstrels and The Vulture sings 'I Wish I Was In Dixie' as a dark memory of the Black and White Minstrels. I shrug the connection off as I watch him crunch away.

I stink. My outside stench makes the stink of my insides evident. I depend on Pete for validation all the fucking time, letting him pick at me because of it. Finally, I go to give myself to him again in a hotel somewhere in France. But he stops me from doing so, asking, 'Ever been at a party that you weren't invited to?'

* * *

After nine turbulent months of sloshing around Caitlin's muscular, pear-shaped organ; after hearing muffled voices of scorn, derision and a little laughter from myself, Caitlin, Willie, Jimmy and other friends, including Dave Sketchley, Eric Random and Lynn Walsh; after constantly being exposed to the music of The Cramps, Suicide and John Coltrane blasting out of the stereo; after I make it back to the hospital just in time for the actual birth, after slipping out for a curry and some pain relief; after Caitlin digs her left leg into my chest for twenty minutes at the call of 'push' and 'breathe', Christina Adamson is born.

I see her face almost pop out in the final push, in a total *ta-daaaa!* moment. Christina smiles at me, as I do at her. I note that, in this moment, she looks exactly like my mum – though my mum tells me, 'Get away with you,' when I call her on the payphone downstairs at the hospital.

But it's difficult to appreciate what should be a joyous reality, with my inner landscape being so bleak. Using heroin and self-hatred walk hand in hand. Even the beauty of Christina being in the world does not, cannot, change that.

I'll attempt to father her in an upright way, without my self-centred nature pushing me in the opposite direction. The problem is, though, that I'm in a battle I can never win. Underneath the denial, it hurts like hell.

We take a much needed break from the three of us being cooped up in our tiny Wheeldon Street dwelling. We drop in on my parents while they holiday in Wales, at the usual caravan park just outside Rhyl. I attempt to rekindle my youth in some ways, trying to connect myself to the present and the future, before drugs and beyond them.

Out of dope, I suggest that we head back to Manchester pronto. But we find the house in a total mess, thanks to a dealer I'd allowed to stay there. She has left the gas and all the electricity on, as well as the taps running, to settle a score.

I'd thought that the dope I was getting was payment for her and her whacked-out girlfriend staying in the spare room for a while. Which was why I felt justified in taking my cereal spoon in to her after breakfast, for breakfast number two. But apparently not.

Christina Maria Louise Adamson. Photo by Will Trotter.

We begin living in a cesspool of darkness, causing us to fight like cat and dog. This leaves me drained and without any sense of who I am.

I begin to destabilise the relationship further by my ever increasing absences. This is the time I spend 'at the shops', acquiring ever increasing amounts of heroin. Our relationship is a process of double devaluation, with each of us pushing the other away.

With the boundaries of love and hurt so profoundly blurred, we decide to get married and keep the shared fantasy of love alive just a little bit longer. It's intended to show our fierce commitment to each other and quieten the *'daughter born out of wedlock?'* voice that loops around my head, courtesy of The Vulture. Which, of course, continues to loop around my head all the time.

* * *

We set a date for the wedding, November the fifth, blissfully ignoring the potentially explosive ramifications:

Remember, remember, the fifth of November
Gunpowder, treason and plot

I'm pleased to be back in London, especially when I bump into Nick Cave on the Portobello Road (*'Dancing like a ballerina / Squirming like a toad'*).

Nick's star quality constantly shines through, even on a day like today when he seems a little worse for wear. I can see, though, that his mind is spinning off its axis with creative ideas, as he pushes past (as well as embraces) any negative concerns that might assault him.

I think about his commitment to himself, to his career, and conclude that nobody is as dedicated to becoming one of the most important people in the history of rock music than him. It's simply what he demands of himself. I don't experience him ever questioning that; anyone perceived as standing in the way of this goal had simply better look out.

In his life, he is literally dancing right on the very edge. If examined, even the edgiest of performers is probably only 'living on the edge of a very plush cushion', as engineer-turned-producer Flood likes to say. Not Nick, though. He really is the real deal.

He talks to me about putting a new band together, amidst the ashes of the Birthday Party's implosion in Berlin. Have I heard of singer-guitarist Blixa Bargeld? I tell him, 'Of course,' enthusing about the band Einstürzende Neubauten he fronts and the gig I saw them play at Heaven. The way they attacked scrap metal with drilling equipment, sparks flying, I thought they might just burn the place down. I tell Nick how remarkable I think they are.

Nick examines me almost like I'm taking a lie detector test and he's the examiner. 'I hear you were working with that guy Pete Shelley. What was that song of his called?' He pauses, as if loading a pistol. '"Homosexuals?"'

I laugh out loud, in a moment worthy of an Oscar, and correct him. '"Homosapien" it's called, Nick.'

'Right...' he says, his eyes fixed onto my neck, unsure of the correction. He thinks for a second or two before looking for something in every pocket. Finding nothing, he says, 'You should come into the studio with me and Mick and Blixa, what do you reckon?'

My face widens with an affirmative.

Nick hops off down the street even cheerier than before, almost like a whirling dervish. I bop in the other direction, unsure of where I'm going, but the road later leads to...

* * *

The Garden Studios, owned by John Foxx, formerly of Ultravox. I have nothing against any members of Ultravox, of course, even the ones who are in Visage. (Denial is the shock absorber of the soul. Remember that...)

There's Mick Harvey on the drums. His unbalanced aggression alone is worth the price of admission. During 'Wings Off Flies', he smashes the kit so hard that I wait for it to fall apart, while I stumble and scratch around, looking for a bass line.

Blixa is in and out of time with a deconstructed blues guitar. My insides light up at the fuck-off of it all. Nick, his star ascending, pulls and pushes, playing hard with that ersatz Southern Gothic.

The Vulture taps a gnarly claw in time to the beat and shudders: '*Ooooh, now that is what I call THE BLUES!*' He winks at me. '*We gone have a fine time up in here, boy.*' He laughs right in my ear.

I exit the cacophony and make use of the bathroom.

'Saint Huck' is being developed. I establish that the bass should just repeat and repeat as if in a world of its own connected to the central character's mind. His rhythm, if you like. The right side of his brain that just keeps going like that old rollin' riverboat Nick is singing about.

There's a beautiful and unnerving chaos as everyone picks their own tempo, as if we are all together playing a score by Krzysztof Penderecki but then decide to throw away the sheet music. This makes the rhythm defunct.

There's a murderous feel about the piece as the bass comes off the rails. The guitar and drums pound away for all their worth before Huck's theme plays almost nonchalantly on. Blixa extracts never-heard-before noises from the guitar and the most brutal of landscapes is created from nothing.

Something quite original is born right before our eyes as Nick tells Huck's story.

When he gets to the line *'a bad-blind nigger at the piano'*, I throw the magic boomerang and step back to compose myself. After a few deep breaths, I make out like, *'Hey, I'm with you guys. ABC, man, Always Be Cool.'*

The truth is the bottom has just fallen out of my stomach. I scramble for justification of that word being used in front of me.

Everybody in the band knows how this is affecting me. (Don't they?) Are Blixa and Mick smirking by coincidence? Are they even smirking? Is Nick doing a really bad impersonation of playing dumb in the face of another man's pain? They have me thinking, *'Jesus, it's just a fucking word!'*

What are we creating, though? Where is Nick going with these songs? Even *I* know that what is happening, right here in the Garden, will forever change the course of musical history. Whether I'm dying in its very arms or not. (It's just a word.)

The Vulture commends my thinking, telling me, *'It's a small price to pay for being a part of that history, fuckface.'*

Before I have a chance to square up to him, The Vulture cocks an eyebrow in the same way Mick Harvey does and quietly says, *'And by the way, don't you have a stupid fucking wedding to attend, Bazzer?'*

* * *

The family all show up to the registry office in Spring Gardens, off Albert Square, plus a few mates and my best man, Will Trotter.

Caitlin also has a couple of mates come over from Australia, Kate and Philippa. Will zeroes in on Philippa and tells me about her giving one of the black guys from schooldays a clump around the head, when he came on to her heavily at a local football match he played in. I fail to mention how Kate, when we went to a shop on Princess Road to buy 'Orgasmatron' cakes (so called because that's what eating one supposedly gives you), semi-innocently commented that if she were ever to marry a nigger, she'd want it to be a real one. (It's just a word...)

As it's our wedding day, though, it's a time to put all negativity and antipodean anthropology aside as we celebrate the betrothal of Barry and Caitlin.

The day plays out under a banner of normality, with my mum questioning Caitlin's choice of hairstyle for her wedding day. I roll my eyes and say, 'Not now, Mum.' She adds that she was 'only saying' and gets in a minor strop about being pulled up for her remark. Will sits on my mum's Kodak camera and prays it still works after the *crack* he hears. But as the photos of me and my dad, me and Our Kid, me, Caitlin and Will himself will testify, he has a very lucky escape.

With the vows, nuptials and formalities sorted, it's off to the Midland Hotel for the reception. Actress Anna Massey, from Michael Powell's film, *Peeping Tom*, sits at an adjacent table, drawing my attention until I put that movie to one side and focus on the plate in front of me.

Then we taxi back to Wheeldon Street for a bit of a knees-up.

At around four in the afternoon, various nefarious 'friends' begin to drop by. In what is almost a reversal of putting the kids to bed, we send the grown-ups home, whip out the drugs, turn up the music and begin to really tie one on – which, as every good Australian will testify, is the right thing to do.

Chapter Twenty-Eight

We honeymoon in Melbourne. A family visit to God's country to let Christina meet her grandma and step-granddad, three aunts and an uncle. It's also a good time (and the first time) for them to meet me.

On arrival at a car park near Caitlin's folks' place, it absolutely pours down on this grey morning. Through the car windows and the tears of rain wobbling against the glass, Melbourne is a different city to the one I came to with Magazine, then returned to for Leigh.

I didn't really have eyes for the place but, without the dazzle of the sun, I can see it's an amazing city. I know Caitlin wants to be here more than she does Moss Side. I mean, who can blame her? Not just because her family and her past are here; the way of life is enviable. Everything is simply larger than life as we know it in England.

But I'm keen to unearth and reconnect with its darker side, which I can feel everywhere pulsating beneath the façade of things. I say nothing as we drive past St Kilda, which is usually lively with its beach and Luna theme park. It's also a hotspot for junkies.

I think back to me and Caitlin screaming at each other on the plane before it took off. '*Makes you doubt yourself, all that stuff,*' quips The Vulture.

We arrive at Caitlin's parents' place and I get even more of it. I'm told why we need to come here for a life that's the complete opposite to, say, living in Manchester. We live in a shoebox compared to where we stand now, surrounded by palm trees and the greenery of the opulent garden.

I meet her mum. She is immediately likeable, with a caring and open face. The stepdad is a shifty, old-school, khaki-covered Australian. He squints hard at me below bushy eyebrows and asks questions like 'Do you Jamaican blokes do anything else besides play cricket?'

Her two sisters (like Caitlin, from her mum's previous marriage) complete a triple act of what we might term wayward punkishness. I gravitate towards them, for some reason.

Her younger stepsister and stepbrother seem nice enough, though the stepbrother might be trouble. I try to keep things on the surface, suspend all judgement and play meet-the-parents as affably as I can.

Family barbies aside, things go awry quickly. I start to go out and party with some of the people I'd met before and some I've not met, in thriving antisocial scenery that is not at all about greenery. I end up one night at Caitlin's sister's boyfriend's house at five in the morning, on the nod from some really strong heroin.

I nod out watching the Jacques Tati film *Playtime*, on the arts channel SBS. The film sticks with me and will forever remind me of returning to the homestead a little later, greeted by the receiver of a wall-mounted telephone smashed into my face as I open the kitchen door. Cartoon music plus the usual circling stars ensue, as I wonder what I've done this time. I plead innocence to the crime of fooling around with her older sister, but as to staying out all night, getting stoned and hanging with Tati, I'm guilty as charged.

* * *

Nick has a bunch of shows arranged while he is also in Australia for the festive season, billed as Nick Cave: Man or Myth. This offers me work after the honeymoon is over.

The Man or Myth shows have an almost celebratory gathering of local musicians. I'm probably the only non-local, as Blixa isn't with us. Mick Harvey tells me that I'm an honorary Australian anyway, but I'm acutely aware that I'm the only (albeit English) black face in a sea of Aussie whiteness.

New material is to be presented. An overweight, oversized piano is brought in so that Nick can lay down the beginnings of what will become a concert trademark and highlight, his solo songwriting, performing here 'A Box For Black Paul'.

With Tracy on bass, I'm left to scratch around on guitar and occasionally play the other keyboard. I forget the words of 'Saint Huck' as I begin thumping out my own rhythmic style over the chorus. I mark out Huck's '*favourite river song*', a leitmotif in the upper registers, and then comes the line, '*And a bad-blind nigger at the piano*'.

I feel as though the whole room is pointing at me. I stand alone. My flaming hubris and I. It is quite a moment.

Knowing Nick a little now, I get that he'll think that this moment is a really great one. The trouble is that *it is*.

Promo poster for the Man or Myth Australian shows.

Back in dear old Blighty in nineteen eighty-four, I'm on the way to London for round two of the recording of Nick Cave's first post-Birthday Party record. I listen to Bowie's *Diamond Dogs* album. Like the books of Hubert Selby Jr, Richard Wright and James Baldwin, Bowie's albums are food for my spirit. I get nourishment from the songs; they stimulate thought and help me work out a sense of purpose.

The song '1984' plays on my brand-new Sony Walkman. It's a pseudo-soul ballad full of futuristic foreboding. But now we're living in the real nineteen eighty-four.

Trident Studios is booked for the recording, with Flood at the helm again. It doesn't seem that long ago (though it could be another lifetime) that I was here with Magazine, when Flood was the seventeen-year-old tape op sat at the back of the studio, making floods of tea for various engineers and producers. Now he is one of them.

He's also one of us, pushing or hacking away at the current boundaries of music to come up with something not heard before. He names the area under the main window and to the far right of the live room, where my bass amp is set up, 'diabetics' corner', for reasons I probably don't have to go into.

The sessions run from some point in the afternoon until dawn the next day, after which I usually end up at Gray's Inn Buildings, at our friends Trish and Rena's place. This sturdy eighteen eighty-eight building in Roseberry Avenue, off Clerkenwell Road, has historical character. It's known as a short-life estate, due to the turnaround of tenants, and there's always a party going on. I, for one, am not put off by tales of drug dealers held up by machete-wielding robbers at all. Besides, in the daytime between studio sessions, the flat is calm and quiet as Rena and Trish head off for their day jobs. It leaves a room free for 'admin work' (as using dope is now called).

The atmospheric structure of the Leonard Cohen song 'Avalanche' is offset by a gnarly low-end vocal, picked up by a rhythm where there ain't no rhythm at all. Nick makes the song his own, squeezing the life out of himself in the process as he jumps up an octave and bares not just his teeth, but his soul:

You who wish to conquer pain
You must learn to serve me well

The tension within and around us is palpable, creating something akin to extraordinary. Whereas Magazine rehearsed to note perfection, here every take is different, experimental and improvisational. You have to keep your wits about you at all times.

The song 'Cabin Fever' is shaping up nicely. But guitarist and fledgling group member Hugo Race seems a little distraught, as though something personal is going on with him. He's not being supported by anyone and is all at sea. I take no pleasure from this, knowing the feeling all too well.

Mick Harvey brings up the idea of a pecking order, and smirks to himself as he wafts it around like a stinking fart for all to sniff. No doubt he is placing himself pretty high up that order, rendering everyone else – well, me anyway, as I read it – with the exception of Nick, to the bottom end. Nick visits me in diabetics' corner during the bass take of 'Cabin Fever' and begins dancing, emulating being on the deck of a ship amidst frightening storms, so I assume. He also makes movements up and down an 'air bass'.

This direction from Nick seems to have the desired effect, as I begin sliding up and down the ropes (the bass strings) that support the mast and keep the mainframe together, using The Moodists' bass player Chris Walsh's fretless bass that he's kindly lent me.

The song 'Well Of Misery' feels like a dull ache at the centre of a wound, with its sparse thud and swinging/not swinging bass which serves as the only anchor. I'm playing as though the ship's rope is now taut and I'm walking across it, mocking the confidence needed to get to the other side. Vocally, we sing antistrophe to Nick's strophe.

I mention something to Nick that a producer might say, like 'maybe add a little more soul?' This creates a noticeable joy in Mick Harvey, who sees it as a line crossed. My card has been marked. Did I just slip further down the pecking order?

Nick's vocal is sublime and the tone of the whole song glows with the tearfulness of hearts taken and broken by his own hands.

My note about 'not enough soul' is proven to be completely unjust and out of accordance with the way Nick evokes a duende that draws you into the narrative, defying conventional ideas about 'what soul is' and how it is evoked in song.

The defining moment of the album is its title track, 'From Her To Eternity'. My respect for Blixa is now unequivocal (though he's yet to bring in loops of Elvis songs to work on – 'In The Ghetto' will be a defining moment for everyone). His playing on this song simply astonishes, adding to an already operatic atmosphere which is laid out right from the beginning. The ominous low piano and drum pattern, with me picking up the slack playing eight beats to the bar, beautifully sets up Nick's haunted narrative. The cinematic nature of his lyric is clear, with words that come to life as a series of images darting across the screen. Or, they linger as you picture the song and all of its senses. This 'sense description' offers the listener an experience: they can immerse themselves into the song aurally and visually, directed by a storyteller who is guiding his audience and demanding that they surrender to the music, as he has.

Nick comes up with a piano line that's also played on pizzicato strings. It's the cinematic icing on the cake for me. Nick throws an Elvis lilt into the title refrain and we quieten down to make room for the next part of the story, then build behind the lyric. Really, though, I'm like a bystander in the song, holding the note and rhythm down until I can take a kind of trademark walk between the vocal lines. It's an amazing collection of moments.

* * *

With the album finished and touring starting in the next breath, I manage to get a few days to be with Christina, and to hear her say her name... 'Deeda.'

With that said, I return to the band, now known as The Cavemen. We push through the deadened air that envelops us and go in hard, sweeping away an already encroaching world weariness until we come off like the coolest people on the planet, marching through song after song.

Setlist after setlist.

Show after show.

Night after night.

City after city.

Country after country, and continent after continent.

Me and Christina. Photo by Caitlin.

There's a density to the work that requires you to be mindful of the tightrope you walk. It just might end up around your neck if you're not careful. This is the place where falling apart often brings with it a coming together. You know that you must push yourself even further, especially when you are beset by the insufferable self.

The alternative is to be swept off your feet into the arms of The Vulture, laughing at you as its claws dig into your back and you yell for help but it falls on deaf ears, dropping you off at the emptiest well when you are most at thirst.

Being on the road offers no respite from the insufferable self. In fact it is the opposite. It is the playground where personal battles (with yourself or otherwise) are either won or lost. The audience has little idea about this, the show often being the only time that there is a little

256

breathing space from this very battle, for an hour or two. That time onstage is all moment to moment, heart and soul.

The road is beautiful and the road is ugly, and those two opposites go hand in hand. Nick knows this all too well. His performances go way beyond the pale as he backflips and lands on the mat with a splat. The crowd lap it up as he screams in their faces, confronting and affirming their demons for them while his own bounce around the room. His going too far, farther than most, is the very thing that makes the difference, drawing them in totally with his charismatic influence.

The shows bristle with a darkness, often devoid of any source of light. We sometimes communicate with an almost psychic ability, knowing what each other is about to play before they've played it, landing squarely between the eyes of the audience. Or else we are a borderline chaotic shambles. Either way, we are the best thing to come out of this whole damn eighties mess. And we know it.

Something squeezes at me, though. I'm starting to have moments where I feel completely under threat of some sort of collapse. Maybe it's simply the precarious nature of being an addict who needs a constant supply of 'whatever you have'. But it's beginning to take a quite real, destructive toll on me.

Chapter Twenty-Nine

I return after six months or so on and off the road. I find Caitlin with two aeroplane tickets in her hand and a taxi ticking over like a time bomb outside, as the cab that dropped me off disappears into the distance.

I try to put a positive spin on things, thinking of how Christina will have a better life in the land of the long weekend. A least that's the way The Vulture reasons.

As the first night alone begins to draw in, a darkening black-and-white sky coalesces over the Moss Side rooftops. The Vulture sings from way up high, circling and belting his filthy, rotten heart out. He sings an old song from the seventies by Hall & Oates, 'She's Gone'.

He soars higher, mocking the emotion by singing off-key. I close the door with a bang as the song continues in an echo. I listen for Deeda. Nothing.

I look inside the fridge for something to eat but there is only a lemon or two. With enough heroin to see me through the night, I take a walk to the Maine road chippie, only a stone's throw away.

On my return, The Vulture is sitting on the chair of a three-piece art deco suite that cost me a fiver from a Sunday furniture sale, legs crossed, smoking a joint.

'*You're* fucken *toast now, mate.*'

I don't engage eye contact but note his Aussie accent. I eat my chips in silence while looking at a colour repro book of paintings by Tamara de Lempicka and pretend I didn't hear what I just imagined I did.

A music show called *The Tube* comes on shortly after I switch on my Sony Triniton colour TV. Ultravox are performing the song 'Vienna'. I feel a nausea as the synth line rolls round in the verses and observe how Billy Currie ('Hot Food', as he calls himself) tries to act all cool, like the fucking kid with the big dick who got the girl. Mine, in fact.

The Vulture sings along to 'Vienna' and suggests I join in; if I want any peace of mind, it should mean nothing to me at all.

I think about the TV show *Rising Damp,* a seventies comedy sitcom starring the genius actor Leonard Rossiter, who plays a miserly landlord called Rigsby. He has a cat called Vienna, which he regularly kicks across the hallways of the shabby bedsits he rents out.

The Ultravox song finishes to rapturous applause. I look out of the window. I know what this means and so does The Vulture, who makes a mock-empathetic face then scowls.

'Fuck her. Oh, sorry, you can't anymore. Can you?'

He catches my quick downward glance of self-pity, then he joins me at the window.

'You know what your problem is? You can't tell people to fuck off. When I think about all the missed opportunities you have just… sat on.'

'Fuck off,' I say.

The Vulture claps its wings. 'See, not difficult, is it? Not like anyone's got their knee on your neck, is it?'

I leave the room to go to bed.

As I climb the stairs, The Vulture puts on a record. Nick Cave & the Bad Seeds' first album, *From Her To Eternity,* was released not long ago. The theme from 'Saint Huck' is audible. After the initial six notes, at the ascending part of the melody The Vulture joins in from the living room and adds the song 'And I Love Her So' by Perry Como. Only an obsessive melody trainspotter would hear them as similar in any way whatsoever. He pisses himself laughing.

I'm off my tits on tiredness. Plum tuckered, I am. I remove the belt from my trousers and tie it around my arm to shoot myself up. Then I drift into a dream…

I am on the seventies TV drama *Crown Court.* The opening theme comprises of two French horns, two trumpets and a string section. It's followed by a panning shot of the sombre white jury members.

A white lawyer in a white wig walks over to the witness stand where I am sat, nodding off. The decor is brown and beige. The lawyer says, 'In the situations you've described, one at school and several at your work, did anybody actually call you a "nigger"? To your face, I mean?'

'Well, not really,' I offer.

The prosecutor turns to the jury, which is now a committee of vultures. He walks over to them and says *slooooowly*, 'Not really?'

My lids are heavy and my head droops as the committee look at each other. He continues: 'Isn't it true that in each of these situations you had the chance to speak up' – he gesticulates – 'to speak out, yet you chose to say… nothing?' He looks at the jury. 'Why was that?'

A silence fills the entire courtroom as everybody is motionless. I search desperately for an answer.

The prosecutor says, 'No further questions, m'lud.'

There are hushed tones coming from the gallery, which I now see is filled with minstrels from the TV show of the same name. They eat chocolate Minstrels and smile vigorously at each other while softly singing the song 'Oh, Dem Golden Slippers'.

My QC, played by Caitlin, who does look rather fetching in her wig and gown, flirts with my solicitor and turns only to quickly fire, 'No other questions, your honour,' before loudly guffawing at the lawyer's crap joke. The judge, who is my dad, shouts, 'Order!' and brings the hammer down, which startles me awake.

I'm alone here in my half-empty bed.

I make my way downstairs, noting the slap, slap, slap of wood beneath my bare feet. I look in the kitchen ahead of entering, just in case Caitlin and Christina have come back and all of it was just a dream.

Like a sci-fi movie where people are projected into a space from another time and another dimension, I think I see Caitlin and Christina moving around; Christina is scuttling across the floor with Caitlin, talking ten to the dozen.

But no. Maybe they're upstairs? I'm sure I just heard Caitlin say, '*Put that down, darling.*'

I make a cuppa tea and take my last hit.

* * *

I decide I will get clean. I can come off the gear at my mum's. I've done it before; that time I stayed at Roseberry Street with Will, I actually managed to stay clean for weeks. The laughter returned. We named the cats in the alleyway Bird, Monk, Trane, Miles and Dizzy, because they were so fucking cool. We'd put on *Giant Steps by* John Coltrane and get *all* of it. Every note. We'd follow Paul Chambers' bass lines as he walked all over town, while Coltrane weaved in and out of his complex chord progressions.

Eric Random and Lynn Walton, who lived with us then, would kick and scream for each other's love. The dinner she made would slide down the wall and she'd go mad on the stairs, calling his name over and over. Me and Will would just be pissing ourselves, passing a joint around before cracking up again.

The sound filters away until all I can hear is a deafening silence and a clock ticking.

I wonder if anyone's up yet. I've forgiven Pinkerton since that episode with the gas, the electricals and everything else. I did get on a train to London to buy a gun to kill her with, but bottled it when I realised what the fuck I was getting myself into.

What about that hippie guy? Or the biker, what's he called? Or that guy in the Crescents with the kid? I'd better get out and pick up some smack as I don't want to get sick while I'm hanging out.

But no. Not again. No fucking way. My mum has suggested I come home and let go of the house; even though it's tiny, she said, there's no point rattling around in there all day and all night. I could get clean there this time. I feel energised now, with some sense of purpose.

The Vulture is engrossed in a copy of the William S Burroughs novel *Junky*, while singing the Magazine song 'My Tulpa':

I suspect you ain't so sweet
As the lust I'm concealing
My skin wants to crawl back home to Ma
I've lost my way in my feelings

'*You know what your problem is?*' says The Vulture as I roll my eyes.

'Not this again,' I deflect, as though it might trip him up.

'Soft as shit you are. Always have been, always will be. Soft as fucking shit.' He tosses the book aside. 'Soft in the head and soft in the belly,' he spits. 'Even your bones are soft. I mean, they're mostly cartilage, right?'

I look down at my legs.

'Caitlin was on to something when she told you to "man up". I mean, look at you, a bloody gutless wonder.'

I grab my keys and wonder what Nick and the rest are doing. Maybe I should call Mick and find out. The tour's soon, I know.

I can't wait to get back to the black moods, the bad moods, the Bad Seeds.

* * *

Oh, the doom, oh, the fucking gloom of it all. The propagation and multiplication of my negative thinking seems so automatic that it consumes my every waking moment. It's ever supported by the endless search for drugs while we're on the road.

I can't even see that I'm not helping matters by scoring backstage off junkies who, when other band members (notably Blixa) return from an early evening pre-show meal, are shooting up in their neck. Who wouldn't be horrified by an act of self-vampirism before their very eyes?

Then there's Mick Harvey giving me the shits with his fucking looks, eyeballing me from behind the kit until I smash my beautiful red Gibson 335 copy (the one I bought for fifteen quid in Moss Side from a junk shop) into smithereens on stage in Athens, letting him know the stage floor is a simulation of his fucking face.

Or being so pissed off when Blixa starts the song 'Blind Lemon Jefferson' in the wrong key, so that when Nick comes in, in quite another key, he's totally off. This is the opening song and nobody seems to notice, except me. Or maybe they're all playing a very good game of conceal-and-don't-reveal. But my blood boils, as I think we look like a bunch of idiots.

Or in Italy, where I'm singled out by this motherfucker who makes his way to the front of the stage with one aim in mind, to launch a full gob on me. I take off my bass and leave the stage, waiting for the others to do the same. They don't.

I get stoned in the dressing-room toilet and try to act calm when the others return backstage. I hold a big glass of orange juice and as the dope kicks in, it slides from my hands and smashes onto the floor into a thousand pieces. So what? Fuck that guy.

I have this slightly paranoid feeling that all these current events are being noted down (by the group *and* the universe) for future reference. It's in a look. A sort of '*Oh, and what do we have here?*' that specifies that somebody (me) is getting way above their designated station.

Nick talks to me about a John Lee Hooker song, 'My First Wife Left Me'; he also mentions 'It Serve You Right To Suffer', which is a particularly powerful song. Much to my shame, I cannot bring myself to admit I know little of the blues idiom, having given the subject a wide berth since birth. I know nothing of the Delta; have no idea who Skip James is; have no understanding of which notes are 'worried' in the blues scale, be they third, fifth or seventh.

The Deep South? Is that Wythenshawe? Robert Johnson? I cannot be lucid about his story at all, though I know fragments. When Marc Bolan plays a twelve-bar, that's a blues surely? But the meanings, the references to depression and withdrawal – whatever that is in relation to, be it person, place or event – are easy to understand. To that I can relate.

What I'm highly aware of is that I'm admitting I have no idea of who I am. That this other hidden part of my identity does not exist, has never existed. That my black heritage has been discarded in favour of literally sucking up to a society that is largely white and indifferent to me, save the people I call my friends: school, college, bands – all white.

When his conversation with me draws a blank, I'm sure Nick senses a bone buried. You know how it is. The very thing you are trying to conceal is often the very thing that reveals itself as you walk into the room.

* * *

Mick tells me the next album will begin recording at Hansa Tonstudio in Berlin on the twenty-fifth of November. I can't wait to get away from my failed marriage, The Vulture, my parents and myself.

I stay at a small hotel within walking distance of the studio. I hop along Köthener Straße, by the Berlin Wall, through the snow, in my newly acquired patent-leather shoes. I arrive in soaking wet feet at this most spectacular of studios.

The live room itself is a sight to behold. Known as the Meistersaal, it was once a venue where SS officers held dances during the Nazi years. But you can still hear the echoes of David Bowie singing 'Heroes' across this very room. Three microphones were set up, one close to him (for his low and quiet vocal), one quite far away (so he could sing at full voice but had to push it) and the last one across the other side of the room, to achieve the end result: calling out in near desperation to be heard and understood.

'The big hall by the wall' is the name Bowie and Iggy Pop gave to Studio Two, two hundred and seventy square metres wide and, unusually, sixty feet away from the control room down a corridor. The control room has a window that overlooks the wall, where there is a lookout (a crow's nest) patrolled by East German border guards who keep watch over the ministerial buildings, in the East.

Nick is recording here because of the freedom it gives him, I'm told. After coming to London, where he feared that some regarded the Birthday Party as a joke, here in Berlin he is heralded as a king. Like Elvis. For Australians there is no '*don't mention the war*' hangover, as there always is with the Brits where Germany is concerned. They are free to fuck around without getting burned.

For me, however, upon my arrival, the stink of displacement moves gently around with me like the faint smell of shit on somebody's shoe. With Caitlin gone and Manchester a million miles away, I find out that heroin is in short supply here – a perfect recipe for my own version of the blues. My inadequate patent-leather shoes have left my toes soaking, as the cold air gathers around my feet.

While I'm determined not to allow myself to be pulled under by being black and blue and British too, I'm gonna play my bass, play my role, keep my head down and try to get something great out of this, like I did on the last record. I mean, just look at this place. What's the worst thing that could happen?

A tightness gathers about my chest as Mick Harvey picks up the bass and begins playing the foundation of what will become 'Tupelo'. He has flipped the bass line to 'Saint Huck' and sits in grandiose fashion, bashing it out as the great hall responds to his every gesture, making the bass sound huge and bombastic.

Inspired and pissed off in equal measures, I move over to the kit and flail out a play on the song 'Bo Diddley'. When Nick sings, '*Distant thunder rumbles,* 'I march out a pattern using the floor tom, against what Mick is playing and what Nick is singing, to try to capture this dense atmosphere.

The walk to the control room is far down the corridor. It feels to me like going from one studio to another. There is always an audience in the room as friends of Nick's stop by, members of Die Haut, Einstürzende Neubauten, Malaria. A guy introduced to me as Christoph Dreher, bass player with the band Die Haut, eyes me up with a slightly psychotic fixed grin. Thomas Wydler, who wants to be a tough guy but finds life so strange that he can only laugh at it, seems okay.

I'd like to look for points of connection here, as a way to blend in, but it ain't gonna happen. I talk mostly to Beate Bartel from Malaria, who I've come to know from playing here a couple of times with the band; otherwise I keep pretty much schtum. Beate tells me her boyfriend is mistreating her. This can only help my case if I make a move on her, which I do.

When the room is clear, Mick and myself notice how hot it is in the control room one snowy evening. He opens the windows, which then sends the room into the freezer. A joke starts up about the temperature outside, with us singing 'Two Below' instead of 'Tupelo'. Mick offers that it's '*Big brass monkeys at two below*'.

I think about how I felt when, with McGeoch in Magazine, we would make light of Howard's lyrics and twist them into nonsense. How this ultimately alienated me, even if it was only in my own mind.

The stakes here are raised, though, to the degree that they seem vertiginous. I consider that Mick might be setting me up for a mighty fall, such is my growing paranoia.

But...

His drumming is really something. Just leave me to play the bass.

I sit at the kit again for 'Say Goodbye To The Little Girl Tree'. I'm shrinking into self-doubt and fear at every turn. Without any heroin to balance the books, I'm going out of my mind as I begin shooting up a synthetic cocaine that's offered to me, known as procaine. This acts on the system in a completely opposite way to heroin, added to which I have no idea as to why I'm shooting it up in the first place. It brings with it a deepening psychosis that I'm now having to work really hard to keep at bay.

The original Bad Seeds: me (foreground); Harvey (background); Bargeld (right).
Photo by Jutta Henglein.

On the walk into the studio one afternoon, I swear I both see and hear The Vulture flying high above Kreuzberg, singing 'Say Goodbye To The Little Girl Tree'. *'Fuck, what's he doing here?'*

I try to retain my sense of normality. The singing is in German but I recognise Mick Harvey's cowboy guitar line, coarsely sung by The Vulture as an introduction. He then swoops down on a small group of schoolgirls.

I panic and start to run towards them. They seem not to notice and when I realise that the swooping figure is merely an older man walking past them in a dark billowing coat, I put the whole episode down to tiredness and the effects of the procaine. Of which I'm going to need some more today, as I haven't slept for nearly five days.

There is a hilarious tape of Eddie Murphy's *Delirious* show, where he does an impression of Stevie Wonder. He plays on the fact that Stevie is so loved by everybody that when he accentuates nuances like the

266

swaying head and eyes moving in different directions, he is able to bring in another character who's really pissed off at the impression.

Finally, he gives voice to this other guy: 'Hey, motherfucker! Leave Stevie alone. Don't you know he's a musical genius? Making Stevie Wonder jokes and shit. I'll kill you, motherfucker.'

Nick is a brilliant cartoonist. He can draw anybody and bring out their traits with the turn of a pencil stroke. While listening to Elvis's album *Just A Closer Walk With Thee*, he draws Stevie Wonder in the studio as a hideous caricature. I become the guy in Eddie Murphy's routine, my face a picture of distortion: '*Stevie Wonder jokes and shit.*'

I decide to teach myself to play some John Lee Hooker songs on the guitar between takes and during the long cold nights when Beate's not around.

The song 'Train Long Suffering' probes at my poor open wound of a soul with a blunt pen. It's a take on the gospel and blues tradition, and here I am on call-and-response backing vocals, my procaine-addled brain trying to distinguish between art and soul and coming up with nothing.

But I'm secretly in awe of Nick's ability to tap into a universe that I don't see him having any connection to, at the ease with which he is able to write lines from within what ought to be my own wound. How is this achieved? It's an idiom that is so far away from a small-town Australian upbringing – not that I've ever visited Warracknabeal, 'the place of big gums shading the water hole', as the aboriginal translation goes.

However, I'm about as uncomfortable as a stranger can be right now. When Mick Harvey does jazz hands while we sing, in my mind evoking those minstrels in blackface and white gloves, it's all I can do not to rip his head off and eat it. Instead I sing: '*The name of the pain is...*'

I try to confide in Flood. He's logical; he's English; I have a history of working with him throughout my entire career; he knows about black and white culture in the UK.

I expose a little darkness. I can see he gets me but there is no way, given the task in hand, that he can be any kind of ally. He has to capture Nick's performances in the moment, on two inches of tape as it whirs between the reels. The snow continues to fall as he talks to me about the only time he ever wanted the ground to open up and swallow him.

I think to myself, 'Steady on, old chap, I'm nowhere near there yet. Am I?'

I manage to get stoned on heroin one night and pull out all the stops on 'Train Long Suffering', adding production and an organ part, embracing the song from another viewpoint altogether. But I'm disappointed at the lack of enthusiasm for what I've done; Nick regards my upbeat mood with suspicion. He is right to.

Once I get some sleep and consult with The Vulture (who now sleeps at the end of the bed... actually I can never tell if he's awake or asleep), I'll be back with a 'Needy Norman' placard hanging around my neck, pretending I'm cool: '*Hey, what song are we doing today, guys?*'

Blixa plays the blues riff to 'Black Crow King', then he curls up like a snake and slithers across the floor towards me. I cannot deny the beauty or the brevity of the lyric, how each line is like a small death for me.

I can't save face so I retreat fully into myself, to a place where I'm now totally enveloped by my own darkness. Centuries of differences I can never accept as the truth haunts me. I do my best to play along (on the piano, or foot stomps). I am close to conceding defeat. But not quite yet...

I go back to the hotel. Beate has tried to help me by explaining that what we're dealing with here isn't just about music. This is happening due to the special nature of things. I lie awake with The Vulture, knowing that at least things cannot get any worse.

I 'act as if' the best that I can; as if I'm happy; as if I'm having a great time; as if my new drug of choice, procaine, is really doing it for me.

The song 'Knockin' On Joe' feels like I wrote the music in my sleep, though I'm never credited for it. To this day, I feel I wrote the chorus in a drug-induced stupor and showed it to Nick, then completely forgot about it. I can sit down at the piano to write verses, then a chorus, and lo and behold... or maybe I dreamt the whole thing up.

Bob Dylan's 'Wanted Man' feels like the Bad Seeds of old, before we became a distortion of the blues. As for 'Blind Lemon Jefferson', it's a song I love and hate, given the way it sits on my chest and squeezes the life out of me. I grow sick of these negative portraits of black men and women.

I make a comment that almost costs me my life, when questioned about adding an instrument: 'It's only a song.' This I know is untrue.

The reality is that every nuance and stroke is of such delicacy, whether the song be a sword or a declaration of love, but I just cannot play the game in this moment.

Flood turns up the bass on 'Blind Lemon Jefferson' really high. I use my boss chorus pedal on the tremelo setting to try to fuel the song with authentic emotion, as it wobbles and sends shivers down the spine. In reality I feel like a complete dick for joining in with these constant negative affirmations.

Mick Harvey continues to take cheap shots at me. His girlfriend, Katy, thinks it's hilarious how easy I am to bait and giggles when Harvey says, 'Every one a lemon,' when something he is trying to get from a food machine doesn't work. It gets a rise from me, as I remember the comic books at school, when the white manager goes around blinding black blues players, his fingers jabbing into their eyes. '*FOIT!*' was the noise made by their eyes jumping out of their skulls.

On the way back to London in a cab with Mick and Katy, I am out of my mind and exhausted. I wish them a merry Christmas, as, after all, it's December the twenty-third.

At Euston Station, I think I've missed the train. I have very little money too. Then there is an announcement that the delayed train to Manchester is leaving in five minutes. I have no ticket. The lady at the barrier reads my desperation and just opens the gate.

I board the train home to my parents.

I can't wait to get home for some rest. On arrival, though, my mum and my dad are standing at the door. They are crying and totally distraught. They tell me that our Carol is in the hospital and has had both of her legs amputated.

Chapter Thirty

My mum backs away from the door, hiding from whatever might come next. It could obliterate her. She cowers in shame, as if to say, '*How could I let this awful thing happen to my firstborn?*'

My dad looks at me to see what kind of man I am, if I am with him now. Sorrow lurches down from the ceiling of the front room in looming, oppressive clouds. The Christmas tree, with its presents beneath, twinkles as I wipe my tears away.

My mum explains that Our Kid went into the hospital for a routine gall bladder removal, but when she woke up both of her legs were black.

So they cut them off. Now there is another issue, in that they cannot stem the blood-flow from her stumps.

They hand me my Christmas present and a card from each of them. Their faces are lit up, awaiting my response. My dad's card reads, 'WE ARE SO PROUD OF YOU' and he wishes me a merry Christmas. My mum pushes me to open my present. The size alone seems to dwarf everything else as I peel off the Christmas tree-patterned paper to reveal quite possibly the world's biggest ghetto blaster.

My mum asks me if that's the right one. I tell her how absolutely brilliant it is; how I've been after one of these for ages; how it has an inbuilt cassette player so I can record music directly from the radio; the speakers are massive, so the bass will be amazing; really, I could not have wished for anything better.

I try not to draw breath or stop talking, to keep us all from thinking about what is really going on here on Christmas Eve, with Christ the master.

The next morning, we visit Carol at the hospital. Merry Christmas, Our Kid...

En route, I feel sick and scared as my body goes into withdrawal. My hands throb and sweat forms on my top lip, which I wipe away, trying not to think about myself so much.

My sister lies in a bed. I see that halfway down her body, her body shape disappears. Only then do I start to believe the horror of what my parents have told me.

As I'm absorbing this fact, her husband David ('Nip') and our Lisa, now seven, follow up behind us. Lisa asks, 'Mummy, where are your legs? Do you have them tucked underneath you?' I chat to David in the stairwell and he braves out the idea of chairlifts and various aids to make Carol's life easier, once she leaves the hospital.

I say goodbye to Our Kid and kiss her on the cheek. She whispers something I can't quite hear, so I move my ear to her mouth to hear her say, 'Can you get me some of that stuff that you take?' My heart begins to break.

Back at my mum and dad's, I vow to never take 'that stuff' again. The pain of what is happening to my sister, the dead calm of Christmas and the drugs leaving my system all conspire to cut me like a knife.

I sweat it all out in the tiny bed next door to the living room for five days, my nights filled with terrors that rip through me: images of passengers on trains, their faces cut off or half hanging on. I wake covered in sweat and change the sheets, as though I've pissed the bed.

My mum brings the odd meal to my pit of doom, which I've turned into a prison. I'm convinced that the endless chicken she brings me is actually pigeons caught outside. I glance out of the window, where The Vulture sits high in a stark midwinter tree nearby, overlooking Dudley Road and the flat, as the days grow colder.

After five crucial days of 'clucking' (street name for withdrawal), I have myself back. My parents are going through hell, so I decide to drive into town to buy them something nice. I know nothing can take their minds off what is happening with Our Kid, but maybe I can show them some appreciation and let them know that I care while they're going through all this, the most awful of times.

I climb behind the wheel and point myself in the direction of town, through Whalley Range and onto Princess Road. I'm thinking that, as I didn't get them anything for Christmas, I could make up for that too. I could get a piece of jewellery for my mum and a jazz record and some Hamlet cigars for my dad. Not just a flat tin of them but the bigger, rounder ones. Sounds good to me.

I pull into the Crescents and park up, thinking that my dad would probably like something by Oscar Peterson. He turned me on to him and his 'C Jam Blues', with Ray Brown on bass, which inspired me to learn the intro note for note on my upright.

I enter the dealer's place. He asks me if I've been away and we both laugh. What about my mum? I'm torn between a necklace and brooch as the needle goes in.

'Good to have you back, lad,' says the dealer. I leave and jump back in the car. I decide on a gold necklace for my mum. Eighteen-carat, I reckon. The stores on Deansgate are buzzing, with everyone spreading the post-Christmas cheer.

*   *   *

My sister is now off the ward and in a room by herself. She is delirious. We're told that this is because of the morphine. We are also told that she has been put on the 'free list', which means she is going to die.

Which is what happens on January the fifth, nineteen eighty-five. She is thirty-five years old.

The days all run into each other without distinction. I used to be able to ground myself in the knowledge that if we're eating lamb chops, then it must be Tuesday. Friday is fish. As for Saturdays, Dickie Davis and tag wrestling, then it's definitely pork chops. It's all like 'Today's Monday' by The Scaffold:

Is everybody happy?
You bet your life we are

I go to the shops with my mum, to help her out. Her indifference towards me grows daily. I can't take her pain away, but she is right when

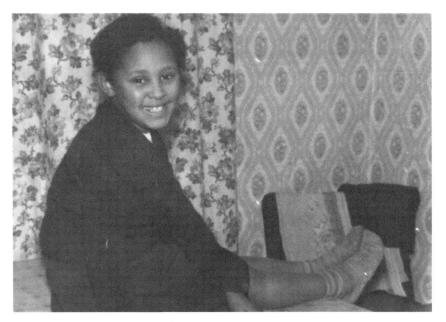

Our Kid, our Carol. Photo by my dad.

she says I can't be there for her at a time like this. I slip into a heroin nod in the middle of the day, whatever day it might be.

She pulls out of Dudley Road and into Withington Road, turning right as a car careers towards us at speed. I'm in the passenger seat watching it hurtle towards me. I manage to alert her to the danger just in time, as two sets of brakes screech out loud. I empathise with the other guy's gob-smacked expression as my mum merely carries on driving to Asda, as though the near-miss didn't happen at all. She seems totally oblivious to the whole moment.

* * *

News from London is that the new Bad Seeds album release is being delayed while permission is sought from Bob Dylan to use our version of his song 'Wanted Man'. Otherwise it's ready to go and will be titled *The Firstborn Is Dead*.

* * *

From my dungeon, I look out of the window to see if I can spy The Vulture. But I see nothing except the bleak, black, arthritic fingers of the trees scratching against an enduring, cold, grey sky. As March and April become the cruellest of months, the spring offers little hope; sunlight on raindrops on the leaves, and all that good stuff, avails me nothing as I sit in silence throughout the days and the nights.

Doped up to the eyeballs, I float back to Pendlebury Children's Hospital in the late sixties. Hovering over an even tinier bed, I see myself wheeled into the theatre. There are machines, pumping and whirring, men and women in gowns and masks. Their voices echo out, loud and assertive. The anaesthetist smiles at me from upside down, her face a bizarre grimace, asking me what my favourite toy is. She then asks me to count down from ten to one. I make it to seven, then all in the room agree that I'm out for the count and ready for my osteotomy, a young person's version of a bone-replacement operation.

The surgeon cuts the side of my legs open and resets the bone, so that in its new position the acetabulum will be enticed to naturally grow a nodule of additional bone that latches onto the femur. This will act as a kind of lever so that I'll be able to walk better in later life. That part done, the plaster casters get to work and cover most of my body, making sure the metal bar, the witch's broom, is in the right place, keeping my legs spread as wide as they can be.

A nurse comes in with an envelope and hands it to the surgeon. 'It's from Central Control, sir.'

The anaesthetist worriedly looks at another surgical team member. 'Is that what I think it is?' The surgeon gives no answer. The anaesthetist asks, 'What has he done?'

'It's not about that this time,' answers the surgeon. The perfusionist adds, 'It's just standard TI monitoring.' Another team member questions, 'Targeted individual? I don't understand.'

'It's not our business as to why or who. All we know is that when this kind of order comes to us, especially when it's a kid, we have to act without question. Now let's just get on with the implant,' says the surgeon in mild annoyance.

The team switches quickly to a mode of professionalism disengaged from any personal emotions as the tiny monitor is brought into theatre in a little glass box by the cardiologist. A hole is drilled into the back of my brain and the Central Control (standard issue) TI Monitor (serial number 06192500666) is implanted. Several checks are made before I am ushered back onto the ward, back into the land of the living.

*   *   *

I visit my sister at the undertakers on Princess Road which the school bus used to drive past; Leech's Funeral Service. I stare at her face for what seems like forever, trying to will her back into existence via some kind of super power. I hope for a breath of air from her nostrils, or a rising of the chest, but she is completely motionless.

I sit with her and fill myself up with memory; the harsh light cuts through the window as life and death go to war with each other. Neither of them will win.

I kiss my beautiful sister on the forehead. Her cold skin against my lips is a shocking discovery, asking me to now fully accept that which I cannot.

I then drive over to the Crescents, fully aware that Central Control are tuned into my implant and are watching me. I go to a dealer who has a kid, a young girl. He's off his trolley. Even now, after Caitlin has taken Christina away, I judge him for that.

He tells me she often says to him, 'Dad, can we watch *Black Bastards?*' I quickly work out that he's referring to the popular game show *Blockbusters*. I'm saddened to the core as I watch him laugh, guffawing his way through his pain as a black man.

Back at the flat, the smell of cabbage wafts throughout. My dad sits in his chair behind the news as my mum sits on the sofa packing labels into cardboard boxes. Central Control don't care about my parents; it's me they're monitoring. No doubt The Vulture (one of their agents, I've now realised) will show up soon and make out like he's my friend. Or maybe he's a double agent?

I've also noticed of late that my senses are becoming more and more unreliable. I heard a John Coltrane record where the saxophone solo actually changed. Yeah, it did, right before my ears.

I've heard the album *Giant Steps* thousands of times and have every chord and solo etched into my very DNA. So, when the phrasing and notes changed, not once but twice, then I knew it was either one of two things: that records are an illusion and when you drop the needle, it sends a signal to Central Control to play the song, which in this instance they got wrong; or they got it wrong on purpose, just to fuck me up and make me feel strange.

Whatever this means, from now on I'm gonna have to pay very close attention to what some might call 'phenomena', which I say is some fucking deadly game at play. Secretly, I'm very worried about this and could probably use The Vulture's take on things, whether he's a double agent or not.

I hear screaming from another flat and ask my parents if they heard it too. They smile at me and say that they didn't, asking if I'm okay. I nod and shield myself.

Upon entering my room, something clicks. They are both in on it.

I scan the details of my life since the operation and up until now, like a sped-up movie. I realise that the order for the monitor to be implanted was issued by the government, for Central Control, but signed off by... my parents. When those two guys came over with the information about the school for the disabled, don't forget, they appeared like vultures.

Fuck.

I look outside.

I flee the house, but up in the trees he is nowhere to be seen.

* * *

I visit Nico from the Velvet Underground, who now lives nearby. We watch a recording of Gil Scott-Heron performing 'The Bottle'. Nico looks at the bass player and then at me, several times. She finally realises (or thinks she does) where she recognises him from. 'Barry, I didn't know you played so good,' she tells me. I let it go without explanation as she jumps onto her harmonium and begins to sing:

The honesty that wants to be lies...

I stop eating the pigeons that my mum brings me and slip out to a burger place, then drop in on Wayne Worm who lives just down the road. I now live in total fear of Central Control's next move, so I'm wary of everything. Wayne's cat tries to tell me I'm not safe as we watch a prison drama movie called *Brubaker*. I realise that the Worm is a part of all this. Even his cat is now eyeing me with suspicion. I get out of there fast.

I go home, where my parents are in the same positions as before. My mum tells me, 'Nick Cave called. I told him to bugger off, messing you about like that.' This is due to my trying to explain the difficulties of being in the group.

'*Shit. What has she done now?*' I think as I scramble to my room.

Is that what really went on, though? Maybe he was checking on how it's going from Central Control and my parents' end? Now they're going to have to rely on the people who brought me into this world to willingly take me out of it.

The Bad Seeds were probably amazed that I even made it back to Manchester. But browbeating, even to such an extent, by Cave and Harvey did not work. Christoph Dreher failed in his mission to finally see me off, having sent me down one blind alley after another when I was down and needed to get myself back on track.

'So Central Control links together everyone from your parents to your work colleagues, maybe the people at school even?' I ask The Vulture.

The Vulture lights a Benson & Hedges cigarette and tosses the Bic lighter to me, so that I can do the same. '*Yep, everyone you have ever known.*'

'Shit... why me?'

The Vulture blows several impressive smoke rings. '*Why not you?*' He rationalises to me that the point of revelation is when you have to enact what Central Control have programmed you to do. If not, then the everyday just gets extraordinarily worse and worse, until you get to the point where you'll want nothing else but to make it stop.

I try to call The Vulture's bluff. 'What is *it?*'

'Oh, I think you know well enough.'

My mum comes into my room. 'Me and your dad are going over to babysit Lisa. You'll be alright, won't you?'

She is deaf to The Vulture, who mocks her voice and winks at me. '*Tell her to fuck off. We don't need her.*'

I try and shut the thing up with a scowl, but then switch expressions to reassure my mum.

'Yeah, no problem. I'll just get a burger for me tea.'

I hear the rustle of my parents' coats and hushed tones from the corridor. I lean in to gauge what they are saying. It's as though they're keeping something from me and not out of good intent.

I hear my mum: '*Shhhhh…*' My dad acts as though he might be worried about giving the game away. But what game, exactly, I'm not sure.

It is then that I realise all events have come down to tonight, and that everyone is involved: Central Control, Pendlebury Hospital, Old Moat Junior, Ducie High School, Stockport College, Magazine, the Bad Seeds. Everyone I have ever known, even down to the lady in the burger shop ('You want chips with your order?'), now lies in wait for me.

They wait for me to finish it all.

There is another scream outside. I dash to the front door, to the tiny annexe where other flats face ours. All I hear is the closing of the door downstairs as my parents leave and the echo that follows, penetrating the stillness of the electric light as a wave of nausea washes over me.

A record begins to play from the front room. The news from the television is deafening. I run back and look out of the window. My parents are standing in the car park, smiling and waving at me in slow motion as Miles Davis plays the solo on 'So What' from the *Kind Of Blue* album, but completely differently to the reassuring sound that I've always had hardwired into my brain.

I think it's better that I leave the house and so I look for my mac, the one I never leave home without. But just then the television speaks of Max Bygraves, the popular entertainer. I realise this is coded information that I'm to be shut down the moment that I escape; 'by graves' is the clue, the man who wears the mac needs to die. Tonight.

The Vulture changes the tape and mocks Coltrane as his soloing goes awry. This is a further clue that the train which carries me is about to crash, coal being its colour.

I look outside as my parents wave to me again. They are crying. I realise then that they really have signed off on the project.

The Vulture assures me that it'll be okay, that he's gonna be with me until the end. I walk to the kitchen and take out a carving knife from the drawer.

I go back into the living room and look out of the window. My parents are gone. The noise from the television is playing backwards now, with canned laughter cutting through my attempt to decipher what is being said. Max sings 'You Need Hands' from nineteen fifty-eight, the year I was born. Now, it seems, it's marking the day I shall die.

The Vulture watches the television and finds it hilarious, side-eyeing me to see how I'm getting on.

The music of Coltrane grinds to a slowing, unrecognisable stop as I hold the knife against my chest with both hands and Max sings:

When you feel nobody wants to know you
You need hands to brush away the tears

I plunge the knife into my chest, hitting bone as a deafening silence ensues.

The Vulture's jaw drops. The picture on the television is frozen on Max as The Vulture holds its breath.

I draw the knife across my left wrist and watch it open up wide. The Vulture rolls its eyes.

I take the knife and hold it against the jugular vein in my neck. As I close in on what will surely happen next, a voice – Carol's? Christina's? Mine? All three? – cuts through the silence and says, '*Please don't.*'

I drop the knife and pick up the brown-and-beige Trimphone, dialling my dad on my sister's number. I tell him that he has to come home and finish the job himself.

Chapter Thirty-One

My dad opens the door to the front room. His face shows disappointment; I apologise to him for being the cause of it. He says, 'We have to go now, Barry lad.' I assume this means to a secret location, where the job will be finally executed.

We drive through the night, through empty streets, arrive at a barren building and walk down a dimly lit corridor, at the end of which I'm taken into a room. A woman in a nurse's uniform arrives. She stitches up my wrist, whispering to me, 'You want to end your life? Well, I wouldn't mind driving the final nail into your coffin.'

I'm taken away down another corridor, where my dad is waiting. He tells me, 'I have to go now, son, but I'll come back and see you tomorrow.'

I'm then approached by Beverley, a young black girl who holds her hands out in front of herself and begins to sing:

Who will buy this wonderful morning?

She is told rather curtly by a nurse to go back to her room as I'm shown into another room with four beds. I undress, put on pyjamas, get into bed and wait for my killer to arrive.

A man opposite me pulls the sheets back and lifts what I assume is a sawn-off shotgun from under his bed. It is in fact a bedpan, so I'm cowering for nothing. I eventually fall asleep in a field of snores while planning my escape.

The next day, I am introduced to Dr Hackett, a male psychiatrist, followed up by Dr Love, a female one. They both talk to me about psychosis as I keep my eye on a Scottish patient, who mutters insults under his breath towards me. Beverley enters the room and bursts into song from her Dickensian repertoire. Today she sings 'Where Is Love?'

It's very astute of Beverley to sing this just as Dr Love leaves the building. Then it's time for us to take our pills and we all queue up as though waiting for the January sales to start. We're each given a range of antipsychotic medicines before returning to the bedroom.

I am genuinely surprised to see my mum and dad arrive later in the day. My mum says her usual, 'Ooh, our Barry, what have you done now?' But it's music to my ears. I try to explain to them what, in my mind, I have actually done. They look at me quizzically as I unpick the lyrics of songs and tell them my theories about what they really mean.

I'm just pleased to see them really.

That night, the classic horror film *The Omen* is on television. Me and the Scot watch it, saying nothing to each other. Later, in the middle of the night, I feel my bed shake and open my eyes to see my new friend lifting the whole thing up, with me in it.

He smashes it down several times, shouting, '*It's him! He's the Antichrist!*'

I remember a sketch on Peter Cook and Dudley Moore's album *Derek And Clive Come Again*, where Dud, in hospital, is overcome by a farting attack and cries out, 'Nurse!' I now do the same (crying out, 'Nurse!', not the farting) until one arrives. The Scotsman is gently talked down from smashing my bed to smithereens and escorted to another room.

Then I meet Alan, a quietly well-spoken chap. I wonder what in hell's name he is doing here. He talks to me about a breakdown at work and I wonder if that's what happened to me. '*But surely that kind of thing only happens to the old?*' I ask myself.

We discuss music and he talks with authority about Martin Denny. I confess to only knowing one instrumental, 'Quiet Village'. He pontificates on all things exotica and is able to discuss one 'fantasy island' theme after another.

The next morning, I wake up with Alan's erect penis pointing at my face. I look him in the eye (the one in his face) and he is full of rage, spitting out at me, '*I like music. I like Marvin Gaye, do you hear me? Gay! Gay!*'

Before I'm able to form the word 'Nurse!' on my lips, not one but two of them enter the room and talk Alan down, literally, and ease him back into his pyjamas as he sobs like a child.

After which, on one quite sunny morning, one of the women from the adjacent ward comes into our males-only room in a see-thru negligee and walks to the window. One of the younger guys flings himself onto his bed face down.

'*She can't bear it!*' screams the woman. The kid starts to grip the edges of the mattress.

'The wreath! The veil! The weight of the cross!' she bellows.

The boy who, like me, is in his early twenties stares at her like a man possessed. As she starts lifting her negligee, he begins humping the bed with everything he's got. We've all been there, of course, but I know what I have to do…

'Nurse!'

Outside, two gardeners are digging a hole. This concerns me. Dr Love comes to see me and asks if I want to go outside, where nearby sit two methodically placed chairs. I think, '*Okay, well, I was just starting to feel at home. But I guess they've had a rethink about my situation.*' My fear of assassination comes hurtling back.

However, the air on my skin and the spring sunshine on my face feel restorative. I now see that, in fact, the holes in the garden have been dug for a variety of plants which the gardeners are tending to.

Dr Love asks me if I want a job.

'What?'

She explains to me that a disabled old lady has been brought in. Perhaps I would consider helping her out? She's unable to feed herself due to her arms being permanently twisted.

I say, 'Yes, of course, I'll do it.'

Come lunchtime, Betty is brought in a wheelchair into the canteen and plonked down next to me. Indeed, she is all twisted up; her neck is also twisted and she cannot speak properly. I begin feeding her with a spoon and mopping up what doesn't go in her mouth.

As the days go by, Betty's body begins to relax and her head starts to face forwards. We have a chat about the weather and I begin to understand what she says. She smiles at me and I smile back.

I start to look forward to mealtimes with Betty. After a month, she is completely untwisted and we are having sparkling conversations about nothing and everything.

*   *   *

Word from London is that the Bad Seeds see my suicide attempt as a cry for help. Tour manager Jessamy Calkin sends her brother Adam to visit me, with information about what he calls 'recovery'. Recovery from addiction.

I struggle with the term 'addict', believing addicts to be filthy rats who live on the streets like beggars, shuffling around and robbing people wherever they can. (Denial is the shock absorber of the soul, remember.)

He offers me some ill-designed pamphlets about a Twelve Steps programme, which I cast aside at first glance, deeming the whole idea to be rather cultish. I add, rather churlishly, that their graphics person ought to be shot.

Adam does have something about him, though, I have to quietly admit. I also relate to all the things he is telling me about being an addict. Like he's been there and now he's not there anymore.

Mick Harvey and his girlfriend, Katy Beale, come to see me too. I'm totally wary of them both, given my experiences in Berlin, and hugely sceptical of their reasons for visiting. Have they been sent by Nick? Is there a tinge of guilt in the air? That a slither of empathy has reasoned them? My perception (being in the midst of psychosis) is awry, and though they express concern, Mick, to my mind, casts a look of disconnection from a somewhat haughty position. Maybe that's just who he is. Katie stares at my bandaged wrist to gauge the extent of the damage. By saying nothing, I don't take the bait.

Howard Devoto and Pete Shelley also pay a visit. It feels good to see them, though somewhat bittersweet, remembering how I idolised them at college, the history of Magazine, my embarrassment at my wretched behaviour towards Pete.

They double-act through their various eccentricities. Howard talks at length about preferring to drive along A-roads for the journey up. Pete hilariously storyboards his imminent marriage to young Carol Morley – sister of the now popular journalist Paul, who once sold me a copy of *Spiral Scratch* – as though it were a scene from *Coronation Street*, with Pete himself as Derek and Carol Morley as Mavis.

I start to get a sense that maybe I'm going to be okay, for the first time in a while.

It's now Easter on Ward PS2, where I've lived for what seems like a lifetime. Beverly continues to breeze through the whole *Oliver!* songbook and I've come to consider myself part of the furniture.

I get a nice surprise when Celia Johnstone comes to visit me with bunch of chocolate eggs. She looked in on me when Howard and Pete were here and has now come back.

I was introduced to Celia, the Johnstone's paint magnate's daughter, at a Bad Seeds gig in London through Jessamy. I was immediately captivated by her perfect sense of style, her emotional openness and free, clean-living attitude. Her presence was like a breath of fresh air. Something inside me saw myself in her. Like me at my best.

Plus, I enjoy the fact that I can easily goad her about not being from Manchester, my argument being that Cheshire isn't actually Manchester at all. ('So don't think you're all that cool, young lady!') This becomes the first in a series of running jokes that we share. She lives in London but was in 'Manchester' to see her folks, then heard I was 'resting' here like some Charlie Parker figure, taking the cure to get 'off the hop'.

We get along like the proverbial house on fire. I see something in her eyes and hear in her tone of voice what just might be called 'hope'.

I guess she hopes I like these Easter eggs – which of course I do, though I'm beginning to doubt everything else. I take a sneaky look to see if there are any hidden cameras in those damn eggs, no longer sure who Celia works for or which side she is on. Or why she is here at all.

Then I tell myself to *stop it*. I have to try to trust that maybe what is happening here isn't about Central Control.

After Celia leaves me with a glow, I am called into the office. I quickly discern that Caitlin is on the phone from Australia, calling in a panic, demanding to speak to me.

The sister covers the phone's speaker with her hand and says, 'It's your wife. She is insistent on talking to you.' I feign surprise. 'I suppose that's okay, even though visiting time is officially over,' she adds.

* * *

Celia and my good self start to see each other a little bit. Once I leave the hospital, I vow to my bad self to only smoke a little bit of dope here and there and have the odd pint of lager from here on out.

My paranoia is still running high, though, and the antipsychotic pill that I've been prescribed, Stelazine, does fuck all. I seem to just hang on each day for dear life, trying not to slip once more into the persecution complex that won't leave me be.

Anyway, my mum seems to like Celia, which is a step in the right direction. She asks her, 'Why the bloody 'ell do you want to go out with him?' To which I raise an eyebrow. 'He's a bloody mumbler is what he is.'

I take offence and begin to say something, but with perfect timing, my mum bellows, 'You what? Speak up, I can't hear you.'

* * *

Back in London, I stay with Celia on the houseboat she shares with her sister, Christine, in Cheyne Walk, Chelsea. Bumping into Mick Jagger in the local pub is an everyday occurrence, as is Concorde flying overhead on a sunny afternoon as I look out across the Thames. By the evening, the Freixenet Cordon Negro Brut will be flowing freely, as it often does in these parts. Every day seems to be Freixenet Friday.

Caitlin somehow catches wind of my new beginnings and my new romantic interest. Thinking that we are still a couple (and best friends to boot, even though she left me months ago), she calls once more from Australia, demanding that I return to my parents' place in Manchester, or else. Or else what, I ponder?

We go to the movies, to gigs and to restaurants on the nearby King's Road or World's End. We see foul-mouthed drag queen Jayne County (formerly Wayne) play at the Electric Ballroom. Because my right eye is giving me gyp, I decide on a look that will offset my baby-blue jacket, crisp white shirt and black crossover tie from the fifties, with an extra added cool effect: a black eye-patch.

Not only does it do away with the eye irritation, it gives me the look of a Bond villain too, which is a bonus. At the gig, we walk past the front of the stage where I cast an eye over Jayne, who takes offence and blurts out, 'Who the fuck are you looking at, *Popeye*?'

On our way back to the houseboat, the taxi driver casts me a sullen look which isn't so far from the stink-eye. I'm used to this and I'm on to him. I've met this mood many times in many taxis. So I'm not too surprised that, when we get out of the cab, he takes a cloth and begins wiping down the back seat where I'd sat. Celia is mortified as I welcome her to my world.

Not that racism and my using are intrinsically connected, but as soon as I'm settling in I begin sniffing out dealers. To score heroin around the World's End pubs and nearby estates.

Work with the Bad Seeds begins again with a tour of Europe. Celia comes to visit me in Rotterdam and is horrified when the door is almost kicked down in the middle of the night by Nico.

Rather than expose how I'm still using, I concoct some story about having to help Nico out. Celia cocks an ear to what seems to be a coded dialogue between Nico and myself.

After 'helping Nico out' I return to the hotel completely out of it, nodding off in the lift the next morning. Celia has a fit as I'm trying to explain that I didn't get much sleep.

After this episode, I'm back to where I was before. Shooting up wherever and whenever I can. Before the tour continues to the USA, I'm particularly cruel to Celia: mocking her for how she's gonna miss me and generally being a dick to her in front of her friends.

It's a mixture of self-hatred and the inability to accept personal responsibility.

In no time I'm in Alphabet City, downtown New York. Junkie Brian, an actor friend of the band, is scoring dope around the corner from where he lives on Avenue A.

The ten-dollar bags of dope come in glassine packets and are stamped on the side with names like 'Life', 'No Pain', 'Special Delivery', 'White Fang', 'Time Bomb', 'Monster Power', 'Deadly Sin', 'The Last Temptation', 'Notorious', 'Outlaw' and 'Game Over'.

They are small wax-coated paper baggies measuring twenty to twenty-two millimetres wide, resembling a tiny paper lunch bag but housing single units of heroin. The bags were originally used to preserve collectible stamps and coins.

Today, walking the streets with Brian, he speaks under his breath, quietly calling to dealers, 'Special Delivery?' Once we collect a few bags, it is back to his place to play shoot-'em-up.

In a derelict area between the houses, some kids are roasting a whole pig on a spit as a cop car drifts by. One cop gives me a look, and for a moment I think he's gonna get out and approach me. I have pockets full of packets. In true *Kojak* style, though, they get a call on the radio and take off somewhere fast.

The six gigs the Bad Seeds play are lost on me. I feel stuck because of what I learned about myself through Adam Calkin and my visit to ward PS2. I have to make sure my denial is kept in place by using more junk than before.

But I feel relief at arriving in Japan, where drugs are so near-impossible to find that they're not on the agenda at all. Plus I've never been here before, so I relish the fact of being somewhere new and exciting.

Which it really is, from the word go. Japan is the only place where I have ever experienced total culture shock, in the most wonderful, disorientating, discombobulating way. There are no signs I can read, no street names or language cues to pick up on.

The only connection with any world I know is when, one afternoon, I wander into a bar where John Coltrane's music is coming up from the basement. I walk downstairs, and there on a huge screen is 'Trane, playing his solo on Miles Davis' tune 'So What', exactly as I remember it.

I begin my withdrawal from heroin which, for the first time in my life, I'm only too happy to. I spend more time with Nick than I've ever done previously. We talk a lot and have quite a fun time.

We go check out one of the venues the night before we play. San Francisco avant-garde band The Residents are performing. Me, Pete Shelley and Francis listened to their album *Fingerprince* over and over at Tony Wilson's house in the late seventies. It's a surreal moment finally meeting them backstage, holding the oversized eyeballs they use to preserve their anonymity.

We play shows in the evening and matinees in the afternoons. A contingent of fans live at the hotel in Tokyo on the floor above ours and the bowing never ends. Then we take the Bullet Train to Kyoto and witness an ancient, slower-paced Japan.

We fly north to a beautifully snow-covered Sapporo, before preparing to end the year in Australia. I feel great now, clean, and although my hope is to see Christina, I'm also looking forward to going home to be with Celia.

* * *

Screamin' Jay Hawkins' 'I Put A Spell On You' is one of the greatest songs ever written or performed. It's one of those timeless classics, right up there in musical history with Peggy Lee's 'Fever'. Everything about it is distinct from any other song, beginning with the brass figures punched out across a brush-slapped snare in three-four tempo (a waltz).

Then of course there's Screamin' Jay's voice of pure gravel and deep-toned dexterity, which cuts through the orchestral arrangement like a blade that there's zero escape from.

Screamin' Jay Hawkins also has a black-magic schtick. The lyrics read like standard blues, but on record they're akin to a voodoo incantation. I'm gobsmacked that he's supporting the Bad Seeds on the Australian leg of the tour. Given that he's sold a million records, surely it should be the other way around?

In Melbourne, it turns out that the girl across the street from the hotel is selling 'pink rocks'. This is heroin from Thailand which comes in the form of little, uh, pink rocks. I figure to buy enough to keep a modicum of control, by dealing them too.

This doesn't go well. I get high off my own supply immediately. When I'm not rehearsing, I waste all my time waiting for the girl to come home from work. I sit by the window, waiting for her to show up at the opposite apartment, and then ring up the moment I see her.

Christina doesn't seem to recognise me, really, which gives me an inroad to get her over to London, to get to know her again.

We end the year recording cover versions for the new album with producer Tony Cohen, whose work is brilliant. He talks of recording 'into the red' and 'limiting the amount of compression' to give it extra punch.

Although I am yet to fully grieve the death of my sister, or the end of my marriage, or to be able to come to terms with my continued dependence on heroin, I enjoy the sessions. In particular, the fact that I'm being musically stretched in another way, that all these different songs demand various ways of playing as, of course, they're not all blues.

* * *

Nineteen eighty-six slides under the door and across the floor of Celia's pink bedroom carpet as she stares, embarrassed, at her name. It's tattooed across my right bicep, on a white band across a big, juicy red heart.

I decided to get the tattoo while I was in Australia. I recall sitting in the chair as Nick and a mate of his walked in, surprised to see I was being inked. The tattoo is Celia's birthday present, along with a super-futuristic radio watch that I bought from Kiddy Land, the biggest toy store in Tokyo.

The Bad Seeds' current activity is centred around Berlin, finishing the album that's now titled *Kicking Against The Pricks*. Back in London, some of Einstürzende Neubauten stay at the houseboat.

I get on with FM Einheit, also known as Mufti, who gives me a cassette tape of various seventies film soundtracks by different composers: Morricone, John Barry, Quincy Jones, Bernard Herrmann. I listen to the tape a lot and reimagine it is as if all of this music was made by one person, instead of many.

The idea is something I keep returning to.

I take some more time out and go to see my mum. The truth is she looks awful. I can see she is wracked by grief and unwarranted guilt about Our Kid, but I don't know what to do for her.

As I leave there is a strange exchange between us, as if this might be the last time we will ever see each other. She tells me, 'Take care of yourself, son,' and her eyes well up. I feel that I should comfort her, but in an almost cruel and condescending manner I volley a quick 'See ya later then, Ma', turn on my heel and bolt down the stairs.

Back at the houseboat we crack open another bottle of Brut, roll a spliff and listen to the new Prince album, *Parade*, with Celia's sister, Christine, and her boyfriend Simeon. I wonder if this is the time to bring up the fact that I know he's been rifling through my porn stash, as some of my magazines (or as Tracy Pew would call them, 'stick books') are missing.

Within days, my dad calls and tells me my mum has died. It hits me like a shotgun blast to the chest. I break down in front of Celia.

We drive to Manchester, where I carry on to Leeches Funeral Service. My mum's face looks so drawn in death as the muscles in her cheeks have collapsed in on themselves. I repeat the process that I went through with my sister, kissing her cold forehead.

I spend a little time with my dad, who now tells me that he has cancer. He has been given only another two years to live. At best.

Days later, I turn off the television and sit alone on the deck of the houseboat, shooting up heroin.

I decide that the time to leave the band is now. I've been thinking a lot about music in films after experiencing an epiphany, of sorts, via the cassette tape that Mufti gave to me.

I intrinsically feel this is something I could do, even though I'm aware the situation is a catch twenty-two. In order to be a film composer, surely I'd have to be making music for film already to best demonstrate my abilities?

I get all itchy again.

At Hansa Tonstudio, I join the Bad Seeds to play what I reckon will be one last bass line, on the song 'Your Funeral My Trial'. I come up with a descending line that takes the verse to the chorus, picturing a metaphorical lowering into the ground, into darkness.

Chapter Thirty-Two

Kid Congo Powers, guitar player, singer-songwriter, ex of The Cramps, right-hand man to Jeffrey Lee Pierce in the Gun Club, is now fronting his own band, Fur Bible. Kid Congo is a warm-hearted, generous human being with the broadest, most infectious of smiles. He is a total joy to be around, except for when, like tonight, his water pistol is pointing in your direction.

It's on… and somehow I have to make it from the bathroom, which is at the front of the houseboat as you come in the front door on the left, and get my arse downstairs to the lower deck, without being drenched by anyone.

I'm loaded. Plus my own water pistol is full and ready to take anyone out who gets in my way. I push myself away from the sink, turn on my left leg and begin to sprint, head bowed, knowing that if I make it past the kitchen, where Celia is hiding, I can career down the wooden staircase where there is no railing, turn a sharp left and bomb it to the front bedroom.

I'm right, goddammit! But the look on Celia's face says she has just realised I'm ahead of the game. I'm able to squirt her right in her eye as I fly by. By the third step, however, out of the corner of my own eye, I see Kid Congo raise up a gun from beneath the kitchen bar.

I'm fucked. I either stop and shoot it out with him or, at more speed than I can muster, push harder and faster and possibly even skip a couple of steps. Like I used to with Our Kid, when heading down the stairs at Upper Medlock Street for the Robertson's marmalade, to get to the Golly.

Or I land without taking one hit or getting the slightest bit wet.

I go for the latter but mistime the fuck out of the jump. 'Splat goes the cat!', as Celia liked to say as a child, when her parents reversed over a bump as the car came out of the driveway.

I land hard. My Ollier's disease awakes as I writhe in agony, ready to go to casualty. I'm bruised up but there's no damage to my hips, as far as they can see. Yet this incident exposes a particular issue that I thought had been conveniently tucked away.

* * *

Deciding that I need to, and I'm able to, become a part of mainstream society, I take a job. It starts on Monday, involves getting up at four in the morning and taking the tube to Hammersmith. Once there, I meet my fellow workers from the agency. We pile into a van and head off to a warehouse in Willesden.

Here we are given orders from hotels, shops and the like for cases of wine. The layout is like a grid, football-field size, divided into vertical lanes A to Z and 1 to 26 across. A typical order form looks like this:

Four boxes	Blue Nun	F22
Ten boxes	Mateus Rosé	G12
Six boxes	Lambrusco	D6
Two boxes	Le Piat d'Or	K11

The pallets that we push around the aisles measure about five feet by seven in length. Once they are stacked up with the order, the pallet is pushed to the end of the 'pitch', ready to be loaded onto the vans.

It is only Wednesday and I can hardly walk. I hear the careers officer's voice from school bleating in my head, telling me, '*A boy in your physical condition is best to look for a sit-down job in an office.*'

As my mood darkens, my bones begin to sing their song of pain and suffering. I talk to one of the guys, who picks up on the way I'm acting, telling me, 'This job is so shit, man.' We get talking about life beyond the job, the weekends, having fun, until we arrive at drugs.

In my head I'm clean, only smoking dope and drinking. If Kojak pulled me over and threw me against the wall, I could roll up my sleeves and say, 'You got nothing on me, man.'

But on the next day, my workmate slips me a wrap of smack. Relieved in all areas, I get through the job.

Celia is working as an assistant to a photographer who I don't trust at all. (Not that I've met him.) I storm past Christine's boyfriend, Simeon, who is dancing to the Prince track 'Mountains'. I head downstairs and ponder my fate before dropping into much needed, bone-resting sleep.

* * *

Thank the good Lord Jesus, then, that I'm able to quit the job to play bass on a string of English and European dates with Kid Congo and Jeffrey in the Gun Club.

Once we set off, I want to blame 'life on the road' for the fact that I immediately fall back into bad behaviour. But I've been following a hollow moral philosophy and the whole sex, drugs, disability and rock'n'roll identity which I've paraded is now a corner I've painted myself into. So I vow to change my ways again.

It's true that there used to be a strange kind of existential pay-off to being a Bad Seed. The last tour before I left saw me in Perth, dope-sick and falling asleep in the hotel pool after waking up in the middle of the night, covered in the most hideously bulbous mosquito bites and needing to cool myself down. Turns out I'd forgotten to pull down the 'mozzy' net. All very Bukowski, all very William S Burroughs, all very me – like Charlie Parker wandering around in my own chaos.

Now, off the back of playing with the Gun Club, I'm offered a job playing bass on the UK and European legs of Iggy Pop's *Blah Blah Blah* tour. I couldn't be more thrilled. I love the album already and know the songs to sing along to. I'm given a setlist and settle in to learn some thirty-four songs over the weekend.

I meet the band: guitarist Kevin Armstrong, MD, responsible for recruiting me; drummer Andy Anderson, a likeable cheeky chappie who likes a drink; and Seamus Beaghen, who very quickly becomes a friend.

Man, what a player. Seamus's skills on the piano and the Hammond organ are just astounding. We also share a sense of humour, taking the piss and impersonating Andy and Kev ('the Rev'), who we playfully tear apart.

I run through the songs with them, before Jim (Mr Pop) arrives. When he walks into the rehearsal studios, he sizes me up. Seamus introduces me and tells him I own a seven-inch single of 'I Got A Right', to which he raises a positive eyebrow. We then play various songs off *Blah Blah Blah* and *The Idiot*. During 'Mass Production', I can see Iggy is struggling with a line, so I walk across to him mid-song and mouth, '*By the way / I'm going for cigarettes.*' Which he then comes in with.

Iggy's voice is unreal. I'd say he's right up there with the greatest singers of all time. He goofs around and sings like Sinatra during a break, and I note how his pitch is so natural, his vocal control so brilliant, as well as being able to blast his lungs out on the rockier Stooges songs.

My initiation over, it looks like I'm in. Jim knows I'm familiar enough with his world, that nothing about the songs needs explaining to me, so he relaxes a little and I feel like a man renewed. He tells great stories about touring with James Brown and life in The Stooges in the late sixties.

I promise myself to stay away from drugs, girls and anything else that might lead me astray. In fact, the only slight lapse I have is getting especially drunk one night and leaving my hotel-room door on the latch. Tour manager Henry McGrogan finds me sprawled out on the bed, naked. I know from my pep talk the next day that this cannot happen again.

After the first show at the Roskilde Festival, we watch a playback and make notes to improve certain songs. I've never even thought about doing this before but it makes sense. I don't like seeing myself, though, as I zero in on my gimpy leg too much, rather than the show itself.

We play Berlin and the Bad Seeds gang turn up. As we blast into the first song, 'I Got A Right', the wireless radio to my bass packs in for about twenty seconds at the start. I can feel Mick Harvey's laughter, but once the sound is back I push even harder, using the feeling of humiliation as a source of strength and determination.

Another night, post-show, Jim approaches me totally naked backstage. I know my main task is to maintain eye contact at all times while he bemoans the prowess of The Cult, who play with us on some of the dates. I reassure him that we are better, much bigger and certainly more powerful than they are.

In Stockholm, we play a sensational afternoon show at the Grona Lunds Tivoli amusement park. Jim is on brilliant form, climbing high

294

above the disabled and wheelchair section at the front, giving them all he has.

That night, with other members of Iggy's band, we go and see Curtis Mayfield play in a small club. The band play so quietly you can hear a pin drop. This could be the most amazing and beautiful gig I've ever been to. The next day, Jim is gutted that he passed on coming to the show, asking me, 'Did he play "Superfly"? Did he play "Freddie's Dead"? "Pusherman"?'

I have to concede yes, yes and yes.

We also play a show with David Bowie, supporting him in Gothenburg, During 'The Passenger', I think it might be cool to whack the bass volume right up. I spin around to hit the volume in mid-phrase and see Bowie leaning on my amp, staring at me. I turn up the volume and spin back around as he checks out my pointed, steel-toecapped cowboy boots from Kensington Market.

After the show we are asked if we want to meet Bowie, maybe get a guitar signed by him? I decline, remembering the *Aladdin Sane* show I saw when I was fourteen, treasuring it. Meeting him now, in a way, is too much for me, beyond what I could ever have imagined.

In Paris, I forget the chord sequence to 'Lust For Life'. I know the figure, but as we haven't played this song, other than in rehearsal, the shift is lost on me. I cue Seamus, who in turn cues me the next chord by mouthing it so I can lip-read him. Then I'm back on the horse without anybody noticing.

After that show I ask Jim, 'What's the encore tonight?' He says these three words: 'Dog' ('I Wanna Be Your Dog'); 'Fun' ('No Fun'); 'Eye' ('TV Eye').

Anyone who loves rock music will tell you that those three words pretty much sum up what is so great, not just about Iggy Pop and indeed The Stooges, but the whole world of rock itself. Walking out onto a stage in front of thousands of people and playing those three songs casts everything else aside.

I leave the stage full to the brim and head to the after-show party. I'm talking to Jim when Tina Weymouth comes over to us. I play down how she has goddess-like status for me when Jim introduces us. She then demonstrates how she thought my playing was really great, in that I use fingers, thumb (like Larry Graham from Sly & the Family Stone), also a pick and play the odd chord too. I play all of this down and simply say thank you.

* * *

As the Bad Seeds are on Mute Records, owner and founder Daniel Miller asks me what I'm going to do now. He offers me a publishing deal, giving me a chance to write music which Mute will get out there to film music supervisors, advertising companies and the like. This is great news. I focus on becoming the next John Barry Adamson.

I spend most of my advance on a keyboard. Not just any keyboard, but the newly marketed Ensoniq Mirage sampler synth: 'A WHOLE ORCHESTRA AT YOUR FINGERTIPS' (my line, not theirs).

* * *

The Mirage is an eight-bit sampler featuring a 61-key velocity-sensitive keyboard, a two-digit LED display, extensive MIDI implementation, analog filters, a 333-event sequencer. It has 128kB of RAM (64kB for each keyboard half) and it is not expandable. Sample rate is variable from 10kHz to 33kHz with available sample time ranging from 2 to 6.5 seconds accordingly (for each keyboard half). It includes a built-in 3.5-inch SS/DD floppy-disk drive, which is used to boot the operating system as well as to store samples and sequences. The keyboard is pre-configured into two halves, each functioning as two independent

The Ensoniq Mirage keyboard.

instruments. This makes it easy to have one sound for the right hand and another for the left. Using a feature called multi-sampling, the Mirage is also capable of assigning multiple samples to different keys across its keyboard.

Using the mighty Mirage, by recording an idea onto a cassette tape and then overdubbing further ideas onto a twin cassette loading machine, I'm able to build track after track. The split keyboard feature makes it possible to play, say, bass on the left hand while also playing a string part with the right hand. This is mind-blowing to me, the very thing I need to express my new ideas.

*   *   *

I visit my dad, who has just got his Jamaican passport renewed and is thinking of taking a trip there. I could not be more pleased for him, knowing it's no doubt the last chance he'll get to 'go home'.

I'm offered a job soundtracking a scene in an arthouse film, *The Last Of England,* by renowned independent director Derek Jarman, starring Tilda Swinton. I put the Mirage to work, creating a bed of textures that bleed into a repeating chaos and adding sampled dialogue, the sounds of war and echoing steel scrapings. I then introduce the theme itself, a sorrowful cello played by Martin McCarrick.

The theme builds as refugees are rounded up by men in balaclavas and killed. The theme is reintroduced before heading off into an insane waltz where the gunmen dance and drink tea in a near-future dystopian nightmare.

I can now call myself a film composer.

My demos are coming along and the pieces start to feel connected, like an album. So I propose to Daniel Miller that maybe Mute could get behind it. Like the man from Delmonte, 'he say yes!'

This will help get me through the cinematic door, allowing my music to be heard by filmmakers. It also enables me to carry on my career as a musician, instead of carrying endless boxes of wine and worrying if I have the strength to go on.

My dad comes to stay on the houseboat and spends a couple of days with me and Celia. Only a month later I go to the hospital with him in Manchester. The news is not good. The cancer is spreading and attacking the lymph nodes in his left armpit. A friend of his,

Photo by Celia Johnstone.

Una, offers to come around and help look after him from time to time.

He will be okay while I go back to London, before I return to move back in with him. Una also talks to me about getting in touch with St Ann's Hospice in Heald Green, as it looks now like the two years left to live might be reduced to only two months.

My addiction has ramped up again. I'm back to full-on using and Celia is beside herself. She will admit to me one day about how her

298

frustration, her powerlessness, caused her to consider driving her car into a wall.

But the idea of stopping, as much as I want to, seems impossible to me. Even though it's what I desire most. So I go to see a dealer, a sound engineer extraordinaire, and pick up enough smack to get me to Manchester.

I go with my dad to St Ann's. The staff reassure me that he will be well looked after. I notice how the weight has dropped from his huge shoulders and his face looks gaunt. I try to get my head around the little time he has left. He gives me instructions on how to pay bills, where his wallet is. I tell him not to worry, that I will take care of it.

I arrive back at the flat, parking in the usual place. I look up at the window and swear I see something moving. A curtain twitching? A flicker of life?

I turn on the hallway light as I enter. The light is cast over the lounge, where the door is open. Shadows shift as I steady myself. My dad's silhouette shimmers behind an invisible newspaper.

I wish he was really there, not just a ghostly reverberation. Next to the sickly green chair that he disappears into nightly, to hide himself away from the world, sits a table that boasts his *Concise Oxford English Dictionary* and *Roget's Thesaurus,* his two best friends after Norman and Bomber. Allies that give him knowledge which enables him, in his own mind, to be a more welcome guest at a party he was never invited to. In his private world of intellectual prowess, the cryptic crossword can be as pleasant as a gentle stroll in the park.

I find said wallet stuffed with twenty-pound notes, plus a notebook with a list of bills. He has no direct debits; they will need paying with cash. I look towards the door and then back at the wallet.

Next to it is a drawer, which I open. I catch my breath as I see bags of 1ml syringes, of the type used by diabetics and heroin addicts.

The phone rings. I pick it up. A woman on the other end is crying.
'Hello?'

'Listen, I've been up all night thinking about you and I really think, y'know, it would be good if we could get together and talk about this thing because I really miss you and I love you.'

'I'm sorry, who is this?'

'I'm out walking with the baby right now and we miss you.'

299

I have no idea who this woman is. Despite having had a drug-induced breakdown in this very same room, this is not another psychotic episode. Of that I can be certain.

She carries on. 'I want you to come home. You know, we were at the park yesterday and I saw you and I thought that you saw me too, but I guess you didn't see me. You were walking straight towards me and I thought you were coming to see us, you know, but you walked right fucking past me.

'*WHAT THE HELL IS GOING ON WITH YOU?* I know you love us, we love you too. Please come home, we miss you. I want it to be like it used to be.'

I'm speechless at this point. I know that I should say, 'Think you've got the wrong number, love,' but then a man's voice comes on the line.

'Good evening, I've got news for you: I saw you with her, I saw you. I keep good track of my girl. I keep good track of my woman. I saw you walking, the way you do. Strutting your stuff. My woman. My baby. I was walking, paying close attention to what she was doing, to what she was doing to you at the park and I don't like it, *I DON'T FUCKING LIKE IT.* So listen... knock that shit off or I'll knock you off, *YOU SHIT!*

I'm sucked right into whatever this head-fuck is. I hear menacing noises in the background before the woman speaks again.

'I don't want to embarrass myself or anything if you don't care anymore, but I had to call. I'm very lonely and frightened and I feel crazy sometimes when I think about this and, you know, I think about it all of the time. I love you, baby. I love you so much.'

She puts the phone down. I listen to the dead tone for some time before putting the receiver back in the cradle.

I make notes about the incident. I think of a way of using it in my work, as that's the only way I can separate myself from feeling quite freaked out. I listen to my demos and realise that the ideas I've been working on are highlighted when I come home.

Maybe when I look out of the window every day, I'm absorbing what is right in front of me – what has always been inside me. The spirit of where I'm from. I get an idea for the title of my first solo album: *Moss Side Story.*

* * *

Back at the hospice I sit outside with my dad, who seems in good spirits. He talks about Jamaica. He tells me about his four brothers and three sisters; coming over to England to join the RAF; missing his brother's death due to TB, as he didn't make it to the hospital in time. The scar on his face seems to fade.

I'm seeing Celia this evening. We talk on the phone and she is distraught. She says, 'If you're stoned, then it's over, Barry.'

I lie my arse off as I'm stoned already. 'I've not used today, honest.'

When she arrives, we have a huge fight and she leaves.

I throw the rest of the stuff down the toilet. She believes me when I tell her, and she eventually comes back.

The next time I visit my dad, he is in a state. Out of his mind and really sweaty. I get some cool water and a cloth, washing him and changing his pyjamas. I sit with him, but we are both sullen. I can tell that he is gripped with the shame of me looking after him.

So he talks about my work. He tells me how he listened to the demo and how he 'gets' the track with the car-chase theme: '*Bwoy, you can see de ting.*' He describes how the first car eventually gets away from the one that is chasing it. I know he is giving me all of his love. I feel grateful and guilty in equal measure.

The nurses pull me to one side and say he might not last much longer – mere days, in fact. 'Why don't you go home and we'll call you when it's looking like the end? Then you can come in.'

I say okay to this, though I want to stay.

The next morning is Sunday. I get the call to come in, as my dad might not make it through the day.

On the way I stop and score, which doesn't take much time at all. When I get to the hospice, though, Una is there crying. My dad's bed is empty.

I am taken next door to where my dad now lies. I'm told he died just a few moments earlier.

Chapter Thirty-Three

After seeing Otto Preminger's movie *The Man With The Golden Arm*, adapted from the novel by Nelson Algren, at the Scala cinema in King's Cross late one night, I decide to make a version of the opening theme as a single. This is prior to the release of my first solo album.

Film composer Elmer Bernstein's arrangement is thrilling and harrowing in equal measure, and I want those two elements to be the main thing people get from my version. I set about this by sampling what in any other idiom would be the main groove. This, in Elmer's original tune, is a figure that comes in after an introductory theme when a hi-hat figure sets said groove.

I then loop it around; the figure repeats a couple of times before the trumpet comes in, making it possible to grab four bars. Once sampled into the mighty Mirage, at middle C on the keyboard, I can now play the key several octaves down. The result being that the loop still plays, but at a really slow speed.

To my ears it sounds amazing. My thinking is that this is a movie about a junkie. Everything in lead character Frankie Machine's world is on junk time, which moves slow. There's a scene where Frankie, played brilliantly by Frank Sinatra, goes for an audition to be the drummer in a band. He's trying to stay straight but is so frazzled from withdrawal that he can't keep up with the other players. I get that.

So, to convey his inner world, I slow everything down. Using the sampler gives it a modern spin; it sounds so cool, completely new and totally irresistible, giving me the necessary impetus to keep developing it. I also add a new drum loop, leaving space for the trumpet to play the theme.

The great thing about the track is that all of it relies on the loop, so apart from instrumental colouring and solos, the flavour of the piece is heard and digested immediately. Keeping in mind that this has got to be both thrilling and harrowing, I put myself in Frankie Machine's shoes. Sitting behind the drums, I play against the loop for all its worth, pulsating the rhythm and going in heavy for the tom-tom breaks. It sounds great.

Next thing is to arrange a down section, still based on the loops figure but with just the bass and John Doyle from Magazine brushing the kit. The Mirage provides a flute sound to play a countermelody before an ascending figure comes in, with Seamus Beaghen playing a cool piano. An ascending string line played by Anni Hogan rises higher and higher, before the song slams back into the main theme and a sampled brass BLAST stops everything.

The tension is held by a sustained Hammond organ. This repeats several times before the track SLAMS back in again, with Seamus continuing the thrill by intercutting each of the solos with the Hammond. The solos are played by Enrico Tommaso on trumpet and Terry Edwards on sax. The entire orchestration is handled by Billy McGee. It's raucous, noisy and has the desired effect.

Now that the arrangement is solid, it's time to mix it. We put down the version as it stands, as a reference to how we want it to sound after we mix the balance of instruments. The only problem is that something doesn't sound right.

Try as we (myself, engineer Paul Kendall and mix engineer John Fryer) might, we just can't get the feeling of the way the track sounded when we finished playing. So we go back to the original version, timecode bleeding all over it, and know that in fact this is the one.

My first single is finished. I'm now a solo artist and a composer of film music, on *The Last Of England*. I stand alone.

* * *

I belligerently take myself off to see Nick and the band, when they play at the Limelight club in London. I have mixed feelings about no longer being a Bad Seed and, let's face it, I can't blame them for my need to use drugs anymore. I drink until drunk and, not being able to see the band, perch myself up on the bar. When I'm told to get off, I tell the barman, 'Go and fuck yourself.'

There's trouble brewing and I want in. Next thing I know, two bouncers are dragging me off the bar and escorting me away from the premises.

There's a side door which they kick open and a flight of stairs which they throw me down. This opens up to the street, into which I fall flat on my face. I'm dazed after landing but fuck them. Who the fuck do they think they are?

I go back to the front entrance, to the three doormen standing on the next step above me, towering over me, and demand to be let back in. Bouncer friction ensues as I push the issue.

One of them pushes me in the chest. I tell him to fuck off. Another bouncer walks behind me and swings his arm fully around, so that his fist connects with my jaw.

This is called a 'king hit'. From the moment the fist connects, I see the ground rushing up to meet me at high speed. I also see flashing images of Christina, my sister, my mum and, finally, my dad.

Katy Beale's face hovers over mine, totally dreamlike. She calls out for help before I pass into unconsciousness, with my jaw completely broken.

The wiring is the most uncomfortable thing. Plus I can't eat. Me and Celia joke about this being a possible new weight-loss regime, 'the Jawbreaker', as now I have to suck up everything through a straw.

I vacillate between feeling like a complete dick and lapping up all the attention, telling the story over and over. I go to the cops to make a statement. They know who did it, but they fob me off with a line about being unable to do anything.

I also tell friends and dealers, 'That is it now, I'm off the stuff.' All of us, even me, believe it to be the truth. I mean, look at me now…

* * *

I get a call from Australian singer Dave Graney. His band, The Moodists, have broken up and so he's going solo with partner Clare Moore. They are making an EP for Fire Records under the name Dave Graney & the Coral Snakes, and ask if I'd be up for producing it. I say yes, after gulping down a full roast dinner that's been put through a blender.

I love The Moodists' first album, *Thirsty's Calling*, so I'm thrilled to be asked to work with him and Clare despite my injuries. Dave is the king of observational noir and has such a great ear for the subterranean.

Both have daytime jobs at this point, so we record over the weekend at Greenhouse Studios in North London. I park my Mercedes-Benz and rattle on in there with a briefcase, like I'm on business.

The case is actually full of antipsychotic pills. Dave notes the car, a silver machine, which I tell him was bought under sad circumstances (from some of the money my dad left me). I go to the bathroom and swallow my guilt, along with a bunch of pills.

There are no issues with the songs or the way they're played, making my job fairly easy. I'm all ears, though. When I ask for more from guitarist Malcolm Ross (ex-Orange Juice and Aztec Camera), not one eyebrow is raised; everyone knows we're all on the same page.

* * *

Work continues on *Moss Side Story*. I begin committing tracks to tape and adding new elements, at the Worldwide International Recording Studio in Collier Street, King's Cross, with Paul Kendall (PK aka Piquet). The studio is above the Rough Trade offices, and we have the mixing desk and the mighty Mirage at our disposal.

Rowland Howard comes in to play a ferocious guitar part on a piece he suggests I should call 'Glittering Blades', but which ends up as 'Autodestruction'. To get the sound he wants, he stands about six inches from the tiniest of amplifiers, turned up to ten, and makes the most incredible noise.

Mick and Katy, Jessamy, Kid Congo and Anita Lane come in and sing back-up, a choir if you will. Saxophonist Gary Barnacle perfectly executes a solo on the 'car-chase' track my dad commented on, which becomes 'Sounds From The Big House'.

I'm completely spent and often stoned, so I struggle sometimes to 'be there' at the sessions. It prompts PK to discuss with Mute Song publisher Roger D'Arcy (Roger the Dodger) the personal grief that I've been going through. Mr D'Arcy comments, 'That's the best time to get 'em.'

Once we move to the Mute studio in the Harrow Road, Diamanda Galas adds her vocal genius to the start of the album, 'On The Wrong Side Of Relaxation'. She finishes the take and enters the control room, moving in close to me to say, 'It's just like Maria Callas and Verdi.'

Celia dons a pair of high heels for the same song. We record her footsteps as she walks along the pavement outside the studio to add a little spookiness at the front of the piece.

Angela Conway, who records as AC Marias, has shot a scintillating video in a pub on the Harrow Road for her song 'Just Talk'. It inspires me to ask her to shoot the video for 'The Man With The Golden Arm'. It will riff on the Frankie Machine story from the original novel/movie, focusing on the theme of obsession.

It is to be shot in Chelsea, in a nightclub and around the streets. Celia, her sister and various friends will be at the club, which we've scripted as a fifties strip club, where I'm the drummer, who's essentially a sort of man outside. My character is obsessed with Kim Novak (who starred in the original fifties film) and I am to play this out in the video. This obsession is then projected onto another woman. The Fall's Marcia Schofield will play the stripper.

While drinking in a bar in Chelsea, I notice a girl who I think would look great on screen, particularly in the video for 'The Man With The Golden Arm'. I ask the eighteen-year-old Minnie Driver to play the role of the girl, she agrees, and the video, no doubt, helps pave her way to Hollywood stardom.

All the vital assets necessary to launch my solo career are now put into place. The sleeve is put together by Malcolm Garrett from the Magazine/post-punk days, who now runs his own company, Assorted Images (AI). Along with Joe Ewart, who works at AI, we come up with the line, *'In a black and white world, murder brings a touch of colour.'*

He takes the concept further, adding photographer Lawrence Watson to the mix and suggesting all three of us drive up to Manchester, to Moss Side, to get shots for the sleeve and other promotional material. I'm over the moon with the results.

So *Moss Side Story* is finished and life is on the up. All I have to do now is try not to fuck it up.

* * *

306

Me and Minnie Driver in the video for 'The Man With The Golden Arm'.

I see a counsellor not too far away from home, at Redcliffe Gardens in Chelsea. Her name is Suzy and she tells me I'm not ready to get clean yet, so I should keep on using until I hit rock bottom. I wonder if I can make a song out of the phrase 'rock bottom', though it's possibly a little too seventies?

But I'm joking with myself, because I can't actually see how much further down I can go. I remember it all so clearly: Berlin, Caitlin, the psych ward, my family dying. Isn't that hitting rock bottom?

Suzy tells me that she can set up a place in a treatment centre, should I decide I want to do it. I must admit to feeling a little confused.

I drive to Edgware Road to see another dealer friend in the music industry. I pick up half a gram of heroin, which should see me right for the evening and the next day. I end up taking it all and go back for more.

It's then that I realise something quite extraordinary. The drugs no longer work. I'm getting stoned but, at the same time, it doesn't feel like I am.

I tell my dealer friend I'm thinking of throwing in the towel. That these slippers I wear, as comfortable as they are, need to be thrown away as they're so old, tired and worn.

I make the call to Suzy, who sets me up to go to Clouds House.

*   *   *

On the bright October morning of my leaving, I admit my doubts about the treatment centre to Celia. I tell her I think this is a bad idea. 'Maybe we should think about it a little more?' I offer. She tells me in no uncertain terms that *we* are going.

Arriving at Clouds, set in the gentle landscape of East Knoyle, Wiltshire, is almost like opening the pages of *Country Life* magazine. If the proprietor was Bryan Ferry, then it would be just perfect.

Celia says, 'Goodbye and good luck.'

Chapter Thirty-Four

I sit in the office at Clouds House in the November of nineteen eighty-eight, filling out a questionnaire. I'm also trying to clock a few of the other residents who pass by the open door. Everyone looks pretty normal.

Then I see a couple a little older than me, carrying folders and files. My crooked mind comes into play as the woman looks at me in a surreptitious manner. She covers her mouth slightly to speak to the guy, who wears a pair of wire-framed spectacles and glances my way over the top of them. They're still looking at me as they walk out of sight.

The secretary suggests I talk to Nick, who is about to leave, and ask him how his time here has been. I walk across the entrance hall and shake hands with fidgety Nick. He looks around both of my shoulders and begins telling me how, at first, he thought the place was a controlled set-up. That they were operating a tailor-made programme for each client and that everyone here was an actor, brought in especially for each case. One of the main cases in question being his, and now mine. I laugh with him, knowing that what he's said is just about conceivable and that he probably still thinks that way.

I'm given a timetable, told that there's no music allowed and shown into a huge 'common area' where about thirty people are chatting in smaller groups. All of them are smoking cigarettes.

It's explained that, on arrival, everyone is appointed a mentor. Then a burly Scot is called over to me. As I'm introduced to Gary, he rolls his

309

eyes and expresses a very clear exasperation. The secretary dismisses it as 'just being his way' and leaves us to it.

Various people look in my direction, whispering to each other. I think of what Nick said about the residents being actors. I imagine that they are discussing where to meet, to go through their lines.

Gary shows me around the place with a disconnected attitude, only coming to life when one of the girls walks by. He swoops down on her, a vulnerable cockney redhead, pinning her against the corridor wall. I assume they are old mates.

She welcomes the attention at first, blushing a little, but then senses she's in some kind of a trap. She tries to push him away, becoming frustrated when she can't escape. He's stripped her of her usual thick-skinned, fuck-off approach to life.

Gary laughs and backs off, pointing at her face. He tells her he'll see her in the chapel at some point, then mutters something under his breath in an aggressive tone.

I ask him where the canteen is so we can get a cuppa, in an attempt to show friendliness. He looks at me as though I've just threatened him, then moves into my space. Right into my face.

'The Stockwell Strangler – that's who you remind me of, pal. He had the cell across from mine in Broadmoor.' He moves even closer. 'Same shitty, half-caste eyes.'

I sit in the main room and pretend that I'm not there. I could definitely use a hit right about now, as I'm starting to cluck. My face is peppery and I feel a nausea in my belly. Sounds are exaggerated and each look in my direction brings an air of menace with it.

As I choke on the tobacco smoke, I see a man leaning against the far wall with a clipboard, suit and tie, eyeing me off in the distance. I take out a cigarette from a packet of Rothmans and light it up as he walks towards me with a fixed gaze.

The counsellor introduces himself and sits over me, perched on the edge of the nearest chair. He has ill-fitting tight slacks, slicked-back black hair and gold-rimmed specs that he keeps pushing up the bridge of his nose. He breathes heavily as he talks to me about getting clean.

'The only way out from addiction is what? Jails, institutions and death, right? And let's face it, what's this place? It's just another institution.'

He smiles as I grapple with the idea that this country estate is no weekend getaway at all. There's no spa. No pampering. Just Clonidine, a piss-weak drug to help you withdraw, which I've already taken today and doesn't seem to be helping me one iota.

Several days in and I want to die.

I go 'to group' and listen to the stories of men battered and broken, of girls selling their bodies and souls for a fix. Of shattered dreams and fractured lives.

I find somewhere quiet to sit afterwards. Another counsellor, the one I saw chatting to the woman when I arrived, asks me if I want to walk with him in the grounds.

I notice that he is mirroring me by limping; he definitely wasn't doing that before. He tells me about his life after using drugs and his past self-hatred, shooting up strychnine.

'Look at me now. I never thought I'd be in the position I am,' he testifies.

'Me neither,' I joke.

We go back inside. I ponder what he has said, noticing that, as awful as I feel, there is a tiny spring to my step.

The next day, I go to the bathroom for a pee. After I finish urinating, completely without any warning, feeling or erotic arousal, a steady stream of ejaculate leaves my body. I am engulfed in shame as I clean myself up, vowing to tell nobody of this unfortunate incident.

However, my body makes sure that I keep schtum, because my jaw has frozen. I cannot talk or physically move the muscles. Maybe it's an after effect of assault and battery? But in all seriousness, I don't think it's because of that.

I'm taken to the nurses' station and given a pill. I don't know what it is, but I'm told it will help me relax. So why don't I go and write down my life story? (I remember now that it was first suggested on the introductory sheet, which I'd forgotten all about.)

I find a quiet spot near the main room and sit with my A4 pad. The counsellor and the woman approach me. She hides the lower half of her face behind a sheet of paper. I can tell by her eyes that she is smiling. He asks how I am and all I can do is nod. He states his hope that I'll start to feel better.

The truth is I'm starting to feel worse. There's something building inside me; some place I've never visited before has constructed itself within me. It just builds and builds.

I find my way downstairs to a side entrance where there is a small door through which I aim to escape. To just run and run and never stop running.

I begin breathing more and more heavily as I reach my destination, my mind spinning. Behind me are two male counsellors who are in pursuit. As they approach, I become enraged. A fury overtakes me, and I begin to roar through my clenched jaw, a guttural bellow. I flail my arms, kicking the door open, and as I do the two men grab hold of me. My jaw finally cracks open and I scream for all my worth: 'YOU DIDN'T HAVE TO CALL IT *THE FIRSTBORN IS DEAD*, ANYTHING BUT THAT, YOU FUCKING CUNT!'

I rage on as the two men try to calm me down by telling me to keep on letting my anger out.

Back inside, the next day, after only two hours of sleep for the first time in days, I make a joke here and there with some of the others. We've formed a little group of our own, so that we can have a laugh, keep up with all the gossip and generally take the piss out of everyone.

We do this with Leonard, 'hairdresser to the stars'. We take the piss out of him because he tells us that he cuts film star Tony Curtis's hair.

We are on our backs with laughter at the old joke: a man goes into a barber's shop and the barber asks him how he wants his haircut. The guy tells him he wants a Tony Curtis. The barber shaves all the guy's hair off and he goes mad: 'I told you I wanted a Tony Curtis! What's this?' The barber says, 'Well, that's what I gave him when he came 'ere.'

This joke gets told over and over as a piss-take in front of Leonard who, bless him, takes it all in his stride.

On visiting day, the lads get together to discuss who's who in the zoo. Now that our visitors have mostly been and gone, I tell the gang about Celia and how we were caught necking outside, on a bench near the side door. A counsellor fired a look at me as if to say, '*What the hell do you think you're playing at?*'

As we piss ourselves about it, I see the faces on some of the other guys suddenly freeze. Then a voice booms out behind me. 'Excuse me, do you happen to know where I might find Leonard?'

Ready for a laugh, I turn around and look directly into the actual face of Hollywood legend Tony Curtis. I limply say, 'I think he might be in the grounds.' Tony says, 'Thank you,' and bows ever so slightly, not unlike his American millionaire character Danny Wilde in hit TV show *The Persuaders.*

I turn back to the group. Somebody says, 'Fuck me!'

*   *   *

My life story, as I read it out to the group, does nothing but seek pity and justify my own woeful actions. I start by announcing my name and the bands that I've been in, adding, 'Of course, you all already know that.' Eyes roll around the room, flustering me somewhat.

The feedback I receive suggests I should open up and trust people more: let them help the real me; let go of my arrogance and grandiosity, which I mask behind a nice-guy image.

One person tells me he was also labelled grandiose and asks if I know about the concept of the 'King Baby'. I want to call out, '*Guards! Off with his head!*', but he goes on. 'It's a term used to describe somebody who always wants what they want, and they want it now.'

So much talk of powerlessness over my addiction. Of having an unmanageable life. At this stage I can't even say, or spell, the word 'unmanageable'. Or even approach the idea that my life has been governed by the will of others, even here at this institution.

People seem to come through the door in a state of collapse and within days appear accepting of the idea of addiction being like a disease. Then they dance and sing on a Friday night, while I hide away in my room with my overcoat over my pyjamas, waiting for somebody to come and teach me how to fucking live. '*Unmanageable, my arse,*' I almost say out loud.

Nearing the end of my stay, I'm taken for the afternoon to a house in Weston-Super-Mare, to be 'assessed'. This is where I am to stay for six months up to a year, to really get into my recovery and become a useful member of society. The atmosphere is horrible. It's as though something strange and quite possibly evil resides here. This may be only my 'clean for one second' paranoia, I reason with myself.

But no. Something is not right. The people here, except for the counsellors, seem really unhappy.

There is a TV on in the lounge, which is empty. Quite suddenly, Public Enemy leap onscreen, performing 'Fight The Power'.

I catch myself for a moment. I see something in me that has been totally missing.

My fucking soul.

Back at Clouds later that day, I set to work on a new record. Excusing myself to have a bath every afternoon, I draw the image of a keyboard on the steamed mirror. Nick Cave told me how the old blues guys used to do this in prison, on the walls next to their cribs, in order to get their ideas down.

I think about my roots: Manchester, Moss Side and the surrounding areas. I get an idea for something I will call 'From Rusholme With Love'; I imagine how it will sound by playing it every day on the imaginary keyboard drawn on the mirror.

* * *

Six weeks pass by in an instant. With my time here done, and with much damage reparation to be undertaken with almost everyone I know, I leave Clouds and head back to London. Celia, full of hope and optimism, asks me how I'm doing. 'Great,' I exclaim and then glance out of the window as the landscape begins to scarily move in towards me. I cannot admit this fear, even to myself.

Expectations are high. When I reach the houseboat, Christine couldn't be happier that I'm clean and sober. We have a drink to celebrate. I take an orange juice, of course. But I notice how I can taste vodka, even though there is none in the glass.

I walk out on deck to take the air, but then I hear a familiar voice.

'Well, well, well. Look what the cat's dragged in.'

The Vulture is perched on the roof. He begins goading me for a response to a myriad of questions, pushing me and pushing me.

'Fuck this for a game of soldiers,' I say under my breath.

The phone rings; it's somebody from the treatment centre. I make the international sign for 'I'm not here' to Celia, waving my fingers under my throat. She goes along with it but eyes me with concern.

The next morning, I get up after staying awake, thinking, all night. Celia goes to work, so I go out and buy several cans of Carlsberg Special Brew. I begin downing them as fast as I can, on a nearby bench on the

314

CHAPTER THIRTY-FOUR

King's Road. Two homeless people sitting look at me with worry. 'Are you okay?'

I stagger around the pre-Christmas shoppers, past those who are now giving me a wide berth. I sit helpless in packed-out bars, trying to strike up conversations with people who might get pissed with, befriend, exploit or just get pissed off with me.

I end up back at the World's End pub on the King's Road. I meet a guy I used to do heroin with while I'm chatting up a woman who has dirty blonde hair. He tells me about some amazing gear being sold in a pub in Shepherd's Bush, so I discard the woman and we go get some.

We score and head back to World's End: to where the community centre is; to where there is also a public toilet.

He takes the first hit.

I go next and the heroin is powerful. Plus, I haven't had any for a few months.

I start to overdose.

The Vulture looks down on me now and says, '*What the fuck are you doing? That's not enough.*'

I'm just about able to tip the last of the heroin into the spoon.

I draw it up the syringe while The Vulture sits atop the stall.

I put the needle to my arm.

'That's it. Right there.'

The Vulture begins to fade into the distance.

* * *

The familiar sights and sounds of hospital monitors and machines are gradually turned up as I open my eyes. A doctor explains to me how lucky I am. It turns out that the guy I was with, upon seeing me slide down the wall, decided to get the hell out as quickly as he could. The caretaker, seeing him hotfoot it out of the place, reckoned that was it for the day. He locked up, unaware that I was heading towards the light at the end of the tunnel in the last cubicle, and headed for home.

On the way home, he noticed he wasn't wearing his watch. Realising he'd left it at work, he turned back to pick it up. Upon entering, he saw my foot sticking out from under the stall door and called an ambulance.

The doctor jokes. 'Seems like, quite literally, it wasn't your time to go.'

A nurse tells me that my girlfriend, Celia, called and told them I'd been to a treatment centre to try to 'get recovery'.

'Well, we can put you on a "script" for life,' says the good doctor, 'or you can go and get some help through the recovery community.' The former means taking methadone daily until you die: the latter means going to meetings to try to stay clean. Living in some kind of hope.

Without skipping a beat, I say, 'I'll go and get help; I'll go to meetings.' For the first time in as long as I can remember, the volume of the discombobulation in my head, the sounds of people living rent-free in the old shed, all the dissonance and negativity lurching around and around, backwards and forwards, slowly and at speed, begins to quieten.

I remember a phrase that was said in the treatment centre – 'Surrender to win', which is what I may possibly be doing, right now.

I go home to tell Celia the great news, but as we all know, the proof of the pudding is in the eating. All she can see is what's on her plate: the messy remains and bare bones of the last squandered meal, with flies buzzing around it.

She and Anita Lane, Nick Cave's former girlfriend and long-term collaborator, suggest that I call to tell him I've relapsed. Maybe he can help me?

I begrudgingly agree to it, not completely believing in my newfound beliefs but recognising that my swallowed anger towards Nick has dissipated somewhat. This could be part of a new way of thinking.

Nick suggests I come into the studio, where he and the Bad Seeds are recording a version of Neil Young's song 'Helpless'. I think to myself that the title sounds like a meaningful coincidence. I decide I will go to two meetings that day instead.

The first one, just around the corner from the houseboat (as they always are, I'll come to learn), is crowded with about ninety or so people. Some of them are quite excited about being there, chatting and (oh God!) hugging each other.

A speaker is introduced. He tells a story about leaving treatment and immediately relapsing. Then he realised that what is said about having no power over drugs and – when it comes to it – no choice is true.

I'm sitting on my hands next to Suzy, the counsellor I first went to see. She begins telling the story of how angry she was last night with her boss, who demanded that she finish off a project at work. This effectively made her miss her Christmas flight out to New York. Then her plane crashed over Lockerbie in Scotland. While she is heartbroken for everyone who died on the plane, she feels incredibly grateful to her boss.

After the meeting, they ask for people to help put the room back as it was found. 'Would somebody sweep the floor?'

'I'll do that,' I say, almost as though I'm a puppet and my strings are being pulled. (At least I don't have to hug anyone.)

The second meeting is in the evening, around another corner. There are only about ten people in a tiny room, who all seem to know each other very well. I feel a million miles away from where they are, but then there is one other chap who says nothing and sits like a statue in the front row.

The speaker this time talks about 'the power of negative thinking' and how she could not stop herself from following an inner voice of self-destruction. I identify with every word that she says; even the statue in the front row starts to move. I feel empowered for some reason.

She also talks about how the obsession and compulsion to use drugs can be removed, and a relief sweeps over me as if this is what is already happening.

I go back to the houseboat and make dinner. I start writing music again and I'm able to finish 'From Rusholme With Love', making sketches of other ideas as the blood begins to course through my veins.

* * *

Moss Side Story has been released to critical acclaim.

I receive a letter from Hubert Selby Jr, the author of my favourite novels: *Requiem For A Dream, Last Exit To Brooklyn, The Room, The Demon.* He states in his letter that he has listened to *Moss Side Story* and really likes it, saying, 'It sounds like a shoot-'em-up, and I love shoot-'em-ups.'

We meet when he is in London. As he lives in Los Angeles, Selby notes how, in London, 'the streets are drunk'. He also tells me, in a knowing way, that when life is good it can feel like 'dancing on the leaves of the trees'.

Off the back of *Moss Side Story*, I receive a call from a company called Dreamsville in Hollywood, asking if I'd be interested in scoring a movie they are working on entitled *Mirage*. (The film's title will later change to *Delusion*.) I read the script and, of course, I accept.

I sit in the departure lounge and wait to board a Virgin Airways flight to Los Angeles. Over the Tannoy I hear, 'Would Mr Adamson please come to the desk?'

Like a more positive kind of cosmic joke, of the type I realise I'd better get used to, I'm offered an upgrade to First Class. 'Thank you.' I accept without hesitation.

As the plane takes off, I look out of the window. There is not a Vulture nor a Central Control agent in sight.

I feel incredibly grateful for the life that has been gifted to me. The joys of a musical career, love and laughter can converge into a smile creeping across my face. All my troubles and woes now seem to fit into a place of acceptance.

The people who have entered into my life thus far have all imprinted themselves onto my mind and into my heart. Be they friend, foe or passer-by, I feel a connection to them all in this moment.

The aeroplane begins to lift off the ground and take flight.

I'm up above the city and down below the stars.

I smile to myself as I hear my mum clearly say, '*Right, you've had your fun. Now bugger off…*'

Acknowledgements

Thanks to Julia Blackburn, teacher and mentor, for lighting the writing fire in my belly.

Serena Catapano for keeping it burning during the process.

Shaun Connon, a greater ally I could not wish for.

Editor Paul Woods for giving it to me straight and steering the ship through countless seas.

Jason Wood for keeping me afloat in the darkness.

Gerri Frame for coaxing me out of the foetal position when writing got tough.

Omnibus' David Barraclough and Imogen Gordon Clark for wise input, patience and care.

Designer Rehan Abdul for going the extra mile.

Those who gave their permission to use their photos and articles. Thank you.

And of course… all who appear in these pages and many more who live between the lines.

Unending gratitude.

Barry Adamson
June 2021

Lyric Credits